THE LOVECRAFT ANNUAL

Edited by S. T. Joshi

Contents

Abbreviations used in the text and notes:

AT   *The Ancient Track* (Hippocampus Press, 2013)
AV   Joshi & Schultz, *Ave atque Vale* (Necronomicon Press, 2018)
CE   *Collected Essays* (Hippocampus Press, 2004–06; 5 vols.)
CF   *Collected Fiction* (Hippocampus Press; 2015–17; 4 vols.)
IAP   Joshi, *I Am Providence: The Life and Times of H. P. Lovecraft* (Hippocampus Press, 2010)
LL   Joshi & Schultz, *Lovecraft's Library: A Catalogue,* 4th rev. ed. (Hippocampus Press, 2017)
SL   *Selected Letters* (Arkham House, 1965–76; 5 vols.)

Copyright © 2020 by Hippocampus Press
Published by Hippocampus Press, P.O. Box 641, New York, NY 10156
www.hippocampuspress.com

Cover illustration by Allen Koszowski. Hippocampus Press logo designed
by Anastasia Damianakos. Cover design by Barbara Briggs Silbert.

Lovecraft Annual is published once a year, in Fall. Articles and letters
should be sent to the editor, S. T. Joshi, % Hippocampus Press, and must
be accompanied by a self-addressed stamped envelope if return is desired.
All reviews are assigned. Literary rights for articles and reviews will reside
with *Lovecraft Annual* for one year after publication, whereupon they will
revert to their respective authors. Payment is in contributor's copies.

ISSN 1935-6102
ISBN 978-1-61498-308-8

National Defense

H. P. Lovecraft and R. H. Barlow

[In the summer of 1935, H. P. Lovecraft spent his second summer at the home of R. H. Barlow and his family in De Land, Florida. It appears that at some point during this stay (9 June–18 August), the two friends took a series of notes on the subject of national defense, as related by Barlow's father, Col. Everett D. Barlow (1881–1952). The first few pages of notes are in Lovecraft's handwriting, the remainder in Barlow's. E. D. Barlow published an essay on "National Defense" in the *Californian* 3, No. 3 (Winter 1935): 79–82. It is likely that the prose in this essay is largely by Lovecraft and/or Barlow. We present here the previously unpublished notes (A.Ms., John Hay Library, Brown University), followed by the published version of the essay.—ED.]

[HPL:]

so that you might not forget, but take it home with you.

Omit reference to figures or statistics of any kind

Make comparison at outset

Fire department—best insurance against disaster of any kind. Maintenance effects a saving—expense much less than that of damage without it would be. Same with warfare. National defence is insurance against the disaster of an unsuccessful war. Have been lucky in past—successful termination of war. No military policy, but good fortune caused success. In world war unprepared, but allies held front so that preparation could be effected. Took year to put troops into field, & even so some arrived untrained. If military policy had existed, taxpayers would have been saved millions—expense of training camps, munitions factories, & machinery of draft. War ended, need of natl. defence manifest.

Natl. defence act law 1920. Provided force large enough to defend country in case of emergency—not large enough for aggression. Young men often say will not fight unless in case of attack. No one has ever proposed any other kind of military policy. Those in charge of country would never stand for war of aggression—future same as past.

Natl. Defence act	(3) Reg. Army
Component parts—	Natl Guard
	Organised Reserves

comprise several field armies depending on type of emergency arising. Key commissions held by civilians preparing selves for possible service. Extension courses _____ by reservists offer promotion.

Reserves made possible by patriotism of civilians who pursue studies in addition to business

Case of War

Reg. arm. and Nat Guard would serve first—hold line until reserves ready. Details of reserve training in file with W. D. 9 areas have plans prepared & consolidated under Natl. Defence scheme. All prepared even blank telegrams for mobilisation. By this plan expensive training camps needless—training already effected by reserve officers & enlisted men. Mobilisations

brigades
divisions　　　sent to threatened areas.
camps
armies

Great saving easily visible. No training camps—no exp. of transportation. Indust. mobilisation in time of peace—methods of procuring equipment—supplies—munitions— Preparation to expedite the supply troops when mobilised. Much in papers about excessive profits in wartime revealed by sen. investigating committee[.] Plan for prep. in peace take profit out of war. Also movement take profits out of all prep. Profitless—war less liable than in past. No doubt of laws against banking loans to belligerents abroad, less warfare—assurance of peace[.] Fire dept. comparison— None unless necessary. Suppose something better for fire protection. Then adopt—but nothing better came. If improvement though[t] of—still use old till perfected.

Pacifists decry war, & rightly. If war eliminated, econ. progress hastened to genl. advantage. But until war can be abolished & broth. love & golden rule prevail—nations not fear—jealousy—envy—greed—inord ambition— Until millennium—no fear outside aggressions—only common sense perfect & perpetuate nat. defence best means protect citizens & country.

Therefore forces as prescribed should be kept up to prescribed level.

Though reg. army incr. 65,000 men, level of all nat. def. not maintained. Reg. only 42%[.] Nat Guard 40%—_____ 69%[.] Cong. should be urged to insist forces kept up to min. level. What use enhance bus. if nat def. neglected?

In closing wish to say—hope we & children & descendants down path time sing. grand anthem "America["] (text given)

[RHB:]
In speaking to you on Nat. Def. I would like to bring the subject to you in a way that you would not forget, but take home with you and sit down and think of the ideas that I have tried to present to you.

I purposely will omit references to figures and statistics of any kind. Let us take, for example, your local fire department—best insurance against disaster of any kind. The expense or maintenance is much less thru prevention of fire than that of damage without it would be. If you did not know that this department was paying for itself, you probably would not retain it. The same is the case with warfare—best defense against war that our country has. Nat. def. is insurance against the disaster of an unsuccessful war. Have been lucky in past—successful termination of war. But that does not mean that in the future every war in which we are engaged

The country has entered in haphazard fashion in every war that has been waged—world war and if we had not had allies to hold the front until we went into it we would have been in a very precarious position. Took year to get troops into field, and even so, some arrived untrained. Now, if we had had a military policy before the w. w. started, tax-payers would have been saved the expense of many training camps—munitions factories, machinery of draft and terrific cost of military training camps.

When the w w ended it became evident that a Nat. Def. policy was much needed. Best minds prepared the N. D. Act, which became a law in 1920. This act provided forces large enough to defend country in case of emergency, but in no case was it large enough to wage wars of aggression. N.D.A. is purely an act for defense, not offense. Young men often say will not fight unless in case of attack. No one has ever proposed any other kind of military policy. Public opposition in this country would never stand a war of aggression any more than it has in the past. You are all well acquainted with what the regular army is National Reserve, which in time of war would be the greatest army in the United States ... number depending on type of emergency which arises. Civilians, through prior training ... in case reserves are called into XXXX Service through taking advantage of full pay ...

These reserves are only made possible by patriotism of civilians who are interested in their daily bread.

If war declared, reg. army and Nat. Guard would be called into immediate action—hold line until reserves ready—given extra training to form brigades, corps, and armies as prescribed by the NDA. Details in regard to mobilizations, concentrations and training of National Reserves are on file in the War Dept. Nine areas have plans prepared and consolidated under Nat'l Def. scheme. All details have been arranged even to blank telegrams for mobilization. By this plan, expensive training camps are needless—training already effected by reserve officers and enlisted men commanded by officers in these (?) reserves and ... enlisted men who also hold positions in those reserve

brigades
divisions   sent to threatened areas
camps
armies

I believe in these few remarks you will be able to see the great saving in dollars and cents due to an industrial mobilization in time of peace that all methods of procuring equipment—supplies, munitions. Preparation is being made to effectively, economically, and in all details supply troops when mobilized. You of course have seen a great deal in the papers about great profits in wartime revealed by sen. investigating committee. Plan for prep. in peace to take profit out of war—move on foot to take profit out of prep. in time of peace, for war. War will be made so that profits become less likely to . . . War less liable than in past.

Prevention of loans—bankers, US, to belligerents—making impossible for firms in US to deliver munitions . . . elim. of war and assurance of peace. Fire dept. comparison.

Suppose you had in view something to prevent the ravages of fire. Would adopt system—but present nothing better than Fire Dept. affords. If improvement thought of, still use old till perfected.

People called pacifists decrying war, and rightly so, because if war can be eliminated, econ. progress hastened to everybody's profit. But until the time comes when wars have been abolished, golden rule practised as well as preached—jealousy, envy, greed . . . ambition[—]nations not fear one another—until the Millennium—no fear of outside aggression—

(Until this) only common sense for our country to preserve and perpetuate NAT DF as the best means of protecting our country. Therefore forces should be kept up to the level prescribed in 1920. Though regular army has been increased (65 000 men) that level is not held at present. Reg. army is only 42% of that strength. Nat. G. is 40% [. . . 69% (?)][1] I believe that every patriotic citizen should urge his congressman to insist forces kept up to min. level. What use enhance business—beautify and protect cities—if N D neglected?

In closing I wish to say that I hope we and our children and their children down the paths of Time as long as time shall last will sing grand anthem

AMERICA

---

1. [Under the bracketed words, RHB has written: "see note HPL"]

National Defense

E. D. Barlow

In giving a few remarks on National Defense I hope to present the subject in such a way that it will be remembered and reflected upon after these paragraphs are laid aside. I will purposely omit all reference to figures, statistics, and technical matters as far as possible, and try to show in a very general and concrete fashion just how the actual problem bears on the average citizen.

The best common comparison I can think of is with a city and its fire protection. An effective fire department is the best possible insurance against costly and prostrating disaster. Its maintenance requires money, but costs much less than the damage which would occur if it were not maintained. Prevention is cheaper than a conflagration. If a city did not know that the fire department paid for itself, it would probably not maintain it.

So with a nation and its military forces of defense. These forces form the best possible insurance against the disaster of an unsuccessful war, and ought, aside from all sentiment, to be maintained as a matter of ordinary business judgment. We have been lucky with our wars in the past—each having been successful despite the almost total lack of a real military policy on our· part. But only through some system of co-ordinated preparation can such successes be made sure. We cannot always rely on the sheer good fortune which has happened to help us before.

The World War amply proved what kind of a disaster might some time befall us. It caught us unprepared, and would have formed a paralyzing blow had no allies been present to hold the front till our own preparation could be effected. A year was required to place our troops in the field, and even so a substantial number reached the front without adequate training. If a proper military policy had existed, the country's taxpayers would have been saved millions—the expense of special training camps, and of all the haste, waste, and in some instances inferior materials resulting when private companies are suddenly called upon for supplies and munitions which they are not prepared to furnish.

When the war was over the need of a real policy of national defense became plainly manifest. The best minds drew up a carefully considered plan, which in 1920 was officially adopted as the National Defense Act. This act authorizes forces large enough to defend the country in any emergency, but not large enough to wage a war of aggression. The purely defensive nature of this plan has perhaps been insufficiently emphasized. Today we often hear high-school and college students, vowing never to bear arms except in case of an attack upon this country—as if any other sort of military policy had ever been proposed! The fact is that those in charge or likely to be in charge of the nation would never sanction a war of aggression. In the future, as in the past, public opinion will always limit our military enterprises to a defense of the territory and the civilization we have.

The forces which the United States would, according to the National Defense Act, put into the field in case of war, consist of three distinct parts—the Regular Army and the National Guard, with whose nature the general public is well acquainted, and the less known but crucially important corps called the Organized Reserves. It is the latter which would, in time of war, form the country's greatest military strength; being a flexible organization capable of adjustment to emergencies of every type and degree of seriousness. This reserve ensures the formation of field armies in any needed quantity and suited to any sort of operation, yet calls for no expensive special staff or feverish eleventh-hour training when the emergency actually comes. Key commissioned and enlisted men's positions are held by civilians trained in peace time and in addition to their regular occupations—largely through extension courses offered by the Regular Army and affording increased opportunities for promotion. This is made possible by the patriotism of citizens who are willing to divert enough time from their business and personal interests to master the exacting studies involved, and to hold the assignments without pay except during an active training period of two weeks—sometimes annual and sometimes biennial according to the funds provided by Congress.

On the coming of a war the Regular Army, National Guard, and Organized Reserves would join to form one vast force—the Armies of the United States—with all three components acting in predetermined harmony through organization into the brigades, divisions, and army corps which constitute the tactical units of that force. The Regular Army, and the National Guard, already organized and intensively trained, would be called into immediate action to hold the line until the Organized Reserves are ready for field duly. Details of this process—concentration, mobilization and training—are on file in the archives of the War Department. The country had previously been divided into nine geographical Corps Areas, each of whose commanders has complete charge in peace time of activities within his area—the training of the Regular Army, the supervision of the training or the National Guard, and the organization and training of the Organized Reserves. The War Department has co-ordinated the plan submitted by the nine Corps Area Commanders into one large mobilization plan for the entire country. So thorough is this plan that it includes even the filing in the War Department of prepared telegrams ready to use in initiating the war-time mobilization of troops according to its provisions. By this plan of the National Defense Act expensive training camps are rendered needless, the training having already been partly affected by Reserve officers and enlisted men under the supervision of Regular Army officers in time of peace, and being completed by the gradual special training of the various units from the smallest to the largest—company, battalion, regiment, brigade, division—as they are formed during the process of concentration and mobilization. As soon as a company is assembled it will receive its training in the tactics of that unit. When that company is grouped into a battalion this new unit will master battalion tactics, and go on upward—the men absorbing without confusion each larger phase of training as they come to it. In effect, this is a progressive system of concurrent concentration, mobilization and training. Finally, brigades, divisions, corps, and armies are mobilized with the least possible delay and sent to the threatened areas.

The great saving in dollars and cents inherent in such a plan ought to be obvious to every reader. There will be no costly training camps, no vast expenses for the transportation of trainees and supplies to those camps, and none of the other sudden and excessive financial drains common in past wars. Instead, there will have been a quiet industrial survey in time of peace—a survey including methods of procuring equipment, supplies, munitions, and everything else necessary. Everything will be ready and co-ordinated when the troops themselves are mobilized.

At present the papers say a great deal about excessive profits on supplies and munitions in war time, as revealed by the Nye Senate Investigating Committee. Much is also said about the disproportionate profits derived from war preparations in time of peace. The spirit of the National Defense Act, if fully applied, would check both of these evils by systematizing all military preparation and making it a regular part of normal national life. War would be made less profitable and therefore less likely to occur—than in the past. Kindred steps would be the prevention of loans by American bankers to foreign belligerents, and a ban on the sale and delivery of American munitions equipment, and supplies to such parties. Thus, through the removal of several powerful incentives to war, the assurance of peace would become greater than ever before.

Once again the fire-department comparison seems appropriate. If there were some way of preventing fires from ever breaking out, or some better way of checking their ravages, we would not need such a department; but since no such ways exist, we cling to that department as the best known means of combating a constant peril. Even if we are working on a new and improved system, we are naturally forced to keep the old system in use until some successor is really perfected.

People called pacifists are constantly decrying war—and rightly. What is not right in the views of some of them is the notion that adequate preparedness tends to provoke or precipitate warfare. Ability to defend oneself certainly involves no temptation to attack others—but on the contrary makes peace more secure by removing from others the temptation to attack oneself. It is a matter of proved fact that every responsible officer of the United States Army from the Chief of Staff down, and every responsible member of the Congressional Committee on Military Affairs, is acutely conscious through experience of the disastrous and disorganizing effects of warfare, and anxious and determined to avoid that calamity in every possible way. The public does not sufficiently realize the large part which proper military and naval strength plays in the preservation of peace—how many times, for example, serious international disorder has been prevented by the timely appearance of an American battleship in the principal port of some excitable nation.

The advocates of National Defense know better than anyone else how the elimination of war would hasten economic progress to everyone's advantage. Not only is war a tragic financial drain during preparation and actual fighting, but also during the tremendously long aftermath when pensions, hospitalization, and similar expenses form a heavy national item and constant burden on every taxpayer. But until war actually can be superseded by the practice as well as preaching of brotherly love, and the Golden Rule, and the nations truly cease to feel envy, jealousy, greed, and inordinate ambition, or to fear outside aggression—until, that is, the coming of the long-wished millennium—it is only common sense that we do all we can to support, perfect, and perpetuate an adequate system of National Defense as the best and indeed the only means of protecting our citizens and our country.

It is, therefore, our immediate civic duty to see that our defensive forces are kept up to the prescribed level of the Defense Act of 1920, below which it has been conclusively proved dangerous to let them fall. Though the Regular Army has recently been increased by 65,000 men, the general level of all national defense forces is sadly below the limit of safety. The Regular Army is now only 42% of the prescribed minimum; the National Guard only 40%; the Organized Reserves only 69%. I believe that every patriotic citizen should urge his Congressman to insist that these components be kept up to the minimum level provided for in the National Defense Act. Of what use is it to enhance and encourage business, or to beautify our cities and countryside, if we neglect the defense of those opportunities and possessions?

In closing, let me express the hope that we, and in turn our children and our children's children, down the path of time, so long as time shall last, may not neglect the responsibilities imposed by citizenship in a great nation. May we and they always be able to sing with pride and untroubled conscience that grand old anthem—

> "My country, 'tis of thee
> Sweet land of liberty,
>   Of thee I sing;
> Land where my fathers died,
> Land of the Pilgrim's pride,
> From every mountainside
>   Let freedom ring."

Briefly Noted

Hippocampus Press will publish in 2020 two volumes of letters of Clark Ashton Smith: *Eccentric, Impractical Devils* (correspondence between Smith and August Derleth) and *Born under Saturn* (correspondence with Samuel Loveman). Smith's correspondence with Derleth is particularly valuable because, besides providing great insight into the work habits of both authors, the reader can see how Arkham House came into being, and how Derleth mostly single-handedly ran a fairly complex publishing operation while still pursuing his own literary career. In the other volume, we note with interest that Smith and Loveman, both longtime friends of H. P. Lovecraft, were friends long before either became acquainted with Lovecraft. Of particular interest is the reading material in which each author indulged. These volumes are valuable resources for those researching their authors and well beyond.

Atmosphere and the Qualitative Analysis of "The Colour out of Space"

Steven J. Mariconda

> . . . the listener, who listens in the snow,
> And, nothing himself, beholds
> Nothing that is not there and the nothing that is.
> —Wallace Stevens, "The Snow Man"

While there are many controversies regarding Lovecraft, few critical lances will break over the proposition that "The Colour out of Space" (1927; CF 2.367–99) is his finest story. Even the author himself agreed (*IAP* 671). The concept of a "best" story is interesting but imprecise. It is enlightening also to consider the ways in which the story is unique in the Lovecraft canon. One element is the high level of artistic finish, which makes it almost impervious to commentary. More important is the innovative aspect of the source of the story's horror—the Colour itself.

In fact, the horror in "The Colour out of Space" may be read as an emblem of Lovecraft's aesthetic of atmosphere in the weird tale. The Colour does not show itself directly but manifests itself in indirect ways. Atmosphere, too, is something intangible that is thrown off by the prose of the story.

The manner in which Lovecraft creates atmosphere in this story is not, as he is often accused of by critics, by the use of adjectives. It is by a variety of rhetorical devices; by emphasis, balance, syntax, sound, and figurative language. Of this last there are certain elements worthy of inventory in an informal qualitative analysis, among them the use of the concept of "nothing," of painterly language and metaphors, of locative prepositions (e.g., "above"), and of descriptions of the literal atmosphere (air and vapor).

14

Atmosphere: Key to Lovecraft

From a literary perspective, the concept of atmosphere is a little slippery. Atmosphere is not narrative; it is a by-product of narrative. It is not description per se, character development, dialogue, or other elements of the story itself. It is a second-order phenomenon produced by prose style—word choice, syntax, and diction. Just as atmosphere is known only by its presence and cannot be defined on any primary dimension, the Colour is known only by its secondary effects. As such, it may be read as a metaphor for weird atmosphere—something we experience but only at arm's length. All we know of the Color is that something fell from the sky. That is the extent of the first-level effect. After the fall, the horror is known by its second-order effects, or epi-phenomena. These include trees that move in the night, strange mutations of vegetation, sapping of the life force out of all living things, and overall graying of the landscape.

In essays and letters, Lovecraft never tired of insisting on the supreme role of atmosphere in weird fiction. In "Supernatural Horror in Literature" he wrote:

> The true weird tale has . . . [a] certain atmosphere of breathless and unexplainable dread. . . . Atmosphere is the all-important thing, for the final criterion of authenticity is . . . the creation of a given sensation. . . . [T]he more completely and unifiedly a story conveys this atmosphere, the better it is as a work of art in the given medium. (28)

On another occasion he wrote specifically about the importance of atmosphere in his own work:

> I, for instance, have an absolute minimum of plot in the formal, academic sense, and depend almost entirely upon atmosphere. But in the end, atmosphere repays cultivation; because it is the final criterion of convincingness or unconvincingness in any tale whose major appeal is to the imagination. (*Letters to Wilfred B. Talman* 58)

Lovecraft's description of "The Colour out of Space" as an "atmospheric study" (*Dawnward Spire* 130) shows that he considered the item as distinctive relative to his other work, and that he spent even more than his usual extreme care with the style.

What Is Atmosphere?

Though Lovecraft advocated the importance of atmosphere in fiction, remarkably little critical work exists on the concept. So, it may be well to start with some basic premises.

In literary terms, atmosphere is sometimes considered to be defined as the narrative's setting and related elements including weather. We have the term for mood in the German word *stimmung*. William Empson, in *Seven Types of Ambiguity*, said that atmosphere might be defined as "[an] undifferentiated mode of being . . . [c]onveyed in some unknown and fundamental way as a byproduct of meaning." But Empson was not able to define atmosphere: "Analysis cannot hope to do anything but ignore it. . . . Criticism can only state that it is there" (17).

Literary atmosphere is sometimes thought to have become prominent in eighteenth-century England, where writers often remarked on the remarkably variable weather of the British Isles. As Samuel Johnson put it, "In our island Everyman goes to sleep, unable to guess whether he shall behold in the morning, a bright or cloudy atmosphere" (cited in Lewis 14). Philosophically, atmosphere acted as a corrective to the Enlightenment's conceptual emphasis on clarity and transparency. Gothic fiction is atmospheric because of its narrative focus on the weather, which it often actively specifies. Lightning, wind, rain, and mist are manifest as in no other genre. These effects postulate a kind of totalizing aesthetic environment. The "tinge" of the air is a painterly construct of landscape, from Poussin to Claude Lorrain to J. M. W. Turner, the first English painter who took the atmospheric effects as his primary subject. Atmosphere at once depicts and affects. It comprises certain narrative elements, yet at the same time evokes in the reader an emotional response that is experienced as secondary to ideation.

Perhaps the simplest statement we can make is that atmosphere is the dominant tone or mood of a work of art. What then is mood? Mood may be considered to denote the reader's internal reactions and emotions. By contrast, literary atmosphere is a characteristic, something that saturates the entire fabric of the work itself. Mood concerns itself with the feelings evoked in the reader, while atmosphere may be said to consist of the feelings that inhere in the work. The atmosphere of a tale calls forth a mood.

Elsewhere the word "atmosphere" is defined as a pervading influence, something with the ability to affect something else indirectly. A related concept in criticism is the tone of the work. Tone, usually evoked in art criticism, is defined in the dictionary not merely as the quality or shade of color, but also as the general quality, effect, or atmosphere of a work of art.

On the literary side, critic Edward Sapir remarked that

> [m]ost words, like practically all elements of consciousness, have an associated feeling-tone, a mild, yet none the less real and at times insidiously powerful, derivative of pleasure or pain. This feeling-tone, however, is not as a rule an inherent value in the word itself; it is rather a sentimental growth on the word's true body, on its conceptual kernel. . . . [It] varies remarkably from individual to individual, according to the personal association of each. (41)

One searches in vain, however, for a compelling definition of literary atmosphere. Thomas Ligotti, in *The Conspiracy against the Human Race*, comes closest: "It is the index of an identifiable consciousness that has been brewed from an amalgam of sensations, memories, emotions, and everything else that makes individuals what they are and predetermines what they will express as artists" (xxx).

Ligotti, a keen student of the weird genre in general and Lovecraft's work in particular, continues that in supernatural horror "[a]tmosphere is created by anything that suggests an ominous state of affairs beyond what our senses perceive, and our minds fully comprehend." He goes on to assay Ann Radcliffe's atmosphere of the sublime and Poe's atmosphere of personal doom, concluding that Lovecraftian atmosphere is keyed to the notion of "a world in which the 'frightful position' [. . . of] human existence could lead to universal madness or extinction."

Reading involves the experiencing of specific moods, which manifest themselves on a continuum. Language itself has the potential to create these moods. But to document them, it seems the best we can do is gesture in their general direction.

Lovecraftian atmosphere is a by-product of his intense attention to detail, mixing of factual information with fantastic imagination, psychological accuracy, the use of "local color," and so on. But style is the fabric of Lovecraft's approach to weird fiction; it creates the effects we perceive but do not observe when we read his stories, and the atmosphere to which we respond. Briefly, the traits characteristic of Lovecraft's style include Latinate vocabulary, various forms of parallelism, inverted syntax, alliteration (repetition of consonant sounds), and assonance (repetition of vowel sounds). Parallel structures are often used to delay the completion of grammatical structure (closure) of the sentences and create a sense of tension. Also important to Lovecraft's atmosphere is prosody—rhythm or cadence.

The Colour as an Emblem of Lovecraft's Concept of Atmosphere

We may read "The Colour out of Space" as a kind of parable, in that the central concept (the Colour) directly reflects Lovecraft's aesthetic of the weird. Atmosphere, as we have noted, is a second-tier phenomenon. It may be understood as a kind of synesthesia that takes effect as a result of a literary work's content. Atmosphere is an oblique affect that replicates the experience of a situation but is created with the essentially musical qualities of words, that is to say, rhythm, assonance, alliteration, and repetition.

Literary atmosphere, like the Colour, is an epiphenomenon. The cosmic entity in "The Colour out of Space" is never directly described. It is manifested as a by-product to the thing in itself. In this way, it is the same as literary atmosphere. The atmosphere of terror suffuses the story much as, in the context of weather, atmosphere suffuses the air. There is no physical monster. There is something that is inimical to man and all life on earth. It is known only by its manifestation.

Lovecraft hints at the existence of a real set of effects, which the sign "Colour" itself is intrinsically incapable of encapsulating. Similarly, atmosphere is the effect of Lovecraft's approach, which is an amalgam of multiple intangible elements that are impossible to articulate completely. For both, there is no diagram or explicit denotation of what causes the related effects.

What Is Colour?

Lovecraft's idea to make "colour" the protagonist of the story is perhaps his most brilliant literary stroke. The concept of color has its own complex and winding history of attempts to define it, both by artists and philosophers. Physicalists hold that colors are physical properties of surfaces. Eliminativists deny that anything is colored and that colors are merely subjective effects in perceivers.

Our sensory systems determine the kinds of experiences we can have, so colors are dependent upon us for their existence or nature. Neither objects nor lights are actually colored in anything like the way we experience them. Colors are sensational properties of experiences. Colors are not properties of objects because they are, in effect, in us. Color is an affective light on our nervous system. Colors are unreal; color experiences are real.

Lovecraft says that the Colour was like nothing anyone had ever seen. But to discover a new color, one would have to discover a new color system, that is, a system of relations among qualities like the one familiar to us. Only then could something be considered a different species of color.[1]

The Nothing That Is

As we have seen, the Colour does not manifest itself directly but makes itself known as a set of consequences. It is instructive to note some of these consequences. Lovecraft does not simply lay on the adjectives. Instead, he circles around the horror using some usual concepts. We may undertake a simple catalogue of some of them here.

Brilliantly, throughout the story Lovecraft makes something out of "nothing." The word appears like a refrain, 26 times over a total of about 12,300 words. Illustrations follow.

- It must, I thought as I viewed it, be the outcome of a fire; but why had *nothing* new ever grown[?] (369)
- It had acted quite unbelievably in that well-ordered laboratory; doing *nothing* at all . . . (372)
- It was *nothing* of this earth, but a piece of the great out-

---

1. For background on linguistic relativity and the color naming debate, see Biggam.

side; and as such dowered with outside properties and obedient to outside laws. (374)

- Six times within an hour the farmer saw the lightning strike the furrow in the front yard, and when the storm was over *nothing* remained . . . (374)
- That fragment lasted a week, at the end of which *nothing* of value had been learned of it. (374)
- Nahum ploughed and sowed the ten-acre pasture and the upland lot, but did *nothing* with the land around the house. (378)
- Something was taken away—she was being drained of something—something was fastening itself on her that ought not to be—someone must make it keep off— *nothing* was ever still in the night . . . (380)
- [Zenas] had come of late to do *nothing* but stare into space and obey what his father told him . . . (383)
- There could have been *nothing* from outside, for the small barred window and locked door were intact . . . (382).
- After that *nothing* would do but that they empty and explore the well immediately. (389)
- No doubt the meteor had poisoned the soil, but the illness of persons and animals who had eaten *nothing* grown in that soil was another matter. (390)
- Meanwhile I hope *nothing* will happen to Ammi. (399)

Lovecraft, who had a truly fiendish sense of humor, cannot refrain from using the work "nothing" in a different context during the ultimate horror, a compelling scene in which the narrator finds semiconscious Nahum Gardner collapsed in a heap of ashy remains.

> "What was it, Nahum—what was it?" he whispered, and the cleft, bulging lips were just able to crackle out a final answer.
> "*Nothin'* . . . *nothin'* . . ." (387)

Painterly Language

Throughout the story Lovecraft uses painterly language, nouns in conjunction with some unusual adjectives: "No sane wholesome colours were anywhere to be seen except in the green grass and leafage; but everywhere those *hectic* and prismatic variants of some diseased, underlying primary *tone* without a place among the known *tints* of earth" (378). In color theory, a *tint* is a mixture of a color with white, which reduces darkness (in contrast with a shade or a mixture with black, which increases darkness). A *tone* is produced either by mixing a color with grey, or by both tinting and shading. Hue is the term for the pure spectrum colors commonly referred to by the "color names"—red, orange, yellow, blue, green, violet—that appear in the hue circle or rainbow. Theoretically all hues can be mixed from three basic hues, known as primaries. In mixing colors hues can be desaturated (reduced in purity, weakened) in one of three ways: mix with white to lighten the value (*tint*), mix with black to darken the value (*shade*), or mix with gray or the complement to either lighten or darken the value (*tone*).

More startling is the use of the word "hectic": that is, marked by intense agitation, from the Middle English *etik* for recurring or consumptive activity. Of interest, too, are the other adjectives indicating a second order effect; for example, *prismatic* (exhibiting spectral colors formed by refraction of light). Elsewhere, similar adjectives that point elsewhere are used; e.g., *iridescent* (producing a display of lustrous, rainbow-like colors), *lustrous* (gleaming or glowing as with brilliant light), and *luminous* (emitting light).

Neither Here nor There

Heavily used in the story are prepositions of location: near/nearby (20), over (17), back (17), up (16), down (16), through (14), under (12), outside (11), around (11), next (10), against (9), upon (9), between (8), behind (8), inside (8), front (7), above (7), beside (6), and below (6). Representative examples include the following.

- There was too much silence in the dim alleys *between* [the trees]. (368)
- . . . [W]hy had nothing new ever grown *over* those five acres of grey desolation that sprawled open to the sky like a great spot eaten by acid in the woods and fields? (369)
- Nitric acid and even aqua regia merely hissed and spattered *against* its torrid invulnerability. (372–73)

- It was nothing of this earth, but a piece of the great *outside*; and as such dowered with *outside* properties and obedient to *outside* laws. (374)
- It left *behind* a hollow spherical space about three inches across. (374)
- He was prepared for almost anything now, and had grown used to the sense of something *near* him waiting to be heard. (378)
- Mrs. Gardner was the next to see it from the window as she watched the swollen boughs of a maple *against* a moonlit sky. (379)
- There was something of stolid resignation about them all, as if they walked half in another world *between* lines of nameless guards to a certain and familiar doom. (381)
- The way they screamed at each other from *behind* their locked doors was very terrible . . . (381–82)

The figurative senses of these prepositions are extended from their spatial denotations into conceptual metaphors. This unique use of locative prepositions is another refutation of the many who have accused Lovecraft of mechanically piling on adjectives to create atmosphere.

Air Apparent

Critic Arden Reed speaks of being in the weather as being adrift in a system of signs that are "unstable, unpredictable, indeterminate," indicative of "something evermore about to be" (cited in Lewis 18). Lovecraft also shows us the Colour in the form of its effects upon the very firmament: "Certainly, however, restlessness was in the air" (377). Restlessness is the quality of being ceaselessly active, here relative to the transparent sky. But soon after:

> Upon everything was a haze of restlessness and oppression; a touch of the unreal and the grotesque, as if some vital element of perspective or chiaroscuro were awry. (369)

Oppression, by way of contrast with *restlessness*, is the state of being immobilized. *Both states are in effect at the same time.* The word "chiaroscuro" contains a similar paradox, literally "light-dark." The Color affects how the contrasts of light convey a sense of volume upon the visual modeling of three-dimensional objects (trees). But it is not only the air that is restless, as the Colour causes not only the trees to move by themselves, but also the progressive impairment of the younger son of the family whose "*restlessness* was worse after the shutting away of the brother who had been his greatest playmate" (382; my emphasis).

The air around us is invisible but becomes the medium in which the Colour manifests. Examples of the 14 uses of the word "air" include:

- Then there had come that white noontide cloud, that string of explosions *in the air*. . . (371)
- The poor woman screamed about things *in the air* which she could not describe. (380)
- Is it fastened to the roots of those trees that claw *the air?* (399)

Vapor is a visible diffused substance floating in the atmosphere and impairing its transparency, as smoke, fog, gas, etc.[2] The seven occurrences include:

- As I walked hurriedly by I saw the tumbled bricks and stones of an old chimney and cellar on my right, and the yawning black maw of an abandoned well whose stagnant *vapours* played strange tricks with the hues of the sunlight. (369)
- While he screamed he thought a momentary cloud eclipsed the window, and a second later he felt himself brushed as if by some hateful current of *vapour*. (385)
- He even thought a scream had been suddenly choked off, and recalled nervously the clammy *vapour* which had brushed by him in that frightful room above. (386)
- It had flashed there a second, and a clammy and hateful current of *vapour* had brushed past him—and then poor

---

2. The word "gas" is probably derived from Greek *khaos* (i.e., chaos; an abyss, that which gapes wide open, that which is vast and empty). The sound of Dutch "g" is roughly equivalent to that of Greek letter chi ("kh"). The word was first used in the 1650s by Flemish chemist J. B. van Helmont, who speculated about a third state aside from liquid and solid; intending to say "chaos," he was understood as saying "gas."

Nahum had been taken by something of that colour. (391)

- He could not but wonder at his gleaning of the same impression from a *vapour* glimpsed in the daytime, against a window opening on the morning sky, and from a nocturnal exhalation seen as a phosphorescent mist against the black and blasted landscape. (391)

- Ammi had restrained the driver on impulse, forgetting how uninjured he himself was after the clammy brushing of that coloured *vapour* in the attic room, but perhaps it is just as well that he acted as he did. (392)

- Through quickly re-closing *vapours* they followed the great morbidity that had vanished, and in another second they had vanished too. (396)

The All-Important Thing

While at first "The Colour out of Space" seems to deflect critical analysis from its highly polished surface, persistent close reading progressively reveals its tremendous depth of artistry. First and foremost is the employment of a simple but multivalent concept—"Colour"—as its motivating phenomenon. Here Lovecraft has hit upon something that not merely makes for an effective source of terror, but also may be read as a metaphor for literary atmosphere itself, what he deemed the "all-important thing" in a weird tale. Corollary to this are the specific tropes Lovecraft employed, directly and indirectly, to show the second-order phenomena indicating the Colour's essence. There is a rich set of word-play centering on relative location and movement. Ultimately the reader is, like the protagonists, confronted with (to paraphrase poet Wallace Stevens) "the nothing that is not there, and the nothing that is."

Works Cited

Biggam, C. P. *The Semantics of Colour: A Historical Approach.* Cambridge: Cambridge University Press, 2012.

Empson, William. *Seven Types of Ambiguity.* New York: New Directions, 1966.

Gumbrecht, Hans Ulrich. *Atmosphere, Mood, Stimmung: On a Hidden Potential of Literature*. Tr. Erik Butler. Stanford: Stanford University Press, 2012.

Lewis, Jayne Elizabeth. *Air's Appearance: Literary Atmosphere in British Fiction, 1660–1794*. Chicago: University of Chicago Press, 2012.

Lovecraft, H. P. *Letters to Wilfred B. Talman and Helen V. and Genevieve Sully*. Ed. David E. Schultz and S. T. Joshi. New York: Hippocampus Press, 2019.

———, and Clark Ashton Smith. *Dawnward Spire, Lonely Hill: The Letters of H. P. Lovecraft and Clark Ashton Smith*. Ed. David E. Schultz and S. T. Joshi. New York: Hippocampus Press, 2017.

Ligotti, Thomas. *The Conspiracy against the Human Race: A Contrivance of Horror*. 2010. New York: Penguin, 2018.

Noe, Alva. *Action in Perception*. Cambridge, MA: MIT Press, 2004.

Pitkin, Walter B. *The Art and the Business of Story Writing*. New York: Macmillan, 1912.

Sapir, Edward. *Language*. Cambridge, MA: Cambridge University Press, 2014.

Uzzell, Thomas H. *Narrative Technique: A Practical Course in Literary Psychology*. New York: Harcourt Brace, 1923.

H. P. Lovecraft's
First Appearance in Print

Richard Bleiler

In a 1916 letter to Rheinhart Kleiner, H. P. Lovecraft stated that ten years earlier, in 1906, "a 'letter to the editor' in the *Prov. Sunday Journal* of 3 June, was my debut before the public" (*SL* 1.40), apparently unaware that his name had appeared in print nearly nine months earlier, on 6 September 1905. This article discusses first the national contest that motivated Lovecraft to write his letter, establishing an historical context for Lovecraft's participation. It then presents and discusses Lovecraft's letter, for although this survives only in fragmentary form, what exists is an unusual and intriguing document in its own right. It offers insight into Lovecraft's adolescent life, particularly his scientific awareness and his knowledge of meteorology; and because it contains strange—counterfactual, even—statements, a reasonable argument may be made that the letter can be considered as a harbinger of Lovecraft's fictional career.

The national contest began as the brainchild and responsibility of Frederick R. Fast, a lawyer in New York City, who was obsessed with predicting the weather. As contemporary news articles revealed, Fast was obviously wealthy, and starting on 25 August 1905, he began to send what eventually became hundreds of letters to newspapers around the United States offering a $100 prize to the person who could most accurately predict the weather for the one month period that concluded on the 15th of November. Although a $100 prize seems miniscule by today's standards, its relative inflated worth today is more than $3,000.00,[1] but this gives no indication of the relative value of

---

1. www.measuringworth.com/dollarvaluetoday/?amount=100&from=1905 (ac-

the dollar. In the New York City of 1905, a sale on 25 × 125 building lots in Long Island meant one could be had for prices starting at $25.00 ("Special Sale"), and the 1000-page *Students New Century Dictionary* could be had for 85¢ ("New York's Greatest Sale"). Closer to Lovecraft, in Pawtucket, a cord of trash wood could be had for $1, and a cord of hardwood cost $5 ("10 bbls."). In 1905, then, a prize of $100 was a significant incentive.

Fast's letters began appearing in Eastern newspapers on 26 August under various headlines; that published in the *Boston Daily Globe* had the headline "Weather Sharps' Chance. Prize of $100 Offered by New York Man, Who Says Government Method Is Faulty":

> Convinced that the forecasting department of the U.S. weather bureau [*sic*] is sadly defective, and wishing to arouse the interest of amateur weather sharps, F. R. Fast, a lawyer of 97 Nassau St, has offered a cash prize of $100 for the one who proves most correct in predicting the weather during the period commencing at midnight Oct 15 and ending at midnight Nov 15.
>
> "For the past 25 years I have made a close study of weather reports, especially those given by the U.S. weather bureau," said Mr. Fast today. "As a result, I find that not more than 47 percent of these reports are correct. It may surprise the public to learn that the rising young prophets from the small towns throughout the country are even more successful in their prediction than the government forecasters.
>
> "This state of affairs seems strange in view of the fact that the government spends annually some millions of dollars in trying to obtain a correct forecast. That is why I am offering a prize to the amateur prophet.
>
> "Of course, I make the stipulation that he must tell just how he came by his calculations."

Over the next week, Fast sent numerous letters to other newspapers, and many appeared with editorial commentary appended. The appearance in the *Boston Journal* of 28 August

cessed 8 April 2020). The site explains that today $100 from 1905 has a relative income worth of $14,338.17, $25,121.79, or $19,035.93, and that today $100 from 1905 has a relative project worth of $74,757.88.

1905 thus had the headline "Guessers Cast Down," and Fast's offer was almost lost, buried in the commentary:

> There is something heroic, and at the same time almost pathetic, in this $100 offer of the New York lawyer, F. R. Fast, to the person who proves most correct in predicting the weather during the period commencing at midnight Oct. 15 and ending at midnight Nov. 15. Heroic, because he ventures to set himself up against a gigantic governmental monopoly, and pathetic because he has lost faith in our official weather sharps. "For the past twenty-five years," he says, "I have made a close study of weather reports, especially those given by the United States Weather Bureau. As a result I find that not more than 47 per cent. of these reports are correct." Certainly a most unsatisfactory state of affairs for gentlemen who have planned to go on picnics, or ladies with new hats to wear.
>
> In our mind's eye, we see all the weather prophets of all the small towns in New England preparing their schedules of things to be expected from Oct. 15 to Nov. 15. A sheet of paper, a few drops of ink, a lively imagination and $100 is as good as won. But stay: here is a damper cast over the glowing enthusiasm of the amateur forecasts. "Of course, I make the stipulation that he must tell just how he came by his calculations," declares Lawyer Fast. Guessers, then, appear to be out of it, unless they can guess how they came to guess right. Some Maine Yankees are shrewd enough even for that.

Fast's challenge was similarly picked up by the *New York Tribune* and printed as one of the letters to the editor, the editor's bracketed last words being longer than the letter itself:

> As an amateur farmer, I am interested in the weather. I have gathered meteorological data for years, but as yet have not found the slightest basis in which to ascertain the state of the weather even twelve hours ahead.
>
> The government weather predictions are very faulty; and as many laymen claim they can predict the weather more accurately than the Weather Bureau, without any of the elaborate apparatus of the government, I hereby appeal to all the weather prophets of this country to enter a thirty day contest for a cash prize of $100, which I will give to whoever predicts the weather

most accurately and will tell for the benefit of the public by what methods he arrived at his conclusions. If The Tribune will kindly publish this and aid in advancing the science of meteorology, I will be grateful.

[Probably no one is more alert to the deficiencies of the present system of government forecasting than the officials who conduct that work. Moreover, those who hold the most responsible posts in the Weather Bureau at Washington believe that the basis will yet be found for improving the service. Now, it is tolerably safe to say that trained scientists are much more likely than amateurs to make the discoveries which will render progress possible. Again, if any really valuable clew has been found by an amateur, it is doubtful whether he would sell the information to rivals for $100. An offer like Mr. Fast's is hardly likely to evoke a response from those best qualified to compete. Finally, to do the most good, a competition of this sort should be conducted under the auspices of a board of trade, a chamber of commerce, or a government bureau, not under those of a private individual.] ("Letters to the Editor")

Finally, the version of the letter that appeared in the *Dallas Morning News* gave some evidence of the methodology Fast would use in his assessment of the entries:

From Smith of Roaring Run, VA., to Bronson of the Upper Saguenay, Thompson, the trapper of Winnipeg; Devoe of Hackensack and Rodriguez, the hermit of Berkley, Cal., [sic] the weather wise six hundred are at last to come into their own. For a prize of $100 they will match their systems, or whatever it may be that they depend upon for their predictions. F. R. Fast, a lawyer at No. 99 Nassau street [sic], has put up the money and the National Government will indirectly determine the winner.

They may scorn anything more scientific than a rooster's crow, their pet corn may be the source of their confidence, the deep burrowing of the humble angleworm may be their dependence, or less acute they may predict storm or calm—it is all the same to Mr. Fast, and to the gaining of the prize.

To all the sharps he could hear of, and they number at least six hundred, he has written, setting forth the terms of the contest and inviting them to compete, as there is no expense involved except a trifle of postage, all are expected to participate.

From Oct. 15 to Nov. 15 will be the period of the test. The sharps must send their forecasts daily to Mr. Faust [*sic*] for the succeeding twenty-four hours, or for several days in advance if they have confidence to warrant it. The predictions will be carefully tabulated, and at the end of the month will be compared with the weather as officially recorded by the Government Weather Bureau.

"I am something of an amateur farmer," said Mr. Fast yesterday, "and have become greatly interested in meteorology. An old farmer can tell you correctly whether there will be sun or rain the next day. I want to find out now what the system of the outside sharps [*sic*] is, if they have any.

"With most of them, I admit it seems to be only instinct. A grizzled farmer will roll his quid to the other side of his mouth, peer at the clouds and sniff the air; maybe he'll rub his knee or rheumatic elbow; then he'll hem and haw a bit and 'reckon we'll have a storm purty close.' But a good many of the sharps have regular systems and the contest will be as profitable as well as interesting. ("Weather Prophet Contest")

In early December 1905, the winner of Fast's contest was announced. The announcing article revealed that more than a thousand people, from every state, had entered the contest, and it had taken "seven clerks six weeks to tabulate the 63,000 facts that had to be considered" ("Weather-Wise Winner").[2] The winner was a traveling salesman from Chicago, Charles S. Fredricks (or Fredericks), who used a barometer, a thermometer, and the phases of the moon to make his predictions. The contest thus having been concluded, the unsuccessful contestants resumed their lives. Nothing appears to have been written about it or Mr. Fredricks/Fredericks, and no comments have been noted about the odd coincidence of the names of the contest's sponsor (Frederick R.) and its winner (S. Fredrick/Frederick).

As the letters reproduced above indicate, Mr. Fast's contest was announced in many sources, the different newspapers choosing to emphasize and report on different aspects of the

---

2. What data were tabulated and how they were assessed are never revealed.

contest.[3] The announcement in the *Amsterdam* [NY] *Evening Recorder and Daily Democrat* thus stated that "six hundred amateur weather prophets" were competing for Fast's prize, and near the conclusion of the article appears the following:

> H. P. Lovecraft, who says he forecasts for Rhode Island, writes to say that he thinks his predictions will reach over into New York and New England.
>
> "It may interest you to know," he writes, "that I have one mercurial thermometer by Spooner, six maximum and minimum thermomemeters [*sic*] by Casella, one psychometrical apparatus, one rain, one hair hygrometer and a wind vane." He spells the name of the thermometer a syllable longer than usual to indicate a superior length of column. ("Long Distance Predictions")

There is significantly more to Lovecraft's response than initially meets the eye, however, and his seemingly informed and technically cognizant catalogue of his possessions is, in fact, ultimately puzzling.

First, there are the unanswerable questions of how Lovecraft learned about the *Amsterdam Evening Recorder and Daily Democrat* and why he chose to write to that newspaper as opposed to some of the more local newspapers he was more likely to have encountered. In the case of the former question, it is reasonable to assume that Lovecraft encountered the newspaper either through the Providence Athenaeum or from somebody in his vicinity having a personal subscription; it is also possible though less likely that a local newsstand carried it. As for the latter question, there is no reason to assume that he wrote only one response, and it is quite possible that Lovecraft did write to the Providence and Boston newspapers but, perhaps for space reasons, they chose not to run his letters.

Lovecraft's letter to the *Amsterdam Evening Recorder and Daily Democrat* begins strongly and factually. Edwin C. Spooner was a nineteenth-century Boston manufacturer of thermometers and barometers who may have been best known for manufacturing

---

3. It is of course possible that the announcements of the contest varied, but if Mr. Fast could employ seven clerks for six weeks, there is every reason to assume that he could afford secretaries and typists who would generate the same letter.

and selling the "Storm King" stick barometer/thermometer, "a
long glass tube holding mercury, with a scale displayed on the
upper portion of the body next to the tube."[4] Various Spooner
thermometers appear to have been widely used and available
during the nineteenth century, and it is quite conceivable that
one was in use in the house lived in by the young Lovecraft.

The Miller-Casella Thermometer, a U-shaped device, was
likewise recognized and well-known for its ability to record temperature extremes. The latter were used by scientists and explorers and figured prominently in scientific exploration; anybody
possessing six of them would be by default a well-funded and serious researcher, and it is most doubtful that young Lovecraft was
such a researcher. It is possible that he learned of their existence
from Dr. Franklin Chase Clark, who had married Lovecraft's
aunt, or Edward Gamwell, his other uncle-in-law. The former, it
will be remembered, was fondly described by Lovecraft as "a
man of vast learning—a graduate of Brown, Harvard Medical
School, & Columbia College, bearing the degree of A. M. besides his ordinary A. B. and professional M.D. He was the author of medical treatises, & an authority of medical ethics . . . ,"
while the latter "was a Cambridge man . . . He had taught me to
rattle off the Greek alphabet when I was six years old . . . [and]
stimulated my editorial tendencies to such an extent that I
founded the *Rhode Island Journal of Astronomy,* to replace the
almost defunct *Scientific Gazette*" (SL 1.38–39). Nevertheless, if
Lovecraft did not learn of the Miller-Casella thermometer from
these men, it is not inconceivable that he encountered the device in such articles as Arthur P. Crouch's "The World beneath
the Ocean" (1897), which states, for example:

In medium depths, owing to the fact that in the sea the coldest water is always at the bottom, an ordinary maximum and

4. www.nps.gov/long/blogs/storm-king-barometer.htm. "Hanging in the central
hallway of the Longfellow House, just outside of Henry Wadsworth Longfellow's study, is this barometer. Probably manufactured in the late nineteenth
century, the barometer is listed in the 1912 inventory of the house's furnishings
as "1 Old 'Storm King' barometer and Thermometer in walnut case."
www.nps.gov/ long/blogs/Storm-King-Barometer.htm. Accessed 16 January 2017.

minimum thermometer will serve the purpose [of measuring temperatures]; but in deep water, where the pressure causes an error of 8° to 10°, and sometimes even bursts the thermometer, a Miller Casella instrument is the best.

It is also possible that Lovecraft encountered Miller-Casella thermometers in a current monograph such as Hugh R. Mill's *The Siege of the South Pole*, which although nominally published in October 1905 was listed as available in September 1905.[5] Not only was this a popular publication, written in an accessible style, its lists of illustrations concludes with two references to the Miller-Casella thermometer: anybody browsing the book would have noticed them. It cannot be proved that Lovecraft was among those browsing the book, of course, but as Joshi and Schultz note in *An H. P. Lovecraft Encyclopedia*, Lovecraft had "a fascination with Antarctica" that culminated in his writing the (now lost) "*Antarctic Atlas: Voyages of Captain Ross, R.N. and Wilkes's Explorations*" (134). Had the adolescent Lovecraft encountered *The Siege of the South Pole* in the Providence Athenaeum and/or bookstores available to him, it would be most improbable for him *not* to have at least examined the volume.

Next, a hair hygrometer used human hair to measure the moisture in the air, and a wind vane (sometimes called a weather vane) needs no explanation. Lovecraft could have learned of them from any number of sources.

The problematic in Lovecraft's list of devices at his disposal is the so-called "psychometrical apparatus." *Psychometry* is the "practice of obtaining information about an object's history, or about people or events with which it has been associated, purely by touching it or through close proximity to it" ("Psychometry"). It was a term predominantly used by spiritualists, and a psychometrical apparatus would presumably be a device that provides information about the people or events with which it was associated. The term, however, was virtually unused in the nineteenth and early twentieth centuries, and but one pre-twentieth century usage has been located, in a translated article by M. Lombard

---

5. The book was listed as available in the *Bookseller, Newsdealer and Stationer* (15 September 1905): 233.

published in the 10 August 1895 issue of *Literary Digest* that was almost certainly unknown to Lovecraft:

> This new orientation of psychology necessitates, as it may be seen without difficulty, a whole system of instruments appropriate to the researches that are to be carried out. If we go to the Pennsylvania State College, for instances, we shall see a curious psychometrical apparatus, a well-balanced wheel a yard in diameter, turning with a speed capable of exact measurement behind an opening whose size may be altered at will; this may serve for the mixture and contrast of colors, for the determination of time necessary to read words or phrases, and for other similar experiments. ("Laboratory Study" 434)

It would seem, then, that no scientific weather forecaster from 1905 would know of or could use a psychometrical apparatus—but somebody making fun of the idea of scientific weather forecasting might create the term as an impressive sounding neologism. If so, there is a sense of adolescent play emergent from this letter, its writer creating a seemingly professional persona, bolstering its existence with a list of seemingly technical references, and at the same time slipping something completely inappropriate into this list to show that he was not being serious and, possibly, that he considered weather-forecasting to be little more than an exercise in superstition.

Questions of content and play aside, one should ask why Lovecraft bothered to write the letter and what were his original claims. As stated above, the letter indicates a sense of adolescent play, but what else did he claim that was omitted upon newspaper publication? The anonymous writer of the article states that Lovecraft "forecasts for Rhode Island." This appears to allude to the fact that Lovecraft, who had already exhibited an interest in meteorology at this time, was indeed making his own weather forecasts. One of his juvenile periodicals, the *Scientific Gazette,* announced the establishment of a "Climatological Station" that "belongs to the publishers [*sic*] of this paper"; it had "6 circular windows with shutters, in case of severe storm. The instruments have not all arrived yet . . . Although the station is not, as yet, fully equipped, it *can* do much practice-work, for the storm glass is very accurate, and the wet-bulb thermometer, which was made by the observer works to perfection" (issue of 24 January 1904). The *Rhode Island Journal of Astronomy*, another of his juvenile periodicals, actually takes note of the Fast contest, adding that his own forecasts "have been right 1/3 more times than the local weather station since October [1904?]" (issue of 3 September 1905; quoted in *IAP* 104).

Next, Lovecraft's sensitivity to cold is well documented. It can reasonably be asserted that the awareness of thermometers is connected to the young Lovecraft's growing awareness of his hypersensitivity. A person who is indifferent to changes in weather is not going to be overly concerned about temperatures.

Finally, if as is likely, Lovecraft shared the letter with his friends and family, what was the reception? It would seem reasonable that Lovecraft was delighted with his youthful jest, but it is not inconceivable that the publication of a deliberate deception caused some distress to his family, however innocent, amusing, or inconsequential the deception. It may be significant that Lovecraft appears never to have made mention of this letter and does not appear to have kept a copy among his possessions, and any interest he had in weather prognostication appears to have largely terminated with this letter, replaced soon thereafter by his better-known and documented interest in astronomy. It is also greatly regretted that only above fragment can be found and that the complete and original letter does not appear to survive.

Works Cited

Crouch, Archer P. "The World beneath the Ocean." *Eclectic Magazine of Foreign Literature, Science and Art* 65 (January 1897): 22.

"Guessers Cast Down." *Boston Journal* (28 August 1905): 6.

Joshi, S. T., and David E. Schultz. *An H. P. Lovecraft Encyclopedia*. Westport, CT: Greenwood Press, 2001.

"Laboratory Study of the Human Mind." *Literary Digest* 11 (10 August 1895): 434.

"Letters to the Editor. Prize for Weather Prediction." *New York Tribune* (2 September 1905): 6.

"Long Distance Predictions. Weather Guessers Willing to Take
    Any Sort of Chances and Trust to Providence." *Amsterdam
    Evening Recorder and Daily Democrat* (6 September 1905).
    Available at: https://fultonhistory.com/.

Mill, Hugh R. *The Siege of the South Pole*. New York: Frederick
    A. Stokes Co., 1905.

"New York's Greatest Sale of School Supplies." *New York Times*
    (30 August 1905): 5.

"Psychometry, n." *Oxford English Dictionary Online*. Accessed 8
    April 2020.

"Special Sale of Building Lots, 25 × 125, at Lakewood Park."
    New York Times (31 August 1905): 12.

"10 bbls. Wood $1.00." *Pawtucket Times* (15 August 1905): 9.

"Weather Prophet Contest. New York Lawyer Offers Prize for
    System Showing Figures Nearest Correct." *Dallas Morning
    News* (3 September 1905): 18.

"Weather Sharps' Chance. Prize of $100 Offered by New York
    Man, Who Says Government Method Is Faulty." *Boston Dai-
    ly Globe* (26 August 1905): 1.

"Weather-Wise Winner. 'For He Can Prophesy with a Wink of
    His Eye.'" *Kansas City Star* (7 December 1905): 8.

Missing the Punchline: The Subversive Nature of H. P. Lovecraft's Occult Detective

Dylan Henderson

More than seventy-five years after H. P. Lovecraft's death in 1937, his weird fiction, some of which is overtly racist, continues to polarize scholars, but if they agree on anything, it is that "The Horror at Red Hook," a short story Lovecraft wrote during the brief period he lived in New York City, constitutes one of his worst works. In his biography, S. T. Joshi, the preeminent Lovecraft scholar, describes the story as "nothing but a shriek of rage and loathing at the 'foreigners' who have taken New York away from the white people to whom it presumably belongs" (*IAP* 589). Elsewhere, Joshi labels it "one of Lovecraft's great failures," summarizing the story as "a tired rehash of hackneyed demonology and a viciously racist story that transmogrifies the immigrants of the area into the members of an evil cult on the underside of American civilization" (*A Subtler Magick* 104). Jason Eckhardt, echoing Joshi, writes that the story "is mostly a shriek of rage at New York's immigrants and modern, bustling character, and its horrors are textbook demons" (91). Donald Tyson concurs, noting in his Lovecraft biography that "it is never ranked among his best work—there is too much venom in it" (142). As Tyson points out, few scholars, if any, consider the story one of Lovecraft's best, nor should they, but as fundamental as racism and xenophobia are to the story's plot, other aspects of the tale, unrelated to its ethnocentrism, deserve analysis. By focusing solely on the story's racist content, scholars have overlooked the subtle ways in which "The Horror at Red Hook" parodies the subgenre of the occult detective, subverting its conventions so that they reflect the cosmic philosophy Love-craft explores in his later works.

The Occult Detective

By 1925, the year Lovecraft wrote "The Horror at Red Hook," the subgenre had ossified, its conventions unchanged since Lovecraft's literary idol, Edgar Allan Poe, established them in 1841. In that year, Poe's short story "The Murders in the Rue Morgue" introduced readers to the fictional detective, C. Auguste Dupin, thus launching the mystery genre and establishing the basic template that later writers would use for their occult detectives. A brilliant but eccentric layman, Dupin possesses a "peculiar analytic ability," which enables him to assess others as easily as if they "wore windows in their bosoms" and thus uncover truths unknown to the casual observer (Poe 401). In the opening pages of the story, he demonstrates this ability by reading the narrator's mind, tracing a Byzantine line of thought triggered by a collision with a fruit vendor. Dupin reasons, correctly as it turns out, that "the larger links of the chain run thus—Chantilly, Orion, Dr. Nichols, Epicurus, Stereotomy, the street stones, the fruiterer" (403). Dupin then applies the same method to a local mystery, a brutal murder which has baffled the police. He does so, not by investigating the crime, but by reconciling the following facts: a mother and daughter were brutally murdered, but not robbed; witnesses overheard someone speaking in a foreign language though they disagree on what that language was; and the murderer did not gain access to the apartment through the door, which was locked from the inside. Realizing that a human being could not have committed the crime, Dupin pins the murders on an orangutan, which had escaped from its owner and entered the apartment through an open window. Modern readers, familiar with the conventions of the detective genre, may find the story unexceptional, but when it first appeared in *Graham's Magazine* its novelty delighted readers and reinforced Poe's image as a "man of genius" (Silverman 173–74). Seeking, perhaps, to capitalize on this success, Poe wrote two more stories involving Dupin: "The Mystery of Marie Rogêt" and "The Purloined Letter," neither of which depart radically from the formula established in "The Murders in the Rue Morgue."

As entertaining as Dupin's process is, Poe's stories of "ratiocination" are noteworthy, not for their elegant solutions, but for the influence they would have on later writers, particularly Lovecraft's boyhood hero, Sir Arthur Conan Doyle.[1] Indeed, the tales of Sherlock Holmes, beginning with *A Study in Scarlet* in 1887, almost mirror those of Dupin. Just as Dr. John Watson narrates the adventures of Holmes, an unnamed narrator serves in an analogous role in Poe's stories, presenting the facts needed to solve the mystery, marveling at Dupin's cleverness, and acting always as an observer rather than a participant. Like Watson, Poe's narrator can explain his friend's process, but because he can never duplicate it, he remains every bit as baffled as the reader until the denouement. As for Holmes and Dupin, the two detectives share an almost supernatural intelligence, capable of deducing, as Dupin does, someone's inner thoughts or erecting theories, which inevitably prove correct, on the scantiest evidence. When Holmes and Watson meet for the first time, for instance, Holmes immediately deduces, apropos of nothing, that Watson has recently visited Afghanistan. Like Dupin, Holmes arrives at this conclusion by reconciling his observations:

> Here is a gentleman of a medical type, but with the air of a military man. Clearly an army doctor, then. He has just come from the tropics, for his face is dark, and that is not the natural tint of his skin, for his wrists are fair. He has undergone hardship and sickness, as his haggard face says clearly. His left arm has been injured. He holds it in a stiff and unnatural manner. Where in the tropics could an English army doctor have seen much hardship and got his arm wounded? Clearly in Afghanistan. (Doyle 24)

The entire exchange, including Watson's amazed reaction, so closely resembles the opening pages of "The Murders in the Rue Morgue" that Doyle himself, through his narrator, calls atten-

---

1. In a letter written to Alfred Galpin in 1918, HPL claimed that as a child he had been "infatuated" with Sherlock Holmes, having read "every Sherlock Holmes story published" (*Letters to Alfred Galpin and Others* 191).

tion to the similarities, blurting out: "you remind me of Edgar
Allan Poe's Dupin" (24). And yet, the two detectives share
more than their methods; they share personality traits as well.

Both are reclusive, eccentric, and cerebral, and despite their
interest in crime, neither work for the police. Indeed, both men
view crime, not with moral indignation, but with excitement,
recognizing, in the words of Dupin, that "an inquiry will afford
us amusement" (Poe 412). In a sense, the greatest difference between the two is the frequency with which they appear in literature: while Poe wrote only three "tales of ratiocination," Doyle
wrote four novels featuring Holmes and five collections of short
stories, the last appearing in print forty years after A *Study in
Scarlet* was published.

Although Poe deserves credit for founding the detective genre and Doyle for popularizing it, two Anglo-Irish writers, J. Sheridan Le Fanu and Bram Stoker, also contributed to it, creating
in the process the first occult detective while simultaneously retaining most of the conventions Poe established. As the title indicates, the occult detective differs from Dupin and Holmes in
that he or she investigates supernatural phenomena or, at the
very least, phenomena that appear to be supernatural. The first
actually predates Holmes, appearing in 1869 in Le Fanu's novella "Green Tea," which Lovecraft considered "better than anything else of Le Fanu's that I have ever seen" (*Dawnward Spire*
342). He is Dr. Hesselius, a medical doctor who, in the course of
his duties as a physician, sometimes encounters inexplicable
phenomena. Unlike Dupin, or Holmes for that matter, Hesselius
is considerably older than the "young enthusiast" who prefaces
his adventures (Le Fanu 5). Wise, elderly, wealthy, and comparatively sedate, he lacks the eccentricities that imbue Dupin and
Holmes with vitality, and in most of the stories in which he appears, he plays a negligible role, existing, not so much as an active participant, but as a commentator on other people's stories.

And yet, Hesselius undoubtedly served as the inspiration for
literature's most famous occult detective, Professor Abraham
Van Helsing of *Dracula* (1897). Both are elderly doctors, and unlike Dupin and Holmes, they solve cases, not with deduction, but
with the aid of occult knowledge. In "Green Tea," for instance,

Hesselius deduces, much as Dupin or Holmes might, that Mr. Jennings, a man he has just met, drinks a lot of green tea, but he does not rely on this method to solve the man's dilemma. No, to do that, he applies his abstruse knowledge of medicine, physiology, and metaphysics, which leads him to believe that Mr. Jennings's delusions are caused by an "inner eye which Mr. Jennings had inadvertently opened" (39). In much the same way, Van Helsing applies his knowledge of "witch and demon cures," which he gleans from the British Museum, to defeat Count Dracula (Stoker 280). Reflecting, perhaps, the rising popularity of Spiritualism, both Le Fanu and Stoker frequently incorporate occult terminology, rituals, symbols, and even philosophy into their works. Hesselius, for instance, quotes from the Swedish mystic Emanuel Swedenborg at length while Van Helsing, keen to prove that "some people see things that others cannot," teases his colleague John Seward about his materialism: "I suppose now you do not believe in corporeal transference. No? Nor in materialisation. No? Nor in astral bodies. No? Nor in the reading of thought. No?" (Stoker 197). This incorporation of occult subject matter constitutes a major innovation, separating the subgenre of the occult detective from its progenitor, but for a materialist like Lovecraft, it also rendered the subgenre fit for satire. To make matters worse, the popularity of Doyle and Stoker's creations, and the number of imitators they engendered, almost guaranteed that the subgenre would decay into banality.

Talented weird writers, including two Englishmen Lovecraft considered masters of the art, continued to dabble in the subgenre, each one creating his own occult detective according to the template created by Poe, popularized by Doyle, and adapted to horror by Le Fanu and Stoker. In his essay "Supernatural Horror in Literature," Lovecraft rhapsodizes over Arthur Machen, the first of these practitioners, claiming that "of living creators of cosmic fear raised to its most artistic pitch, few if any can hope to equal the versatile Arthur Machen" (81). Indeed, Machen is one of only four writers, the others being Algernon Blackwood, M. R. James, and Lord Dunsany, Lovecraft deems a "modern master" (80–96). Though Machen created only one occult detective, who appears in a single book, the subgenre suited him, for Machen, unlike Lovecraft, considered himself a mystic, a devout Catholic whose "whole work is inspired by one idea and one only: the awesome and utterly unfathomable mystery of the universe" (Joshi, *Weird Tale* 13). His sole occult detective, Mr. Dyson, witnesses these mysteries or "transmutations" in Machen's episodic novel *The Three Impostors* (1895). Like Hesselius in Le Fanu's collection *In a Glass Darkly*, Dyson exists not so much as a character or protagonist, but as a framing device: he and his antithesis, Charles Phillipps, listen to a series of tales, falsehoods really, told by three villains who are trying to garner information about a "young man with spectacles." Unlike Hesselius, however, Dyson makes no attempt to solve or explain the mysteries he uncovers: "not that I shall need to seek; rather adventure will seek me; I shall be like a spider in the midst of his web, responsive to every movement, and ever on the alert" (Machen 111). Investigation, in other words, will bring him nothing: by simply accepting, as Phillips does not, the possibility of the miraculous, Dyson immerses himself in the mysteries that are continually forming and unraveling all around him. To probe further, as other occult detectives do, would actually undermine Machen's goal "to restore the sense of wonder and mystery into our perception of the world" (Joshi, *Weird Tale* 16).

Algernon Blackwood, Lovecraft's second "modern master" and Machen's fellow mystic, incorporated his own beliefs into the tales of John Silence, a "psychic doctor" who, despite his belief in supernatural phenomena, closely resembles Dupin and Holmes. Unlike Dyson, however, Silence actively investigates psychic phenomena, often employing occult methods in the process. In "A Psychical Invasion," for instance, Silence spends the night in a haunted house accompanied by Smoke and Flame, a cat and dog who prove, as Silence had predicted, able to detect an "intensely active Force" that Silence cannot see (Blackwood 32). Once alerted to its presence, Silence confronts the ghostly force in a battle of wills, ultimately calling upon "the spiritual alchemy that can transmute evil forces by raising them into higher channels" (40). As active as Silence is in that tale, in others, he retreats into the background, oscillating, so to speak, between being an active combatant, much like Van Helsing, and being a passive observer, a framing device for a series of otherwise disjointed weird tales. In "Ancient Sorceries," for instance, Silence appears only at the beginning and at the end of the tale, the bulk of the story being the account of one of Silence's clients, a tourist named Arthur Vezin.

At first glance, the occult terminology Silence employs differentiates him from his materialist counterparts, Dupin and Holmes, but in actuality, the characters share a great deal, for Silence is yet another brilliant and wealthy "eccentric" who possesses an "intuitive knowledge of what goes on in other people's minds" and investigates only those "cases that interested him for some very special reason" (1–2). Though Silence lacks a companion to narrate his adventures, the third-person narrator who tells his stories admires Silence in much the same way Watson admires Holmes, remarking frequently on his wisdom, intelligence, and goodwill and presenting him to the reader as an object of wonder. Like Holmes, he seems almost infallible, capable of instantly grasping the nature of seemingly inexplicable phenomena. In that sense, he represents the subgenre at its worst, for he exists, not as a believable or even likable character, but as a "know-it-all" who interrupts every story "with a prosy explanation of the phenomena" and thus "introduces a fatal element of rationalism into something that should not be rationalized" (Joshi, *Weird Tale* 115).

Even though, by Lovecraft's time, the occult detective had degenerated into a stock character, an increasingly clichéd device unchanged since the days of Poe and Le Fanu, the subgenre continued to attract readers, and despite Lovecraft's dismissal of it, his own contemporaries, including his close friend August Derleth, continued to contribute to it. In 1928, three years after Lovecraft wrote "The Horror at Red Hook," Derleth wrote "The Adventure of the Black Narcissus," the first of his tales to feature Solar Pons, a detective closely modeled on Sherlock Holmes. Over the course of his long career, Derleth wrote more than seventy stories involving Pons, but as both Lovecraft and Derleth recognized, they are little more than pastiches. In their correspondence, Lovecraft even refers to them as Derleth's "Sherlock Holmes tales" (*Essential Solitude* 119). Pons even resembles his famous counterpart, so much so that Derleth refers to Pons in his preface as "The Sherlock Holmes of Praed Street" (xi). As in so many detective stories, Pons's adventures are narrated by a close friend and confidant, Dr. Lyndon Parker, who even rooms with Pons, just as Watson does with Holmes, in London.

Another one of Lovecraft's contemporaries, the largely forgotten Seabury Quinn, created a similar character, Jules de Grandin, whose popularity in *Weird Tales* eclipsed Lovecraft's more innovative creations. According to Robert A. W. Lowndes, from 1925 to 1936 Quinn's occult detective appeared in *Weird Tales* a total of sixty-three times, thus cementing Quinn's status as one of the magazine's most popular contributors (11). De Grandin dominated the cover of the magazine as well, appearing dozens of times, an honor Lovecraft received only once.[2] As for the tales themselves, they warrant little discussion, for Quinn, like Derleth, closely adheres to Doyle's formula. In "Terror on the Links" (1925), for instance, Quinn introduces the reader to two familiar characters: Dr. Trowbridge, who narrates the tale, and the brilliant de Grandin, a layman who combines "the vocation of the *savant* with the avocation of criminologist" (21). Though de Grandin does, over the course of the series, encounter all manner of imaginative horrors, including ghosts and other supernatural entities, the first of de Grandin's adventures borrows a great deal from Poe's "The Murders in the Rue Morgue" and presents the reader with yet another brutal murder committed by a great ape or, to be exact, an ape who changes into a man after being injected with a serum. Although both de Grandin and Pons appeared in print after Lovecraft had written "The Horror at Red Hook," one can imagine the chagrin Lovecraft must have felt when he saw an archetype he had lampooned enjoy far more success than his own efforts. Indeed, one wonders if the contempt he later expressed towards the subgenre stemmed, in part, from his contemporaries' success.

---

2. By my count, Seabury Quinn's stories, most of which involved de Grandin, appeared on the cover of *Weird Tales* forty-two times. HPL's "Imprisoned with the Pharaohs" ("Under the Pyramids") appeared on the cover of the May–June–July 1924 issue, but Harry Houdini, for whom HPL had ghostwritten the story, received credit for it.

Lovecraft's Critique of the Subgenre

Such a supposition is not ill founded, for Lovecraft criticized the subgenre repeatedly, especially in his essay "Supernatural Horror in Literature," which never fails to point out the subgenre's flaws. In 1927, two years after he had written "The Horror at Red Hook," Lovecraft finished this landmark review of weird fiction. In it, he credits Poe, the only author to whom he devotes an entire chapter, with initiating "a literary dawn directly affecting not only the history of the weird tale, but that of short fiction as a whole; and indirectly moulding the trends and fortunes of a great European aesthetic school" (54). As for Poe's mysteries, however, Lovecraft dismisses all three, claiming that "the tales of logic and ratiocination, forerunners of the modern detective story, are not to be included at all in weird literature" (57). Elsewhere, he dismisses both Le Fanu and Doyle as part of a "romantic, semi-Gothic, quasi-moral tradition," which addresses "the intellect rather than the impressionistic imagination" (48). Lovecraft's rejection stems, in part, from his novel division of literature into three branches: realism, which appeals to the intellect, romanticism, which appeals to the emotions, and weird fiction, which appeals to the imagination (CE 2.47). By crafting a work of supernatural horror that appeals to "the intellect rather than the impressionistic imagination," these writers are, from Lovecraft's perspective, creating an unwieldy amalgam, a clumsy tale that tries to analyze that which is, by nature, unknowable. As a result, not even Blackwood, whom Lovecraft considers one of the "modern masters" of the weird tale, escapes censure. Though praising *John Silence—Physician Extraordinary* for producing "an illusion at once emphatic and lasting," Lovecraft considers it "marred only be traces of the popular and conventional detective-story atmosphere" (*Supernatural Horror* 89). In a passage added in 1934 after Lovecraft had read the works of William Hope Hodgson, he also criticizes Hodgson's occult detective, Thomas Carnacki, whom he considers "a more or less conventional stock figure of the 'infallible detective' type—the progeny of M. Dupin and Sherlock Holmes, and the close kin of Algernon Blackwood's John Silence" (79). Lovecraft's contempt could not be more explicit: clearly, he considers the occult detective a hackneyed device, the mainstay of "insincere hacks" who "continue to concoct phony ghosts & vampires & space-ships & occult detectives" and the antithesis of the bold, original fiction that he was struggling to create (*RB* 279).

"The Horror at Red Hook" as Parody

And yet, as often as Lovecraft attacks the occult detective in print, his greatest criticism of its vapid conventions remains his much-maligned short story "The Horror at Red Hook." Indeed, the story does more than depart from those conventions: it inverts them. While every Dupin and Holmes story ends in triumph, Malone's tale ends in failure. In a sense, the story must end that way, for Malone seeks, not to solve a single crime, but to restore Red Hook to its "former happiness" when "a brighter picture dwelt, with clear-eyed mariners on the lower streets and homes of taste and substance where the larger houses line the hill" (*CF* 1.484). Red Hook, in other words, symbolizes everything Lovecraft, the conservative antiquarian, despises: drunkenness, poverty, modernity, and racial diversity. Its existence galls Lovecraft, who perceives the city's modern character as a renunciation of its colonial past. That "lovely old city" now lies "beneath the foul claws of the mongrel and misshapen foreign colossus that gibbers and howls vulgarly and dreamlessly on its site" (*Lord of a Visible World* 198). As virulent and racist as Lovecraft's descriptions of Red Hook are, they underscore the hopelessness of Malone's undertaking. He cannot restore Red Hook to its former state any more than Holmes could remake London or Dupin Paris. In the end, Malone himself recognizes, not only that he has failed, but that he was destined to fail, for "who are we to combat poisons older than history and mankind?" (*CF* 1.484). In that sense, Lovecraft has created a world far more dangerous than the one inhabited by, say, Silence, for Lovecraft's world is not one in which supernatural horror occasionally intrudes, as it does in "A Psychical Invasion," but a world shaped by horror, a realm in which "the soul of the beast is omnipresent and triumphant" (*CF* 1.504). The horrors confronted by Hesselius, Van Helsing, Dyson, and others are, in comparison, trite, commonplace, and insignificant.

As a result, Malone's reaction to the mystery he uncovers differs considerably from the comparatively staid reaction of his fellow occult detectives. After Hesselius, for instance, hears Mr. Jennings's disturbing tale, in which an apparition only he can see repeatedly urges him to commit suicide, he responds with a homily, informing Mr. Jennings that "he had evidence of God's care and love" (Le Fanu 33). Possessing the same self-confidence, Silence recovers, almost instantly, from his brush with the supernatural. A week after the events described in "A Psychical Invasion," Silence is laughing about the ordeal with the owner of the haunted house, a local author who, though he was once unnerved by his experiences, is "on the way to recovery and already busy again with his writing" (Blackwood 41). As for Van Helsing, Jonathan Harker seems to be alluding to him, among others, when he observes that "the happiness of some of us since then is, we think, well worth the pain we endured" (Stoker 382). Malone, however, is so shattered by the revelations he has uncovered that he collapses in the street when he encounters an innocuous row of brick buildings that remind him of Red Hook's warrens. Given his sensitivity, it seems unlikely that Malone will ever return to either the police force or New York City. "Mental specialists," in any case, have forbidden him "the sight of such things for an indefinite period" (CF 1.481). While other occult detectives shake off the horrors they confront, Malone declines precipitously after a single encounter with the supernatural. Indeed, his sanity is shaken, perhaps irrevocably, the very instant he enters the nightmarish catacombs beneath Suydam's property, a transformation reflected by the narrative itself, which, from that point on, recounts nothing more than a series of vague impressions. Unlike Silence, or Van Helsing, who analyzes his sensations even as he slaughters the Brides of Dracula, Malone is "delirious and hazy, and doubtful of his place in this or in any world" (CF 1.500). His reaction, histrionic though it may seem, reinforces Lovecraft's critique of weird fiction in which the supernatural "does not extend far into the fabric" of the tale and thus engenders "the artificial weirdness of the fireside tale and the Victorian ghost story" (Lord of a Visible World 209). Lovecraft could not, in other words, con-

ceive of a story in which a character responds with equanimity
to the violation of natural law as anything but puerile. In a
world governed by what Lovecraft calls "the eternal & madden-
ing rigidity of cosmic law" (SL 5.19), any encounter with the supernatural would be psychologically overwhelming, a fact
conveniently overlooked by other contributors to the subgenre.

And yet, Lovecraft's critique does not end there, for not only
does Malone fail in his undertaking to reform Red Hook, an endeavor that ultimately deprives him of his reason, he does not
even succeed in his role as a detective. True, he uncovers the
hideous rites being practiced beneath Suydam's properties, but
he does so by accident. In that sense, he discovers nothing
though discoveries are revealed to him. Even when he tries to
investigate the cellar beneath Parker Place, fate denies him an
active role: as soon as he smashes the cellar door, a "sucking
force not of earth or heaven [. . .] dragged him through the ap-
erture" (CF 1.498). Once inside, he can only watch and listen as
the bizarre scene unfolds before him. When the procession departs with Suydam's corpse, Malone attempts to follow, but his
will, shaky as it is, almost immediately dissolves:

> Malone staggered after them a few steps, delirious and hazy, and
> doubtful of his place in this or in any world. Then he turned,
> faltered, and sank down on the cold damp stone, gasping and
> shivering as the daemon organ croaked on, and the howling and
> drumming and tinkling of the mad procession grew fainter and
> fainter. (CF 1.500)

Being stationary, he witnesses only those events that occur within
his line of sight, like the unloading of Suydam's corpse and the
toppling of Lilith's throne, and remains ignorant of those outside
of his range of vision, such as Suydam's reanimation. He is, at the
most crucial point in the story, no more than a passive observer, a
witness to unholy and uncanny proceedings. Unlike Dupin or
Holmes, he gains nothing by deduction, and unlike Hesselius or
Van Helsing, he lacks the occult knowledge needed to contex-
tualize what he has witnessed. Even at the end of the story,
Malone knows almost nothing, and questions that the reader
might have about Lilith's nature, Suydam's research into the oc-

cult, his role in the creation of the cult, and the reason for his murder and resurrection remain unanswered. The fact that Malone is, unlike other occult detectives, an actual policeman only adds to the irony, for Malone resembles nothing so much as one of the baffled members of Scotland Yard that Holmes and his brethren so often encounter.

Malone also differs from other occult detectives in that he is alone, for unlike Dupin or Holmes, Malone has no one to narrate his story or admire his abilities. In "The Horror at Red Hook," an impersonal and omniscient third-person narrator fills the role established by Dupin's nameless friend and later immortalized by Watson. By replacing this stock character with a third-person narrator, Lovecraft departs from one of the genre's most recognizable conventions, for a similar character, fulfilling a similar function, appears in the stories of almost every occult detective, including Hesselius, Pons, and de Grandin. Even Dyson, who differs so considerably from other occult detectives, has Phillipps, and the dynamic between the two, the result of one being a mystic and the other a rationalist, resembles the tension between Holmes, who understands so much, and Watson, who understands so little. Malone, by comparison, has no one, and if he has friends or family or lovers, Lovecraft does not mention them. After his ordeal in Red Hook, he retires to Chepachet, that "quaint hamlet of wooden colonial houses" in bucolic Rhode Island, not because he has family there, but because a doctor has suggested it as a suitable place for his "psychological convalescence" (CF 1.481). Malone, whose very name contains the word "alone," exists in almost complete isolation, for there are only a few named characters in the entire tale: namely, Malone, Suydam, Miss Cornelia Gerritsen, and Lilith herself. As for dialogue, aside from a few chants, which Lovecraft quotes, there is none. The sense of isolation that this conveys reinforces the impression that Malone is alone in a city contaminated by supernatural horror. Whereas, in other tales, the supernatural intrudes upon our everyday world, in this instance, the reverse has occurred: Malone has intruded upon the supernatural. Despite his fulminations against immigration, he is the true alien in Red Hook.

By subverting the conventions of the occult detective in this way, Lovecraft does more than parody a hackneyed genre, he infuses it with the cosmic philosophy he would explore in his later works. Most scholars believe that Lovecraft's writing improved dramatically in 1926, the year he left his wife and the city that he loathed and came home to Providence. Lovecraft's return to Rhode Island, and the research he did for "Supernatural Horror in Literature," gave him "a new lease on his life and his work" and inspired him to write his most characteristic stories, beginning with "The Call of Cthulhu" in the summer of 1926 (Joshi, *Evolution of the Weird Tale* 95). By far his most famous tale, "The Call of Cthulhu," incorporates Lovecraft's theory of "cosmicism," the belief that the size and age of the cosmos render humanity insignificant. The godless cosmos does not, in other words, give a "damn one way or the other about the especial wants and ultimate welfare of mosquitoes, rats, lice, dogs, men, horses, pterodactyls, trees, fungi, dodo, or other forms of biological energy" (*SL* 3.39).

In its depiction of a gargantuan, malevolent god who awakens from hibernation to terrorize the Earth, "The Call of Cthulhu" expresses this theme as satisfactorily as any story Lovecraft ever wrote. And yet, in many ways, "The Horror at Red Hook," which was written the year before, captures the same sentiments, and it does so by encouraging the reader to juxtapose the experiences of Malone with the comparatively quotidian adventures of other occult detectives. Unlike Van Helsing, who confronts a single vampire, or Silence, who investigates a single house, Malone uncovers an entire culture on the underside of civilization, an ancient and massive cult dedicated to the worship of entities, like Lilith, beyond human conception. Instead of encountering a single ghost or an isolated monster, Malone stumbles upon "a contagion destined to sicken and swallow cities," a pestilence capable of destroying all humanity:

> Satan here held his Babylonish court, and in the blood of stainless childhood the leprous limbs of phosphorescent Lilith were laved. Incubi and succubae howled praise to Hecate, and headless moon-calves bleated to the Magna Mater. Goats leaped to the sound of thin accursed flutes, and Ægipans chased endlessly

after misshapen fauns over rocks twisted like swollen toads. Mo-
loch and Ashtaroth were not absent; for in this quintessence of
all damnation the bounds of consciousness were let down, and
man's fancy lay open to vistas of every realm of horror and every
forbidden dimension that evil had power to mould. (CF 1.499)

If less satisfactory a symbol than great Cthulhu, Lovecraft's iconic god, this plethora of demonic figures, which includes entities
culled from both Christian and pagan mythologies, expresses the
same truth: on the edge of humanity's ken, malevolent forces
have existed for millennia, biding their time as "decay spreads
over the tottering cities of men" (CF 2.55).

And yet, it is fitting that the story will, most likely, always
remain one of Lovecraft's least popular. More so than any of
Lovecraft's other works, "The Horror at Red Hook" incorporates his ethnocentric beliefs. As Michel Houellebecq speculates, writing it provided Lovecraft, who was living in poverty in
a Brooklyn slum, an opportunity to express his frustration by
pouring his hatred of New York and its diverse multitudes onto
the page (105–7). As cathartic as this may have been for Lovecraft, this outpouring of animosity inflates his prose until it bor-
ders upon histrionic. Even Lovecraft considered the story poor:
in one of his letters, written shortly after finishing "The Horror
at Red Hook," he states that "the tale is rather long and ram-
bling, and I don't think it is very good" (SL 2.20). To make matters worse, the racism, both overt and covert, that courses
through the story nullifies whatever good qualities the tale may
possess and renders it anathema to modern readers. As the
United States grows increasingly diverse and multiculturalism
becomes increasingly integral to American society, interest in
Lovecraft, which has been growing for decades, may wane. If it
does, "The Horror at Red Hook" deserves much of the blame,
for it is, as Charlotte Montague claims, a "racist rant aimed
squarely at the 'foreigners' that have 'stolen' New York from
people of white Anglo-Saxon stock" (101). If the story deserves
to be remembered at all, it is for the novel ways in which it subverts the subgenre of the occult detective, a beloved character
that was, by Lovecraft's time, ripe for satire.

Works Cited

Blackwood, Algernon. *The Complete John Silence Stories.* Ed. S. T. Joshi. Mineola, NY: Dover, 1997.

Derleth, August. "Preface." In *Regarding Sherlock Holmes: The Adventures of Solar Pons.* 1945. New York: Pinnacle, 1975. xi–xiii.

Doyle, Arthur Conan. *The Complete Sherlock Holmes.* Volume 1. Garden City, NY; Doubleday and Company, 1930.

Eckhardt, Jason C. "The Cosmic Yankee." In David E. Schultz and S. T. Joshi, ed. *An Epicure in the Terrible: A Centennial Anthology of Essays in Honor of H. P. Lovecraft.* 1991. New York: Hippocampus Press, 2011. 77–99.

Houellebecq, Michel. *H. P. Lovecraft: Against the World, Against Life.* Tr. Dorna Khazeni. London: Gollancz, 2008.

Joshi, S. T. *The Evolution of the Weird Tale.* New York: Hippocampus Press, 2004.

———. *A Subtler Magick: The Writings and Philosophy of H. P. Lovecraft.* San Bernardino, CA: Borgo Press, 1996.

———. *The Weird Tale.* Austin: University of Texas Press, 1990.

Le Fanu, J. Sheridan. *In a Glass Darkly.* Ed. Robert Tracy. London: Oxford University Press, 1993.

Lovecraft, H. P. *The Annotated Supernatural Horror in Literature.* Ed. S. T. Joshi. 2nd ed. New York: Hippocampus Press, 2012.

———. *Dawnward Spire, Lonely Hill: The Letters of H. P. Lovecraft and Clark Ashton Smith.* Ed. David E. Schultz and S. T. Joshi. New York: Hippocampus Press, 2017.

———. *Essential Solitude: The Letters of H. P. Lovecraft and August Derleth.* Ed. David E. Schultz and S. T. Joshi. New York: Hippocampus Press, 2008.

———. *Letters to Alfred Galpin and Others.* Ed. S. T. Joshi and David E. Schultz. New York: Hippocampus Press, 2020.

———. *Lord of a Visible World: An Autobiography in Letters.* Ed. S. T. Joshi and David E. Schultz. Athens: Ohio University Press, 2000. New York: Hippocampus Press, 2019.

Lowndes, Robert A. W. "Introduction." In *The Casebook of Jules de Grandin* by Seabury Quinn. New York: Popular Library, 1976. 9–13.

Machen, Arthur. *The Three Impostors and Other Stories.* Ed. S. T. Joshi. Oakland, CA: Chaosium, 2007.

Montague, Charlotte. *H. P. Lovecraft: The Mysterious Man Behind the Darkness.* New York: Chartwell Books, 2015.

Poe, Edgar Allan. *Poetry and Tales.* New York: Library of America, 1984.

Quinn, Seabury. *The Adventures of Jules de Grandin.* New York: Popular Library, 1976.

Silverman, Kenneth. *Edgar A. Poe: Mournful and Never-ending Remembrance.* New York: HarperCollins, 1991.

Stoker, Bram. *Dracula.* 1897. New York: Signet Classic, 1965.

Tyson, Donald. *The Dream World of H. P. Lovecraft: His Life, His Demons, His Universe.* Woodbury, MN: Llewellyn, 2010.

Briefly Noted

This fall Hippocampus Press will publish another volume of H. P. Lovecraft's collected letters. *Letters to Rheinhart Kleiner and Others* will publish for the first time Lovecraft's letters to Arthur Harris (Welsh amateur journalist, who published Lovecraft's first "separate" publication), James Larkin Pearson (amateur journalist and long-time poet laureate of North Carolina), Arthur Leeds (Kalem Club member and photoplay writer), Winifred V. Jackson (prolific amateur journalist, rumored to have a romance with Lovecraft), and Paul J. Campbell (prominent amateur journalist and founder of the Fraternity of the Wooden Leg). The book teems with selections of the writings of all these writers.

Still other titles are due to be published in 2021.

Yuletide Horror: "Festival" and "The Messenger"

This paper will discuss two of Lovecraft's shorter horror poems, "Festival" and "The Messenger." The first appears to be a parody of a traditional Christmas carol, while the second utilizes the form of the traditional sonnet to create a tight and effective micro-horror. One poem was custom written as a weird Christmas greeting, while the other developed from an in-joke with one of Lovecraft's publishing peers, but this personal touch does not detract from the uncanny mood each narrative generates.

I recently had a parody of "God Rest Ye Merry Gentlemen" published as "A Carol" in *Eerie Christmas*, a seasonal horror anthology by Black Hare Press. The editors chose to preface the volume with "Yule Horror" by H. P. Lovecraft, which made me very happy, because I was in exalted company. It also made me realize that Lovecraft's poem might be a parody of "There's a Song in the Air," a traditional carol with lyrics by Josiah G. Holland.

The poem, otherwise known as "Festival," was written in December 1925 and first published as "Yule Horror" in *Weird Tales* the following Christmas, December 1926. The theme harks back to pre-Christian winter celebrations, and while it might not be archaeologically precise, it represents a liberation of the holiday season from modern trappings, both religious and commercial.

According to hynmary.org, the carol I am suggesting "Festival" parodies was published in church hymnals dating back as far as 1874. In 1919 it was available in *The Excelsior Hymnal*, and in 1921 it was revised in *Worship and Song*. The most "representative text," currently found in the *United Methodist Hymnal*, has four verses (see Plantiga), and so does Lovecraft's poem.

Verse 1 of "Festival" (*AT* 75) commences "There is snow on the ground," creating an earth-bound parallel to the carol, which commences "There's a song in the air!" Line 2 focuses on the chill of winter: "And the valleys are cold," while the carol continues its airy theme: "There's a star in the sky!" Line 3, "And a midnight profound," compares with "There's a mother's deep prayer" in the carol. "Profound" is a synonym for "deep," but Lovecraft is not into prayers, except as poems to beauty, so it is his midnight that is profound. Line 4 personifies the midnight into a brooding monster ("Blackly squats o'er the wold"), while the carol introduces the Christ child: "and a baby's low cry!" Line 5 is suddenly a long one, and introduces the action: there is a "light" on the hill and pagan feast being celebrated. This line actually replaces lines 5 to 8 in the representative text of the carol, although different versions change these lines and include more repetition.

Metrically, the carol scans 6.6.6.6.12.12, which is interesting because the very last line of Lovecraft's poem mentions "the sign of the beast," traditionally thought to be 666 (see Revelation 13:18). Lovecraft's poem scans 6.6.6.7.18, although I expect he meant "o'er" to be said with one beat (even though that is difficult), making the poem scan 6.6.6.6.18. Not only does this reflect the carol quite closely, but the final line has 18 beats, which is 6×3 or 666.

The total number of beats in the poem are 42, which breaks up into four and two. $4 + 2 = 6$, the number ending the first four lines, and also in Hebrew numerology—the number of man and sin. (See Genesis 1:26–31, the human species is created on the "sixth day"; Exodus 21:2 and Deuteronomy 15:12, 18—a slave serves "six years"; Revelation 16:12–14, the bowl of the "sixth Angel" brought forth "unclean spirits" from the "dragon," "beast" and "false prophet.") The number 42 does have some positive associations in Hebrew numerology, but it is also the number of boys cursed to be killed by the female bears (2 Kings 2:24), the number killed in battle on several occasions (Judges 12:6, 2 Kings 10:14), and the amount of time the nations will tread the temple court under foot (Revelation 11:2).

Now that this paper has established a comparison between the poem and the carol, it will concentrate on Lovecraft's poem, which has an eerie charm in its own right. Suffice it to say that in verse 2 there is "death" (l. 1) and "fear" (l. 2) where the carol had "joy." Verse 3 of "Festival" summons an unnatural wind, "No gale of earth's kind" (l. 1) to blow through the "oak" (l. 2), along with "sick boughs (l. 3) and "mad mistletoes" (l. 4) as ancient Druids rise from the grave (l. 5).

Verse 4 is more apocalyptically occult than Lovecraft's cosmic writings. In line 3, the reference to "abbot and priest" would make most sense if it encompassed both Catholic abbot and pagan priest. This would mean all religions had "cannibal greeds" (l. 4), whether for human flesh or monetary offerings. In these final lines, Lovecraft appears to say that whichever way we celebrate Christmas, we are "shewing dimly" (l. 5) the mark of the beast, which is ironic, and a nice bit of creepy weird fantasy.

Even if we dismiss religion, the modern commercialized Christmas of secular feasting, costumed Santas, and presents under the tree is a season of greed. The number 666 was also King Solomon's annual income, "six hundred and sixty-six talents of gold" (1 Kings 10:14); and King Solomon, with his thousands of horses and concubines, generally functions as a symbol of conspicuous consumption. This point is possibly more relevant to us today than in 1925, during the lean years between the two world wars.

So did Lovecraft hate Christmas? According to the letters, and some other seasonal poems, the answer is generally no. K. M. Alexander writes on his blog: "A lot of people don't realize Lovecraft had a sentimental side" and sent his friends custom written Christmas poems.

Letters written around Christmases report a prodigious amount of writing completed over the holiday season in the early years—perhaps a sign of indifference at the worst. However, in 1925 Christmas was spent with the Longs, and Lovecraft writes happily of presents and games (*SL* 2.34–35). In 1928 he spent Christmas with Mrs. Gamwell and reported that the weather was almost as mild as 1903, when he rode his bicycle to visit Mrs. Clark (*SL* 2.254). In 1933, he reports dividing his Christmas time between his aunts and the Longs, and scoring two Christmas dinners (*SL* 4.127–30)! In 1934, Christmas was spent with Mrs. Gamwell, with visits to Loveman and Wandrei (*SL* 4.340–41).

S. T. Joshi explains in his notes for "Festival" that the poem actually started life as a Christmas greeting to Farnsworth Wright (AT 512). This makes sense. Most of the Christmas greeting poems were personalized to suit the recipient. Farnsworth Wright was editor of *Weird Tales*, so he would have liked a weird poem. Apparently, he liked it so much that after receiving it for Christmas 1925, he presumably removed the dedication and published the first three verses as "Yule Horror" in the following year's Christmas issue.

Knowing the poem "Festival" was once actually a greeting does not remove the shiver it provokes, but does make it a little less like an epistle from the notorious Grinch! Considering it a parody of "There's a Song in the Air" makes it seem even cleverer, and opens up interesting numerological insights.

"The Messenger" (AT 80) was written several years later, in 1929. The poem is addressed "To Bertrand K. Hart, Esq.," so in its way it is also a greeting. According to Joshi and Schultz (29, 105), the poem was the subject of an inside joke, as Hart had threatened to send a ghost to scare Lovecraft. Setting such background trivia aside, and considering the poem on its own merits, it generates fairly good horror (see also AT 525).

The poem is a sonnet, written in iambic pentameter, meaning there are ten syllables to a line. The first eight lines, also known as the octet, follow the Petrarchan pattern, with an AB-BA-ABBA rhyming configuration. The second verse consists of six lines, making it a sestet. The sestet follows a CDDCEE pattern, more like the Spenserian sonnet, but not exactly. The sonnet form is often used in classical poetry, so adopting it for a weird poem is risky and adventurous, but in this case it works.

"The Messenger" also contains sound patterning in the form of alliteration. The first line of the octet contains the sound *th* four times, in addition to a couple of *t* sounds (l. 1). The sound *t* continues to be prominent throughout the verse, complimented by *f* and *ch* (l. 2). In the last line of the octet, "fumbling forms" emphasizes the creepy imagery (l. 8), and the sound pattern mirrors the action in the fourth line of the octet where the "firelight faded" (l. 12) as the creatures of darkness are set "free" (l. 8). Despite the attention to sound patterning, it is worth noting that the poem narrates almost as smoothly as prose.

The opening line, "The thing, he said, would come," evokes

images of a patriarch telling folk tales. "That night at three" has a
nice melodic tone to it. Midnight might be the traditional witching
hour, but "three" sounds out like a bell (l. 1) and has folk magic
associations, for example, Shakespeare's three witches in *Macbeth*
(1.1.1): "Thrice to thine and thrice to mine / And thrice again, to
make up nine. / Peace! The charm's wound up" (1.3.36–38). The
number 3 is used also ritually in in Lovecraft's novel *The Case of
Charles Dexter Ward*: "saye yᵉ ninth Uerse thrice" (CF 2.268, 282).

Line 2 sets the scene: "From the old churchyard on the hill
below," which is a suggestive place for a monster to emerge
from. Churchyards are full of graves, and perhaps in an old
churchyard the sanctity of hallowed ground might be wearing
thin. Line 3 goes into the protagonist's denial. This is a phase
the speaker shares in common with the narrator of many of the
stories. He sits by the comfort of "an oak fire's wholesome glow,"
and in the safety of light and warmth he attempts to assure himself "it could not be."

Lines 4 to 8 include the explanation for the denial: the patriarch who predicted the arrival of the monster "did not truly
know / The Elder Sign." This ties in with the mythos Lovecraft
had been creating through multiple stories, and had even invited other writers to share (Joshi and Schultz 51–52). The "Elder
Sign, bequeathed from long ago," is mentioned in "The Descend-
ant" a story fragment written in 1927 (Joshi and Schultz 66); but
also brings to mind summonings such as in *The Case of Charles
Dexter Ward*, where Curwen "Rais'd Yog-Sothoth" (CF 2.344).

In line 8, "the fumbling forms of darkness" reminds one of
the monster, also referred to as "the thing," that shambled
around below the well in Curwen's Pawtucket catacomb (CF
2.334–35). Even for the reader who is not familiar with the other works of Lovecraft, the associations of night and unnamable
monsters emerging from graveyards are sufficient to arouse a
thrilling sense of anticipation.

The sestet commences with a reference to the in-joke, "He
had not meant it" (l. 9), but the reference is not obvious enough
to spoil the fantasy of the poem. The protagonist goes along with
the sense of fear, lighting "Another lamp" to assure himself he is
safe (l. 10). Then come three portents: one in the sky ("starry

Leo climbed"), the second an indication of time ("a steeple chimed"), and the third, "the firelight faded." Note that the word "Three," which has been a significant number throughout the poem, is capitalized as it is positioned to begin a line.

The ultimate lines of the sonnet are a final couplet and contain the climax: "Then at the door that cautious rattling came— / And the mad truth devoured me like a flame!" (ll. 13–14). The reader is not told exactly what came, but it might be fiery— which sets it apart from some of Lovecraft's other ghouls, which are decayed or aquatic. Sometimes in horror, such manifestations are best left to the imagination. The poem somehow got finished while the protagonist was being devoured—but little slips in logic are allowable so we can enjoy the thrill of the writing.

In conclusion, in both "Festival" and "The Messenger" the trappings of poetic form do not detract from the weirdness, but contribute to an evocation of preternatural mood. The constrictions of form are tight, as "Festival" parodies a traditional carol, using strict rhyming form and beat, while "The Messenger" utilizes the inflexible form of a sonnet. "Festival" is composed around the number 6, evoking the symbolism of the "beast"; while "The Messenger" plays more loosely with the symbolism of the number 3 in folk magic and mythology. Both poems were originally addressed to members of Lovecraft's community of friends and peers, but both still work as micro-horrors.

Works Cited

Alexander, K. M. "More of H. P. Lovecraft's Silly Christmas Poems." *I Make Stories*, blog.kmalexander.com/2015/12/21/more-of-h-p-lovecrafts-silly-christmas-poems/.

Joshi, S. T., and David E. Schultz. *An H. P. Lovecraft Encyclopedia*. Westport, CT: Greenwood Press, 2001.

Lovecraft, H. P. "Yule Horror." In Ben Thomas and D. Kershaw, ed. *Eerie Christmas*. Melbourne: Black Hare Press, 2019.

Plantinga, Harry. "There's a Song in the Air." *Hymnary.org.*, Christian Classics Ethereal Library, Calvin Institute of Christian Worship, Calvin University, The Hymn Society, National Endowment for the Humanities, hymnary.org/text/ theres_a_ song_in_the_air_theres_a_star [Accessed 2 January 2020].

The Doomed Lovecrafts of Rochester

Will Murray

"Life is a hideous thing, and from the background behind what we know of it peer demoniacal hints of truth that make it sometimes a thousandfold more hideous" (CF 1.171). So wrote H. P. Lovecraft in his 1920 story "Facts concerning the Late Arthur Jermyn and His Family." This tale of tainted ancestry, miscegenation, and generational horror may have been Lovecraft's most personal story, although it was not in any sense autobiographical.

Not directly.

A scholar of Lovecraft's ancestry might be moved to wonder if the unfortunate fate of his father, Winfield Scott Lovecraft, inspired the story. Or at least its theme. Of course, Lovecraft's father was not a product of delving into lost cities in the African interior. But a horrible secret may have impressed his son, even if he only understood it imperfectly.

Winfield Scott Lovecraft was one of the Rochester Lovecrafts descended from Thomas Lovecraft and his son, Joseph S. Lovecraft, who came to America from Great Britain circa 1827. The sons of Joseph S. Lovecraft were businessman and they lived prosperous and outwardly respectable lives. The six children of Joseph S. Lovecraft (1775–1850) appear to have lived full lives, most them reaching their sixties, with the youngest son, Aaron, passing away prematurely at age fifty-three due to lung congestion. The others were John Full Lovecraft, Joseph Lovecraft, Jr., George Lovecraft, and William Lovecraft. A single daughter, Mary Lovecraft, lived to the age of seventy-nine. She bore nine children, of whom eight did not live to see their eighth birthday—although one, Robert Bell Brown, was still alive in Lovecraft's time. He seemed to be an exception. Their male children were not so fortunate, however. All passed in their mid forties or early fifties, and at least three of them under similar tragic circumstances.

Sidney J. Lovecraft, whose parents were John Full Lovecraft and Eleanor Gaskin, died on 3 October 1890, at age fifty-three, of an unspecified lung disease at home. Reports were that he had been ill since the previous March, but went into a decline only days before his passing. The *Rochester Democrat and Chronicle* for 18 January 1889 reported that he gave a banquet in his capacity as deputy grand chancellor of the Knights of Pythias, so he appeared to be in good health at the beginning of that year. [1]

Three more would soon follow. Sidney's mother, Eleanor, died at home at the age of eighty-four on 13 October 1890. So while her passing ten days after that her son is suggestive, it is not necessarily unusual. Sidney Lovecraft had survived an earlier tragedy in September of 1873, when he, his wife, cousin Joshua Lovecraft and his wife, and two other couples went camping on Sodus Point, Lake Ontario, some thirty miles from Rochester. Joshua Lovecraft and another couple left early. Mr. and Mrs. Sidney Lovecraft, Mrs. Joshua Lovecraft and a fourth couple sailed onto the lake in Sidney's sailboat, the *Peerless*.

At four in the afternoon, a sudden squall caused the boat to capsize. All five passengers were thrown into the water. All succeeded in clinging to the overturned hull and mast, but their calls for help went unheard. The men managed to partially right the hull, but that was all. All night and into the next morning, they struggled to stay alive. Exhaustion set in. Becoming deranged, the other couple fell off the hull the following morning and succumbed. A few hours later, Electa Lovecraft lost her grip and drowned. Sidney and his wife were close to giving up when rescue finally came after thirty-six harrowing hours off Webster Point.

Sidney later worked as a planer at Joseph Lovecraft & Son, alongside Joshua. George Elliott Lovecraft kept the books. He was born in 1868, but the date of his death his unknown. More

---

1. Brothers Sidney and Silas Lovecraft joined the Union Army during the Civil War. Silas returned from a three-year hitch in July 1863. He died on 14 February 1863 at his parents' Rochester home, at the age of seventeen. The cause of death was "debility" brought on by the horrors of war. His brother, Sidney, deserted and fled to Canada for the duration of the conflict.

on him later. Winfield's father, George Lovecraft, was a harness-maker who was forced to retire due to a nervous ailment, according to Lovecraft. Malaria is said to have been the actual reason.

The horror that ultimately overtook the Lovecrafts of Rochester seems to have commenced with Winfield Scott Lovecraft, who began acting peculiarly early during the year 1892. A traveling salesman, he lived the hectic and bohemian lifestyle of a traveling drummer. The story of how Winfield Lovecraft was suddenly consumed by hallucinations while staying at a Chicago hotel in April 1893 is well known to Lovecraftians. Reportedly he claimed his wife was being assaulted in an upstairs room and had to be restrained. Winfield's condition was so extreme that he was committed to Butler Hospital in Providence. The following years were difficult. Winfield was soon judged insane, although his mental deterioration was not altogether downward. The unfortunate man experienced periods in which he seemed to improve.

Winfield Scott Lovecraft ultimately succumbed in July 1898 at the age of forty-five. The medical diagnosis was paresis, which was understood to be a result of contracting syphilis in his past. Inasmuch as the incubation stage can range from a decade to twenty years, it is not certain when he was first exposed, only that the mental deterioration observed at that time led his doctors to assume that syphilis lay at the root of his misfortunes and subsequent death.

How much of this young H. P. Lovecraft was told at that time or learned later is undiscoverable at this point. It is unlikely his Victorian mother revealed to him the whole truth. He was too young, being only five or six when his father passed. Two entries in Lovecraft's commonplace book, apparently dating to 1928, are suggestive:

Ultimate horror—grandfather returns from strange trip—mystery in house—wind and darkness—grandf. and mother engulfed—questions forbidden—somnolence—investigation—cataclysm—screams overheard—

Boy rear'd in the atmosphere of considerable mystery. Believes father died. Suddenly informed that father is about to return. Strange preparations—consequences. (CE 5.229)

We don't know that young Lovecraft was actually told that his father was deceased prior to his demise, but Lovecraft was at a tender age when the death occurred. That alone might have hung in his memory as a moment of horror which he much later considered exploiting.

The death of Winfield Scott Lovecraft and the surrounding circumstances would have been enough to leave a mark on young H. P. But Winfield was not the only Lovecraft of his generation to decline into madness and distraction. There were others.

Frederick Aaron Lovecraft was the son of Aaron Lovecraft, who died in 1870 at the age of sixty-three. With an inheritance of $10,000, the twenty-year-old son relocated to New York City, worked as bookkeeper for a time, and eventually made a killing on Wall Street. He lost it all, but rebuilt his fortune through business ventures. Handsome and a man about town with professional connections to the theatre and the Coney Island Jockey Club, he was living a comfortable lifestyle when in July 1893 his mood and personality changed irrevocably, causing his physician, Dr. Thomas S. Roberson, to diagnose his patient as suffering from "nervous prostration" due to overwork.

Frederick A. Lovecraft (from *San Francisco Chronicle*, 17 February 1894, p. 5).

Frederick Aaron Lovecraft harbored ambitions to become a millionaire. He was significantly on his way when the Panic of 1893, which commenced that May, wiped out many fortunes. Evidently, Lovecraft's was one of them. He grew despondent. This was a scant three months after Winfield Scott Lovecraft's breakdown in Chicago. The two men were not far apart in age, Frederick having been born in 1850 and Winfield in 1853. No doubt the first cousins grew up together in Rochester and shared many experiences.

One can readily imagine that Frederick had been informed by the family of the decline of cousin Winfield and his removal to Butler Hospital. One wonders if that might not have played a role—if only psychological—in Frederick's rapid deterioration.

At first, Frederick's emotional decline might be ascribed to financial losses, but soon it was apparent that something more sinister was at work. His brother-in-law, Robert H. Salmons, stated that Lovecraft had developed a fear of streetcars and became so paranoid that he "walked around a block to get rid of an imaginary crowd of men who were following him."[2] Lovecraft reportedly confided, "They are trying to do me up."[3] He was particularly paranoid about the friend who had moved into his sumptuous Broadway apartment to keep on eye on him. "Is Colonel Kearney following me?" he asked George Lovecraft on one occasion.[4]

Colonel Henry S. Kearney was a Tammany Hall man who worked an an engineer with New York's Board of Electrical Control and was a close friend. Friends and family implored Lovecraft to sail with Colonel Kearney to Europe and find rest. He refused. Pleas that he relocate to Rochester to live with the family of his sister, Florence, and brother-in-law, Robert, were also rebuffed. As his mental derangement worsened, fears that Lovecraft might take his life grew. Finally, the family convinced him to take a temporary rest cure at a sanitarium. He was to depart on October 26 of that year. But this consent was only a ruse.

His insanity showed itself in his cunningly pretending to accept his friends' proposition and at the same time secretly planning to take his own life. He had a horror of asylums and was afraid if he went simply to an ordinary "home" he would soon find himself in a madhouse.[5]

2. "F. A. Lovecraft's Estate," *New York Herald Tribune* (14 March 1894).

3. Ibid.

4. "Fred. Lovecraft's Will," *Rochester Democrat and Chronicle* (13 March 1894).

5. "Her Faith in Signs," *San Francisco Chronicle* (17 February 1894).

"I don't see how I can go to a sanitarium," Lovecraft reportedly confided. "I haven't got money enough. I am a pauper. I don't know what I am going to do."[6]

Other witnesses gave conflicting accounts of his mood the day before his death, some saying that he was alternately listless and nervous, and often stared off into space. Under questioning later, Dr. Thomas S. Robertson averred, "His head was hanging over to one side and he was wringing his hands as if in despair. He was not rational. He had no mental capacity."[7]

That morning, after refusing breakfast, Frederick Aaron Lovecraft drank a bottle of carbolic acid and placed a Smith & Wesson .38-calibre revolver to his head, firing several times. Three bullets went awry, and failed to penetrate his skull. These gunshots alerted the household. An ambulance was called. But Frederick Aaron Lovecraft died en route to the hospital as a result of carbolic acid poisoning.

As one of Gotham's most prominent businessmen, Lovecraft's suicide shocked the city. The *New York Times* summed up his precipitous decline in a single paragraph:

> For sometime previous it had been known to Mr. Lovecraft's close friends that his nervous system was seriously affected. For years he had worked incessantly night and day to accumulate a fortune, his hours usually extending from 8 o'clock in the morning until long after midnight, and the strain finally told on him. His physician advised absolute rest, but Mr. Lovecraft declined to give up his business affairs, and finally melancholia set in. His friends were advised that he was undoubtedly insane, and that unless he could be prevailed to take a long rest he would become a hopeless lunatic.[8]

A. M. Palmer expanded on this for the *New York Evening World*. "Lovecraft told me six months ago that he had $150,000 to the good. But he was ambitious to be a millionaire. He might easily have saved an independent fortune in twenty years from his large salaries, but he speculated and worried. He lost heavily in

---

6. "Driven Crazy by His Losses," *New York Times* (27 October 1893).

7. "Lovecraft a Mental Wreck," *New York Times* (15 March 1894).

8. "Mother and Sisters Sue," *New York Times* (23 January 1894).

the late panic and worried till he was down sick."[9]

During a subsequent trial contesting his will, which he had drafted on August 29 to benefit his roommate, the wealthy Colonel Kearney, rather than his aged mother and sisters— Lovecraft was a widower—facts concerning his state of mind between July and October came to light via his personal physician. When asked if Frederick Lovecraft had suffered any hallucinations, his physician, Dr. Robertson replied, "He dreaded poverty and said things financially were going all wrong. I don't know whether these ideas were founded on fact or not."[10] Under close questioning, Dr. Robertson described a man falling into a deep depression. He employed such terms as "persistent melancholia," "acute dementia," "nervous prostration" and "delusions."[11] Yet the official autopsy also included a more telling diagnosis. As reported the *Evening World* of New York, "Temporary aberration of mind due to incipient paresis is said to have been the cause of his act."[12]

In the aftermath of Lovecraft's death, controversy raged over the true state of his affairs. For, despite his financial reversals, Frederick Lovecraft held numerous business interests, some quite sound. His mentor, Palmer's Theatre owner Theodore Moss, told one reporter: "Lovecraft was crazy. I met him first when he was a young man employed about the Academy of Music, eighteen years ago. He has been with me ever since, and I always found him to be steady, faithful and honest. He had no bad habits. His accounts are in perfect order."[13] M. Palmer, manager of Palmer's Theatre, added: "Needless mental worry caused it. Prior to the late financial trouble I know he was worth $150,000. He lost money, and when we found how this was preying on his mind we had Colonel Kearney go over his accounts a week ago. He found that Mr. Lovecraft was still worth about $60,000. We could not make him believe that, however."[14]

---

9. "Poison and Pistol," *New York Evening World* (26 October 1893).

10. "Lovecraft a Mental Wreck."

11. Ibid.

12. "Paresis and a Shot," *New York Evening World* (26 October 1893).

13. "Crazy for Riches," *New York World* (27 October 1893).

14. Ibid.

Lovecraft's family sued to contest the will, but the decision of the court was that Lovecraft was sane at the time of his suicide. Further, the judge found that Colonel Kearney did not apply undue influence on the befuddled man, and thus inherited his estate, freezing out Lovecraft's mother and sister, and another important person, whose name surfaced later. Through it all, Dr. Robertson blamed Colonel Kearney for Lovecraft's death. At Robertson's suggestion, Kearney had moved into Lovecraft's flat for the express purpose of keeping an eye on him after Lovecraft had threatened to kill himself.

The deaths of two Lovecraft cousins who went into a severe mental decline in the same year suggest a hereditary cause. Frederick Aaron was forty-three, only three years older than Winfield. One newspaper account speculated that the immediate cause of Frederick Aaron's suicide was his growing suspicion that concerned friends were secretly planning to commit him to the Middletown Insane Asylum, near Syracuse. This was, in fact, true. If Frederick knew of Winfield's contemporaneous circumstances, his concern was perhaps understandable.

As Frederick Lovecraft was being buried, a business confident who preferred not to be named offered a more elaborate explanation:

> It was annoying complications and abuses of confidence in the business of his advertising agency which culminated in the death of his manager, that more than anything else led to the unsettling of Lovecraft's mind. He had invested a considerable sum in the advertising agency. A few months ago he took into his employ a bookkeeper who embezzled a large amount. This was a great shock to Lovecraft who was already fretting over his financial affairs. He found that his bookkeeper's wife owned valuable lots in Bedford Park. This property she transferred to Lovecraft toward making good her husband's stealings.
>
> The manager of the advertising agency was Oscar Schoenfeld. The most confidential of business relations existed between him and Lovecraft. One day last week Schoenfeld started for Bedford Park, to meet a man who was to purchase the lots. In crossing the railroad track after leaving his train he was run over by another train and killed. The news of this came to Lovecraft

through the newspapers, and the shock was a terrible one to him. After this the advertising business seemed to be a terror to him, and he was anxious to dispose of it. About a month ago he sold the business for a good sum in cash, and something like his old cheerfulness returned to him. A day or two before his suicide he received notice that a former employee, to whom he had been especially kind, had begun suit against him and the agency to recover a large sum which he alleged was due. This threatened to throw Lovecraft back into the complications of the advertising agency, and re-open all troubles and memories. He looked over it and killed himself to escape at all.[15]

The Allen Advertising Agency had been purchased by Colonel Kearney, who promised Lovecraft that he would liquidate the concern for him, settling all outstanding debts. The treacherous former employee, Issac Liebman, told the *World* that before his gruesome on July 20, Shoenfeld spoke of killing himself. Shoenfeld's untimely death seemed to trigger Lovecraft's emotional decline, which by all accounts commenced that July. When Liebman attempted to collect the supposed debt from Colonel Kearney after Lovecraft's passing, Kearney had Liebman arrested.

In addition to that tragedy, one of Lovecraft's close friends, millionaire merchant Nathan Strauss, had shot himself to death two days before, owing to heavy losses at the racetrack. Lovecraft was said to have brooded over the suicide during his final days. So it would seem that a convergence of financial reversals, as well as personal disappointments, led up to and influenced the suicide. But more would come out in the months following his death.

F. A. Lovecraft—as he was styled in the New York press— lived a life as far removed from that of H. P. Lovecraft as might be imagined. As the secretary of the Jockey Club, he was frequently quoted in print on the state of Gotham's race tracks, then in decline. One description might have fit H.P.L.: "Lovecraft was a tall, pale and studious man, spare of figure, deliberate

---

15. "His Body Brought Back," *Rochester Democrat and Chronicle* (28 October 1893).

of speech, with a quiet, musical voice, and reserved almost to reticence on business matters."[16] Another acquaintance described Fred Lovecraft as possessing "a sunny nature which made him many friends."[17] Yet after Lovecraft was gone, his doctor portrayed his patient with a sentence that fit Howard Lovecraft during his most difficult days. "He was exceedingly pale, and complained of insomnia and nervousness."[18]

The suicide of Frederick Aaron was not the end of it. The doom that followed the grandchildren of Joseph S. Lovecraft next split into two branches. Subsequently, it was revealed that Frederick Aaron Lovecraft was secretly engaged to an acclaimed British actress May Brooklyn, of the Palmer Stock Company, with which he was affiliated. May Brooklyn understandably mourned the tragic passing of her fiancé.

On 16 February 1894, four months after the loss of Frederick Aaron Lovecraft, and as the trial over his contested will was making headlines, while on tour in San Francisco, May Brooklyn drank carbolic acid in a final macabre toast to her lost love. She perished. Buried with great public fanfare under her stage name, Brooklyn's birth name went to the grave with her. Found among her effects was a final communication from Lovecraft: "Pardon neglect: am improving slowly. Do not blame me." It was dated October 24, two days before his suicide.[19]

In addition, evidence surfaced that Brooklyn shared an interest in the occult with close friends, and believed in astrology. Eerily, one newspaper reported an astrological chart with a notation to avoid something in the month of February. As the *Boston Globe* reported, "Letters and papers left by the dead woman show plainly that in her grief over the death of Lovecraft she had dabbled in spiritualism, and had finally reached the conclusion that her only chance at happiness lay in joining her lover in the other world."[20] During a table-tipping session, a friend re-

---

16. "Crazy for Riches."
17. "Her Faith in Signs."
18. "Lovecraft a Mental Wreck."
19. "Driven to Death. May Brooklyn Followed Her Lover," *Boston Globe* (17 February 1894).
20. Ibid.

called, "Mary, Fred is calling you." Brooklyn responded, "If I thought he was, I'd go to him."[21] But in her last days, the despondent actress confided that she had been in communication with her lover, presumably through a spiritual medium she frequented.

Friends described the actress as becoming mentally unbalanced after the suicide of Lovecraft. Her omission from her fiancé's will must have come as a shock. It was also said that her life savings had been depleted through bad investments made by her late paramour, who had lost a good deal of her earnings in the ill-fated Allen Advertising Agency. This underscores the psychological impact of the agency's failure on Lovecraft the previous July.

One thespian who knew them both told the *San Francisco Chronicle* that Lovecraft and Brooklyn had been living together for some seven years. One assumes that the two lovers had been intimate prior to their deaths. And so one could also theorize that May Brooklyn fully understood the diagnosis of incipient paresis, and what it truly portended: that she had been exposed to the syphilis virus through her fiancé.

We can hardly claim certain knowledge of what was in the British actress's mind in her last days, for she left no suicide note. But her suicide did not break the chain. At least not as it related to the Palmer's Theatre.

The following year, on 11 September 1895, Will Palmer committed suicide by gunshot in St. Louis. Newspaper accounts at the time noted that this was the third suicide in two years connected to the theatre troupe. A troubled man given to drink and fired the year before by his brother, A. M. Palmer, he had been rehired as the traveling manager for the troupe the year before. Was Palmer Frederick Aaron's successor as May Brooklyn's paramour? Could this explain his actions?

This suicide would not seem to be connected to the other two unless one postulates that Palmer had also been intimate with May Brooklyn and realized his exposure too late. But that is rank speculation and only worth putting forth inasmuch as the suicide of Palmer was never explained. He was forty-five at

---

21. "Under the Rose," *Boston Globe* (10 March 1894).

the time of his death, and married with two children.

On 11 September 1895, the *New York Sun* stated, "Mr. Palmer was a man of prepossessing appearance and very quiet manner, and he had a great number of friends, who can assign no motive for his self-destruction other than temporary mental disorder. He was a warm personal friend of Fredrick Lovecraft, Manager Palmer's confidential man, who also committed suicide."[22]

Back on the Lovecraft branch of the unfolding tragedy, we come to Joshua Elliot Lovecraft, born in 1845, the son of George Lovecraft and Helen Allgood. George had passed away in 1895 at the age of eighty-one, while his wife pre-deceased him in 1881. After the drowning of first wife Elizabeth, Joshua remarried. Alice D. Ward was his second wife's maiden name.

Tragedy overtook Joshua Elliot Lovecraft in 20 April 1896. Then fifty years old, he was admitted to the Rochester State Hospital as an insane person. "Business anxiety" was said to prey on him, but his diagnosis was initially described as "chronic dementia" (Squires 26). He had been running his father's barrel-making enterprise, Joseph Lovecraft & Son, for several years. The company listing vanishes from the Rochester city directory in 1897. Whether the Panic of 1893–97 played a role in the dissolution of the business is unknown. What is discoverable is that no later than January 1898, Joshua Lovecraft had lost control of his affairs, and had been declared "an incompetent person."[23] This abrupt turn of affairs mirrors in an uncanny way Frederick Aaron Lovecraft's own personal disintegration.

Joshua Lovecraft began exhibiting strange behaviors. He was in the habit of going in and out of his bank without transacting any business. In his home, he neglectfully failed to fire up his furnace, and yet remained oblivious to the indoor temperature of 54 degrees. Delusions of power and wealth alternated with apathetic bouts and excessive sleeping. One of his habits was to pick up pieces of paper when indoors and fallen leaves when out-of-doors and stuff them into his pockets. His business fell into ruin from neglect. Once committed, tremors and ataxic gait manifested

---

22. "Suicide of W. B. Palmer," *New York Sun* (11 September 1895).

23. "An Accounting Filed," *Rochester Democrat and Chronicle* (19 January 1898).

themselves as his mind became increasingly feeble. As Lovecraft gained weight, he grew more incoherent and was considered to be insane.

Compare that with the odd behavior reported of Frederick Lovecraft. In court, George Lovecraft recounted one meeting with Frederick:

> I went to his office and he was acting strangely. . . . His eyes were staring, his hands were shaking and he was in a worse state than I had ever seen him. He was in an awful state. His eyes had a vacant stare, he had a tottering gait, and his hands were continually clasped, and if any one spoke to him his hand was passing over his forehead continually.[24]

Joshua Lovecraft was fifty-four when he passed away on 7 November 1898. The official cause of death was "general paralysis"—another term for general paresis of the insane. His obituary was spare of details, saying only that the deceased had been ill for some months. No monument was erected to mark his burial spot (Squires 28). The next year, the family mill was seized for back taxes.

But there we have it: three Lovecraftian cousins, all of whom had grown up in Rochester, New York, passing away at comparatively young ages within a few short years of one another in the decade of the 1890s. Joshua proved to be the last male Lovecraft who resided in Rochester. Once again, Winfield Scott Lovecraft seemed to have led the way. His death in July 1898 foreshadowed that of Joshua Elliot in October of that year. It has been theorized that during the blank period in Winfield's life—1874 to 1889—he lived in New York and worked for Frederick. If true, they must have been close when in their twenties. In the case of Frederick, his financial reversals appeared to coincide with his mental breakdown to a degree where one might dismiss the theory of syphilis were it not for the severity and specificity of his symptoms, specifically the numerous persons who described his listlessness, vacant stares, and unsteady and tottering gait.

Yet it must be pointed out that Dr. Roberson did not ad-

---

24. "Lovecraft's Will Contested," *New York Times* (13 March 1894).

vance paresis as contributing to Lovecraft's decline in court. Robertson was known to have been suspicious of the will written by Lovecraft in his final weeks, and had a strong motivation for portraying his patient as insane at the time he signed that questionable testament. Before May Brooklyn's suicide, Robertson wrote her a letter stating, "You and I can fix him. He was no friend of yours and did fear me. I am arranging things now so that you will not be forgotten."[25] If Dr. Robertson withheld a diagnosis of paresis while insisting that Frederick Lovecraft was not in his right mind in order to protect the dead man's reputation, this may have contributed to his failure to thwart Colonel Kearney.

One mystery remains: the fate of Joshua's son, George Elliott Lovecraft. Poor George led a challenging life. His mother, Joshua's first wife, Elizabeth Vandervort, drowned when he was five. Growing up, he went to work for his father as a bookkeeper for a time in the 1880s. Within a year of marrying Cecelia Marchand around 1890, the couple moved to New York City where George went to work for his second cousin, the doomed Frederick Lovecraft.

Unfortunately, in July 1893 Cecelia died of acute peritonitis. George accompanied her body back to Rochester for burial. But that was just the beginning of his misfortunes. Three months later, he found himself unemployed after the suicide of Frederick. Newspaper accounts of the legal wrangling over Frederick's will cite George's involvement in the vexing issue. George testified at trial that he had first met Frederick Lovecraft in 1891 and had been fired from Lovecraft's businesses by Colonel Kearney.

Returning to Rochester, George and his father Joshua became partners in a mill in Olean. George moved to Olean to oversee operations. After Joshua died, the mill had to be sold to settle business debts George shared with his late father. Once again unemployed, he was likely near-destitute. The last record of George Lovecraft dates to the years 1899–1900, where he was involved in several legal issues relating to his personal finances and that of his late father. Thereafter, George disappears. An

---

25. "Nothing for May Brooklyn," *New York Sun* (17 February 1894).

only child, he had no other immediate blood-ties in Rochester. His step-mother married Rochester businessman William Williams in 1900, but was widowed four years later.

H. P. Lovecraft reported that George was believed to have gone west, but he asserted that the date was the 1880s. If this was true, it would have no earlier than 1900. No trace of him has ever been discovered. His life ruined, and only in his early thirties, George Lovecraft may have changed his name in order to escape publicity, for the deaths of Frederick Lovecraft and May Brooklyn made national headlines, the joint tragedy invoked by the press for years afterward. Beyond this, it is pointless to speculate further.

All these Lovecrafts passed away while H. P. Lovecraft was between the ages of three and eight. How many of these tragedies came to his attention in later life cannot be known today. Perhaps he heard of them piecemeal and assembled what he knew into a skein of speculation. One hardly expects his prim mother to have told him the whole truth. And well into adulthood it does not seem as if Lovecraft had much to do with the paternal side of his family. Indeed, the male grandchildren of Joseph S. Lovecraft did not survive into the twentieth century in any significant number. The granddaughters seem to have fared much better, at least to the degree their fortunes can be ascertained.

The possibility that some taint of hereditary madness burst forth in the last half of the nineteenth century is a tantalizing one. The fact that there is more than one instance of a Lovecraft marrying a first cousin adds to that theory. But married cousins also exist upon the maternal branch of Lovecraft's forebears.

However, exposure to syphilis—which in these pre-penicillin days was incurable—is the more likely scenario. All three Lovecraft cousins, coming from prosperous families, and who either married later in life or were widowed in their prime, might well have frequented the same house of prostitution, if not coming to contact with the same infected night walker. It may be far-fetched to imagine a single source of infection, but the houses of ill repute in that era would be an exceedingly dangerous place to frequent. Yet people frequented them. Did Winfield Scott Lovecraft, Joshua Eliot Lovecraft and Fredrick Aaron Lovecraft all three contract syphilis during their twenties, only to fall victim in their mid-forties to early fifties? That is one plausible explanation.

Then there is the delicate matter of Sarah Susan Lovecraft, Howard's mother.

Like her husband before her, she ended her days consigned to Butler Hospital for the Insane in Providence, Rhode Island. Her official diagnosis was psychosis brought on, it was believed, by her encroaching expectation of poverty. Neither she nor her adult son worked for a living and they were living off a modest and dwindling inheritance.

A friend of Sarah's, Clara Hess, visited her during this financial decline and observed:

> She was considered then to be getting rather odd. My call was pleasant enough but the house had a strange and shutup air and the atmosphere seemed weird and Mrs. Lovecraft talked continuously of her unfortunate son who was so hideous that he hid from everyone and did not like to walk upon the streets where people could gaze at him. (AV 165–66)

When Hess suggested that the latter was an exaggeration, Sarah Lovecraft bestowed upon her a "pitiful look" (AV 166).

Sarah's condition gradually worsened. Again, Clara Hess evokes her mental decline: "I remember that Mrs. Lovecraft spoke to me about weird and fantastic creatures that rushed out from behind buildings and from corners at dark, and that she shivered and looked about apprehensively as she told her story" (AV 167). This strikingly recalls Frederick Aaron Lovecraft's paranoid fears of being followed, just as the dread of impending financial ruin haunted both persons.

Hess went on to say, "The last time I saw Mrs. Lovecraft we were both going 'down street' on the Butler Avenue car. She was excited and apparently did not know where she was. She attracted the attention of everyone. I was greatly embarrassed as I was the object of all her attention" (AV 167). What appears to be a nervous breakdown took place in January, 1919 when Sarah Lovecraft vacated her dwelling, leaving her sister Lillian to take over all household responsibilities. By March, Sarah was admitted to Butler Hospital. There she lingered for two years before passing on in the same institution where her husband died some twenty years previously. Complications of gallbladder surgery led her to declare a desire to die, stating, "I will only live to suffer." She died the next day (*IAP* 390).

While her patient records no longer exist, they had been examined prior to their destruction and no diagnosis of general paresis was made. Mental and physical exhaustion were described, as well as bouts of weeping, which also manifested during Frederick Lovecraft's last days, and conceivably those of the other doomed Rochester Lovecrafts.

At the age of thirty, H. P. Lovecraft found himself the orphaned only son of two deceased insane persons. No doubt this was a sobering realization by itself. But compounded by at least some grasp of the fates of his largely extinct Lovecraftian forebears, he could be excused for doubting any future prospects for a normal life.

What Lovecraft understood about all this is something to ponder. Surely by adulthood, he had some of the essential facts at his disposal. Possibly shielded from the rawest truths, he might have privately speculated on the subject of hereditary madness, and wondered if he carried some dreadful ancestral taint?

One would hope that even if he feared such a fate, a more mature and analytical Lovecraft would have correctly deduced the truth. Either way, the themes of madness, incest, familial secrets and hereditary doom drove some of his most potent stories, from "Facts concerning the Late Arthur Jermyn and His Family" to "The Shadow over Innsmouth." Did they express some of his deepest fears, or were they merely fictional expressions to cloak unsavory and socially unacceptable truths?

I am reminded of another Lovecraftian quotation: "The most merciful thing in the world, I think, is the inability of the human mind to correlate all its contents" (CF 2.21).

Works Cited

Squires, Richard D. *Stern Fathers 'neath the Mould: The Lovecraft Family in Rochester*. West Warwick, RI: Necronomicon Press, 1995.

How to Read Lovecraft

A Column by Steven J. Mariconda

Number 4: Incompetence or Irony?

As discussed in prior columns, we may enhance our understanding and enjoyment of Lovecraft by approaching his fiction from a specific perspective—the perspective of play.

I do not mean that readers should keep authorial intent in mind. When we read the first line of a poem, we unconsciously adopt a certain mindset—one differing from that with which we read the first line of a short story. I suggest Lovecraft is something of a genre unto himself, and we as readers do well to consider this upon opening the cover of his book. Other authors who have created "a genre unto himself/herself" include Damon Runyon, P. G. Wodehouse, Jack Kerouac, and Gertrude Stein. We should not approach the prose of these authors with the same perspective with which we approach, say, Jack London or H. G. Wells.

My thesis, then: the concept of *play* is central to Lovecraft's art, and without engaging his work in this spirit we can find ourselves, as readers, at odds. We have seen how Lovecraft's sense of play grew out of his solitary childhood, when he learned to amuse himself in a distinctive manner. This involved setting up a series of pretend worlds (or paracosms), using a series of props, and conducting a loosely connected series of episodes over an extended period. Lovecraft started with tabletop dioramas and theaters and progressed to extensive outdoor "villages" complete with buildings, vehicles, and landscaping. As an aspiring writer, he "published" for a few family members installments of hectographed newsletters—as many as *three titles a day* over ten years—that mixed straight content with puns and inside jokes.

This set of imaginative constructs—which served a "self-preserving" function for the young Lovecraft as his father lost his mind and died, his home was lost, and even his pet cat ran away—was something he developed (as one expert put it) "to maintain an experience of wholeness through contact with a continuous self-object" (Konkin 4).

Just as Lovecraft's notion of art was based in play, it was also infused with elements of theatricality and the performative. We saw how Lovecraft the boy was deeply involved in the theatre, through both keen observation of local performances and re-enactment of plays. Later, he was fond of singing popular songs of the turn of the century, reciting soliloquies, and entertaining his friends in the manner of a ham actor.

Also important to understanding Lovecraft's posture toward art is his period of seclusion (roughly 1908–13), when he realized he was no longer a child but struggled to formulate how he might function as an adult. During these years, I suggest that Lovecraft consolidated his idiosyncrasies and neuroses and codified a sense of himself both as a spirited child and as a wise old man. When he emerged, he had constructed the persona of the eighteenth-century gentleman—a persona of great strength, almost like a psychological "carapace"—that incorporated his juvenile and adolescent concepts of play.

Many of Lovecraft's friends were quick to pick up on his sense of play. Edward H. Cole, an amateur journalist colleague from 1914 onward, observed: "It was an amusing part of Lovecraft's *game of life* that he loved to transport himself back to pre-revolutionary days" (AV 113; my emphasis). Other acquaintances made similar comments; one of the sharpest was Wilfred B. Talman, who saw much of Lovecraft in the 1920s. Thirty-five years after Lovecraft's death, Talman finally put pen to paper for a memoir of the writer; his comments on Lovecraft's "psychological carapace" of a persona were especially astute:

> HPL's extent of genius is most evident in the individualistic personality he made of himself. One of lesser ability, given the handicaps under which he grew up, could well have become a disturbed youth or a crotchety old man. He surmounted this likelihood. . . . For anyone to think it odd for a person to identify with and to hone to sharpness whatever aids might enhance

his individuality would be strange indeed. . . . He was little concerned about being misunderstood; it was others' fault if they did not understand. Unfortunately, there were few of his kind, his wife included, who could populate his world. (AV 109–11)

In fiction as in life: those pundits who insist Lovecraft is a terrible writer do not seem equipped or inclined to *populate his world.* Lovecraft's artistry in fiction flowed directly from what he perceived to be his artistry in persona; his perceptive best friend, brilliant Harvard lawyer and polymath James F. Morton, put the question directly to the man: "I remember that I once told [Lovecraft] frankly that some of his particularly extreme justification and admiration of the 18th century was palpably a pose. He laughed and answered: but isn't it an artistic pose?" (AV 30). Similarly, Lovecraft's letters often reference *amusement* relative to art. When he broached to subject of art and play to an elderly correspondent—who wrote "ladies' verse" in a conventional Edwardian style—he apparently caused her some alarm, hastening to explain:

About the nature of poetry—I surely did not mean to belittle it by calling it "simply an elegant amusement," because I believe that nothing in existence is more important than elegant amusement. . . . Real amusement is the sort which is based on a knowledge of real needs, & which therefore hits the spot. *This latter kind of amusement is what art is*—& there is nothing more important in the universe. (HPL to Elizabeth Toldridge, 3 September 1929; 100)

At first hand, a local friend, Muriel Eddy, was quicker to grasp the impish nature of Lovecraft's art:

He started to read this creepy yarn ["The Rats in the Walls," 1923] to us at midnight—and continued placing special emphasis on certain words as he read, his facial expressions changing as he became so absorbed in what he was reading aloud that it seemed he was actually living the story, making it come alive . . . (AV 214)

She declared: "Lovecraft could very easily have become an actor, because he read the manuscript with real effect. He imitated the characters, taking on the voices as he pictured them. . . . He even laughed the insane laugh of the cannibalistic character, adding to the horror of the whole thing' (Eddy 10). But after all, Lovecraft was just having some fun, as the artist confessed: "*He chuckled a little* when he explained that he liked to use such phrases as 'unnamable monster' and 'eldritch horror,' as it made the reader wonder what it was all about" (Eddy 8).

My emphasis, of course, and most probative of my assertion here. The discerning Talman confirms Lovecraft's playful posture, with a circumspect recollection:

> Sometimes mischievous Kalems [Lovecraft's New York friends] would lead HPL into some angles of his own mythology, which now and then he closed out in guttural Clulu language—in effect quoting himself in a way only he understood—either with an amused twinkle in his eye or a self-conscious deadpan expression. (AV 113)

So we come back to one reason that I (humorously) named this column "How to Read Lovecraft." I am struck by the notion that most commentators who say Lovecraft was a poor or incompetent artist are approaching him on the wrong basis. To say Lovecraft was incapable of writing well is akin to saying that Picasso had problems modeling the human figure. Some commentators who dislike Lovecraft seem to be unable to distinguish among Lovecraft's narrators, Lovecraft the artist, and Lovecraft the man. They have not caught on to the game. Could it be that ignorant pundits have overlooked the ironic component of Lovecraft's narrative voice?

Irony is a contradiction between appearance or expectation and reality, when a writer's meaning is different from what is stated. Relative to Lovecraft, I refer not to *dramatic* or *situational irony*—not of that irony which O. Henry raised to new levels of triteness in "The Gift of the Magi" and elsewhere. I am speaking of *verbal irony*. Wayne C. Booth advises that "[i]f a speaker's style departs notably from whatever the reader considers the normal way of saying a thing, or the way normal for this speaker, the reader may suspect irony" (67). Further: "If the author did not intend irony, it would be odd, or outlandish, or inept, or stupid of him to do things in this way. . . . Every clue [to the presence of verbal irony] thus depends for its validity on norms (generally unspoken) which the reader embraces and which he infers, rightly or wrongly, that his author intends" (52–53).

Reread Lovecraft with an eye for the irony and you will be surprised at his occasional boldness, or instances where he lets his narrative guard down—as he almost chuckles aloud in the page, as he did in person with Mrs. Eddy.

"Facts concerning the Late Arthur Jermyn and His Family" (1920) offers an example. It is a good story, a central illustration of how Lovecraft feared the primitive nature of the human unconscious. It is this fear—the fear of being human, the fear of the human *self*—that Lovecraft would work to much greater result in "The Shadow over Innsmouth" (1931). The tale implies that the protagonist's great-great-great-grandfather, while exploring the Congo, conceived a son as a result of (shall I speak plainly?) sexual activity with an ape. Disturbing stuff.

Lovecraft the author (in deadly serious third-person narrative voice) contrives an anecdote regarding Alfred Jermyn, the protagonist's father, meant to foreshadow the terrible revelation. The anecdote is (to follow Booth) odd, or outlandish, or inept, or stupid to use in the context of a serious effort. It seems that father Alfred, a baronet, ran away from his family to join "an itinerant American circus" (CF 1.176). Fascinated by a gorilla on exhibit, Alfred undertakes to train it for a sideshow. The third-person narrator (not Lovecraft the man) recounts: "One morning in Chicago, as the gorilla and Alfred Jermyn were rehearsing an exceedingly clever boxing match, the former [the gorilla] delivered a blow of more than usual force, hurting both the body and dignity of the amateur trainer [Alfred]" (CF 1.176). Alfred attacks the animal, which then kills him. Horrible, to be sure. But before providing an exceptionally grisly description of the gorilla mauling Alfred, the narrator hesitates: "Of what followed, members of 'The Greatest Show on Earth' do not like to speak" (CF 1.176). Odd, or outlandish, or inept, or stupid to use in context? Incompetence or irony? I continue without editorial, while you let that soak in.

When we begin a Lovecraft story, we are aware of a unique quality in the narration, from the very first sentence. I believe a commentator once put it something like this: Lovecraft, having invited us to climb into his machine, straightaway embarks into his own unique reality. Turn to any of his tales and read the first paragraph; the narrator is (my own attempt at humor now) "eminently Lovecraftian," as those of Runyon, Wodehouse, Kerouac, and Stein are, in their respective self-created genres. Take the opening of "The Statement of Randolph Carter" (1919): "I repeat to you, gentlemen, that your inquisition is fruitless. Detain me here forever if you will; confine or execute me if you must have a victim to propitiate the illusion you call justice; but I can say no more than I have said already" (CF 1.132). What are we to make of this narrative voice? Certainly, the speaker is something of a pompous ass. Do you, reader, think this voice is that of Lovecraft the man—or that of Lovecraft the lousy writer—letting his own grandiloquence get the better of him? Or, is it the voice of a first-person narrator that Lovecraft the author has crafted, a smile upon his face, to set you up?

As you read on, note the first-person narrator uses the pronoun "I" nearly a hundred times over seven typed pages. Is this bad prose, or is it Lovecraft the author doing the job? Before answering, reconsider the tableau: a man in a cemetery at night making a phone call into a crypt; and consider again the final sentence, where Lovecraft the author confirms that the bombastic first-person narrator "I" is actually a *"FOOL"* (CF 1.139).

But of course you and I, who understand how to read Lovecraft, are not fools.

Works Cited

Booth, Wayne C. *A Rhetoric of Irony*. Chicago: University of Chicago Press, 1974.

Eddy, Muriel. *The Gentleman from Angell Street: Memories of H. P. Lovecraft*. Narragansett RI: Fenham Publishing, 2001.

Konkin, Serena. *Between Worlds: Paracosms as Imaginal Liminality in Response to Trauma*. Carpinteria CA: Pacifica Graduate Institute, 2014.

Lovecraft, H. P. *Letters to Elizabeth Toldridge and Anne Tillery Renshaw*. Edited by David E. Schultz and S. T. Joshi. New York: Hippocampus Press, 2014.

John Osborne Austin's Seven Club Tales: Did They Inspire Lovecraft?

Ken Faig, Jr.

John Osborne Austin (1849–1918) is primarily remembered as an author of genealogical works, most notably *The Genealogical Dictionary of Rhode Island* (1887). However, he was also an author of fiction. His book-length works of fiction are listed in the appendix, "Works of Fiction by John Osborne Austin." Three of these books, as indicated in the appendix, were owned by H. P. Lovecraft—at least one of them an inheritance from his uncle Franklin C. Clark. It is these works of fiction that constitute the link between Austin and Lovecraft. I will begin with a short sketch of Austin's life and then discuss his fictional works and their possible influence on Lovecraft. I am grateful to the Rhode Island State Archives for some of the information concerning Austin and his relatives and to David E. Schultz for several citations of Lovecraft letters, but I remain solely responsible for any errors and all opinions in this paper.

The Life of John O. Austin

In his paternal line, Austin was of the seventh generation in descent from Robert Austin, of Kingstown, Rhode Island, in 1661. The four generations of paternal ancestors preceding John Osborne Austin were all members of the Quaker faith. His father, Samuel Austin (1816–1897), was born in Nantucket, Massachusetts, but came to Providence in 1828. He was a teacher at the Friends' School in Providence as early as 1838. He married Elizabeth Hanson (1820–1899) in Smithfield, Rhode Island, in 1843. From 1847 to 1868, he conducted the Union Hall School in Providence. From 1868 until his retirement in 1874, he served as agent for the Rhode Island Educational Union, which promoted the establishment of evening schools and public libraries in manufacturing villages.

John Osborne Austin had siblings Katharine Hanson Austin (1844–1926),[1] Mary Louise Austin (1847–1936),[2] William Samuel Austin (1854–1874),[3] and Rachel Austin (1859–1917). None of his siblings ever married. By 1872, Samuel Austin lived at 85 Congdon Street in Providence.[4] His daughters continued to live there into the 1930s.

John Osborne Austin married Helen Augusta Whitaker (1853–1916), the daughter of William and Emma Louise (Barker) Whitaker, in 1878. They had two children, a son, Richard Sisson Austin (1885–1948),[5] and a daughter, Rosamond Whitaker Austin (1879–1949).[6]

---

1. In 1870–74, Katharine H. Austin was a teacher at the Friends' School on Hope Street; in 1884, she was principal of the Rhode Island School for the Deaf. She boarded with her father Samuel Austin at 56 Congdon Street in 1870–71 and at 85 Congdon Street in 1872 and later. The 1896 Providence House Directory listed Miss Katharine H. Austin as a member of the Providence Art Club. Her given name is also spelled Catharine and Catherine.

2. Mary L. Austin taught Latin, English branches, and history at Swarthmore College from 1870 to 1885. She was a teacher of Latin and History in 1870–71, a teacher of Latin and English Branches in 1871–72, an instructor in Latin and English Branches in 1872–75, an instructor in Latin in 1875–78, and Assistant Professor of Latin in 1878–85. Her death certificate indicates that she retired from thirty-five years of teaching in 1911, but 1885 was evidently her final year at Swarthmore. See *Swarthmore College Bulletin: The Register of Swarthmore College 1862–1920* 17, No. 4 (1920): 18.

3. William Samuel Austin worked as a lumber yard clerk. He died of typhus. He was buried with his parents and his sisters in the Quaker section of the North Burial Ground in Providence.

4. As early as 1847, he had lived at 60 Congdon Street. Later addresses included 56 Congdon (1857–71) and 85 Congdon (1872–97).

5. Richard was a graduate of Brown University (1907) and of Harvard Medical School. He became a bacteriologist and lived in Brookline, Massachusetts, in 1925 and in Cincinnati, Ohio, in 1930 and 1940. He died in Cincinnati in 1948. He married Ada Dexter Westcott (1883–1976), the daughter of Oren and Caroline (Hapwood) Westcott. His widow lived at 268 President Avenue in Providence in 1964.

6. Rosamond never married. She lived in Providence for many years, sharing a

John Osborne Austin

1893

household with Helen G. Wheeler (1876–1955), the daughter of Baptist cler-
gyman Nelson J. Wheeler (1833–1919) and his wife Annie E. (Sweet)
Wheeler. Her final address was 257 Benefit Street.

Helen Augusta (Whitaker)
Austin (1853–1916),
from frontispiece of
A Modern Love Chase/Peggy Rog-
ers/An Incompetent (1916).

Richard Sisson Austin
(1885–1948).

The Austin family home at 85 Congdon Street, Providence.

A biographical sketch of John Osborne Austin appeared in *Representative Men and Old Families of Rhode Island* (Chicago: J. H. Beers & Co., 1908, 1.99–100). I extract the following passages, omitting the description of Austin's foreign travels in 1872–73 and 1893:

> John Osborne Austin, as stated in the foregoing, was born Dec. 28, 1849, in Providence, R.I. He received his education at the Primary, Intermediate and Grammar schools, leaving the latter after a few months, and then attending for some years the Union Hall School, on Westminster street, kept by his father. In 1866 he took a clerkship with the firm of Brownell & Rathbone, wool dealers, three years later becoming bookkeeper and salesman for D. L. Brownell. In 1871 he commenced business for himself as a wool dealer. Closing his business out in 1872 he took passage from New York to Glasgow in the steamer "Anglia . . ."
>
> In 1873 Mr. Austin resumed the wool business,[7] purchasing on commission in Maine that season, the next year on joint account in New York State, and in subsequent years on commission in Maine, New Hampshire, Vermont, New York, Georgia and Virginia. Spare intervals of his time (including many evenings) were used between 1873 and 1883, in preparing a family history of his own ancestors and later of his wife's ancestry, her father having left papers which showed an attempt in the same direction. During 1883 and nine subsequent years his time was devoted to the genealogy of Rhode Island families, resulting in the publication, in 1887, of "The Genealogical Dictionary of Rhode Island," in 1889 of "The Ancestry of Thirty-three Rhode Islanders," and in 1891 of "The Ancestral Dictionary." Much time was also given during the latter part of this period to developing the sale of these books. Contributions were frequently made to magazines, on genealogical subjects, and to newspapers advocating broader suffrage.

Helen (Whitaker) Austin died on 4 April 1916. Her husband

---

7. He was a broker at 121 Dyer in 1872. He was a wool dealer at 25 South Water in 1874 and 23 South Water in 1877. He later kept offices as a publisher at 27 Custom House Street (1887) and 96 Westminster Street (1895–1914).

followed her in death on 27 October 1918. They were both buried in Swan Point Cemetery in Providence.[8] In 1880, John O. Austin and his family lived with his mother-in-law, Mrs. William Whitaker, at 33 High Street in Providence; he was the householder there as late as 1887. However, by 1901 he and his wife and children had removed to 113 George Street.[9] After the death of his wife in 1916, he joined his sisters in the family home at 85 Congdon Street for the rest of his life.

The Fiction of John Osborne Austin

While Lovecraft also owned a copy of *Philip and Philippa* (1901), it was Austin's first two published book-length works of fiction, *The Journal of William Jefferay, Gentleman* (1899) and *More Seven Club Tales* (1900), which would have been of primary interest to him. His copy of *The Journal of William Jefferay, Gentleman* had originally been presented to his uncle Franklin C. Clark (1847–1915) by the author.[10] Clark, a noted antiquary in his own right, was the contemporary not only of Austin but of other Rhode Is-

---

8. Their son, Richard Sisson Austin, and their daughter, Rosamond Whitaker Austin, are also buried at Swan Point.

9. This dwelling was demolished when Brown University constructed its Wriston Quadrangle.

10. This copy was offered for sale by California Book Auction Galleries in their catalogue *Science Fiction & Fantasy With Manuscripts & Original Art*, item 584. The auction sale (number 218) was held on 4 May 1985. The item, estimated at $80–$120, actually sold for $37.50. The detailed description ran as follows: "584 [Lovecraft, Howard Phillips, his copy] Austin, John Osborne, ed. (but actually the author) THE JOURNAL OF WILLIAM JEFFERAY, GENTLE-MAN ... A DIARY THAT MIGHT HAVE BEEN. Rebound in cloth. First edition. (Providence: E. L. Freeman, 1909) This copy presented by the author to Lovecraft's uncle F. C. Clark, with presentation letter inserted before title; with Lovecraft's signature & address on front free endpaper, his bookplate on front pastedown. Dampstained throughout, seriously to title page & letter but curiously not affecting front endpapers, which are darkening, the free one split halfway up gutter edge; otherwise a good copy only." Collectors are often quite particular about condition, and perhaps this book's defects accounted for its relatively low hammer price. The bookseller's dating to 1909 is curious: I have not seen copies of this book as published by Austin (and printed for him by E. L. Freeman) dated other than 1899.

land historians such as Sidney S. Rider (1833–1917), James N. Arnold (1844–1927),[11] and Thomas W. Bicknell (1834–1925). Whether Lovecraft himself ever had the occasion to meet Austin is not known. It would certainly have been natural that some of these local historians might have foregathered from time to time to discuss their research, but whether Dr. Clark's nephew was ever invited as a guest—even to a session held at Dr. Clark's final home at 38 Barnes Street—may be doubted.[12]

There seem to be no references to Austin's fiction in Lovecraft's surviving letters. The only reference to Austin's work is to Lovecraft's consulting a copy of *The Genealogical Dictionary of Rhode Island* at the Rhode Island Historical Society cabinet on Waterman Street in his letter to Wilfred B. Talman dated 19 March 1929 (*Letters to Wilfred B. Talman* 108–9).[13] Considering his strong interest in Rhode Island history, there is little doubt that Lovecraft delved into *The Journal of William Jefferay, Gentleman* and *More Seven Club Tales*. If he ever glanced over *Philip and Philippa* (1901), he would likely have been disappointed: two remotely related cousins fall in love, and chase each other over the globe until they find each other. Austin's other two subsequent volumes, *A Week's Wooing and Dolph and Dolly* (1902) and *A Modern Love Chase/Peggy Rogers/An Incompetent* (1916), are much the same sort of stuff, like the romances of Fred Jackson that Lovecraft excoriated in the letter column of *Argosy*.

The Journal of William Jefferay, Gentleman is woven around the life of early Rhode Island settler William Jefferay (1591–1675), who came to the New World in 1623. He settled first in Weymouth and married Mary Gould in 1640, but disagreeing

---

11 Arnold dedicated the first volume of his *Vital Record of Rhode Island* to Dr. Clark.

12 I posited such a meeting at Dr. Clark's home in 1912 or 1913 in my story "Collectors the Sixth and Seventh" in Kenneth W. Faig, Jr., *Lovecraft's Pillow and Other Strange Stories* (New York: Hippocampus Press, 2013), 107–28.

13 HPL indicated that he had never consulted this work before. He consulted it as part of researching his Casey line. Austin believed that HPL's Casey ancestors were of English origin, while other authorities such as John O'Hart (*Irish Pedigrees: or, The Origin and Stem of the Irish Nation* [New York: Murphy & McCarthy, 1923]) believed them to be of Irish origin.

with the Bay's harsh treatment of dissenters, he removed to
Newport, Rhode Island, by 1641. He was encouraged by his wife
to commence the keeping of a diary, which Austin has reconstructed from its beginning through its final entry made on 1
January 1675, the day before Jefferay expired. If there is a fictional personage in *The Journal of William Jefferay, Gentleman*, I
have not succeeded in identifying him or her. Jefferay records all
the notable New England events of the day, including the excess-
es of the Quaker persecution, culminating in the hanging of Mary
Dyer in 1660. However, it is sometimes his more domestic notes
which touch the hearts of modern readers. A topical index (*Jefferay* 165–79) is a great aid in finding some of the more appealing
passages. For example, Jefferay records the results of a blackber-
ry-picking expedition:

> [1654] Sep. 1, Friday. Blackberrying with my wife, and brother
> Daniel Gould, and his wife. The berries are most large and
> sweet this year, the weather having favoured their growing. My
> wife gave us part of them in a pudding, for supper, her brother
> and his wife staying with us to help eat it. They agreed, as did all
> of us, that it was the best they had tasted, being of very light
> crust, with the berries massed together inside, and served with a
> sweet creamy sauce. (*Jefferay* 41)

Not all bounty came from the land:

> [1654] Mar. 27. . . . In coming home from the cliffs where I had
> fished, I stopped upon the beach, and found that the late gale
> had thrown upon the shore some great sea clams, that though
> not fit for baking (like the smaller kind upon our bay), yet
> make a most excellent broth which my wife relisheth much. She
> hath not seemed of her usual health for a day or two, and this
> broth may hearten her. I had caught a few chogsets also in my
> fishing, which, though little esteemed by most, do make the best
> of chowder, from their sweetness, though 'tis true they be ex-
> ceeding bony. (*Jefferay* 39–40)

Some of the most notable nature writing in *Jefferay* can be found
in "The Rock Excursion" (47–50),[14] "The Woods Excursion"

---

14. Part of the "rock excursion" was a visit to Purgatory Chasm, where accord-

(50–53), and "The Bird Excursion" (53–56).

But the central interest for Lovecraft in *Jefferay* must have been the group of tales with which Jefferay and six of his acquaintances, dubbed the Seven Club from their number, regaled themselves at weekly intervals in their respective homes, beginning on New Year's Day 1669. Jefferay himself explained the origin of the tale-telling:

> As the books we have are now mostly read, and some due unto us from England still delayed in the coming, it hath been proposed, this winter, that, for the next seven weeks, meetings shall be held of a Friday evening at seven of the clock, each member telling a tale at his own house. So now we are met, this New Year's Even, at my house, being somewhat the elder, and thus to tell the first tale. (*Jefferay* 80)

Mr. Jefferay[15] begins with "The Sea Serpent; or, The Strange Visitor" (*Jefferay* 80–86). On a fishing expedition to the Isles of Shoals,[16] he and his friends are visited by a strange man of nautical appearance, with a large ring in his left ear only, who after

---

ing to legend an Indian maiden was murdered: "Coming now to the great fissure close by the western end of Sachuest Beach, my son would fain try to jump where the Indian maid did meet her fate; but this must not be, now or hereafter, as I shortly told him" (*Jefferay* 48). The site overlooks Sachuest [Second] Beach in Middletown, Rhode Island. The trailhead is on Tuckerman Avenue at 41° 29' 14.47" N, 71° 16' 9.89" W. A 0.3-mile trail leads to the chasm. A small pedestrian bridge allows viewing of the chasm. (Note: There is another Purgatory Chasm, with its own legend, in Sutton, Massachusetts.) Middletown's Purgatory Chasm is not among the places HPL mentions visiting during the visit of E. Hoffmann Price in early July 1933 (*Letters to James F. Morton* 332–33; *IAP* 854), but HPL did subsequently visit Purgatory Chasm, when Robert E. Moe visited on 27–28 April 1935 (see HPL to E. Hoffmann Price, 4–7 May 1935, and HPL to Richard F. Searight, 31 May 1935). In both these letters he mentions visiting (on Saturday, 27 April 1935) "the strange rock cleft called 'Purgatory,' where the ocean ['sea' in the letter to Searight] pounds thunderously in."

15. William Jefferay, born 1591, died 2 January 1675. See Jefferay 142–43 and GDRI 111.

16. The Isles of Shoals are a group of small islands and tidal ledges about six miles off the coast of the border of Maine and New Hampshire.

demanding a pipe of tobacco, tells his tale in a haze of smoke. He warns Jefferay and his companions to depart before the end of the following day, lest they be eaten by a sea-serpent that lives in a cavern directly below them. The narrator had saved himself from drowning by floating on one of the serpent's scales, which rubbed off when the serpent squeezed into the hole leading to its den. He witnessed the serpent devour a group of mermaids: "Me thinks I can hear their shrieks now, and the noise of his crunching of them; and they of such exceeding beauty, and pretty, playful ways in their gambolling, that it seemed more the pity to have such a fate. It almost makes me weep, the thought of it." To this narration, Jefferay adds: "Yet I perceived not that he did weep, except a queer sniffling be that" (*Jefferay* 84). When Jefferay challenges the visitor with the suggestion that he might be trying to scare them away from his own fishing grounds, only the same sounds of oars which had announced the visitor's appearance announces his departure.

Mr. Arnold[17] follows with the second tale on Jan. 8, "The Goblin Land; or, The Devil's Healing" (*Jefferay* 86–91). The narrator encountered on one of his trading missions a Mohawk sachem who begged leave to accompany him home to Narragansett. While the narrator's cargo is being loaded, the sachem accompanies him to view the awesome falls at Niagara. The sachem tells him the story of an ancient Indian, who is kidnapped by another tribe from his home near Niagara. Carried far west by his captors, he falls ill, and they (having grown fond of him) propose to take him to be healed by a hot spring in the "Goblin Land," or "Land of the Wicked Spirits." Traveling through snow-capped mountains, they come to a lush region, where he is quickly cured by bathing in the hot springs. He witnesses "great spouting springs" that recall for the modern reader the geysers of Yellowstone. Below the springs lives a ferocious goblin who loves to torture and then to devour his victims. The goblin bellows with rage when the visitors would fain escape from his domain, but their "spirits grew strong, and they hastened away from the cursed enchantment of a region which, on-

---

17. Benedict Arnold, born 21 December 1615, died 19 June 1678. See Jefferay 142 and GDRI 242.

ly for the goblins, would be a wonder well worth a pilgrimage to try and find."

Mr. Coddington[18] follows with "The Secret Meeting; or, How a Good Baking May Come From a Cold Oven" (*Jefferay* 92–95) on January 15. In Boston, Lincolnshire, England, dissenters have to meet in secret during the days of King James I. The narrator's father helped to plan these secret meetings. Their strategy was as follows: "To hold one meeting, by a few, in a seeming secret place (but not unreadily found); while another, for the rest to worship, should be the real secret." The real secret meeting is held at the workplace of a baker belonging to the dissenters, who because of his connection with the group must keep one of his two large ovens cold on account of lack of patronage. The disused oven is the real secret meeting place. Feeling hungry, one of the sheriff's officers proposes to visit the dissenting baker, but eventually dismisses the sounds he hears from the disused oven as rats. The hungry official nearly loses his office as a result of his buying bread from the dissenting baker, so all the sheriff's men avoid future visits to the site of the secret meetings.

Mr. Brenton[19] follows with "The Witch of Hammersmith; or, How an Ill-Advised Journey Gained Not Honour or Profit" (*Jefferay* 95–102) on January 22. As an ambitious young man in Hammersmith, in Old England, the narrator makes bold to visit an evil witch to elicit knowledge as to what his future might be. When he comes to her dwelling at dusk, he refuses an invitation to drink from her evil brew and is dismissed with no prophecy, but with the command to circle a not too-distant oak tree three times, and if greeted with "To-whit! To-whit!" by the attending owl, to dig for a ring on the south side of the tree. He hears the owl's cries as predicted by the witch and recovers the ring, which bears the inscription "Go forth and prosper." So, with his father's permission, he ventures forth to the Levant, but prospers not, and returns only to find his dear father deceased for a

---

18. William Coddington, born 1601, died 1 November 1678. See Jefferay 142 and GDRI 276.

19. William Brenton, died 1 December 1674. See Jefferay 138–39 and GDRI 212.

month. He concludes by showing his ring to his fellow Seven
Club members.

Mr. Brinley[20] follows with "The Ghostly Revel; or, The Fair
Nun's Gift" (*Jefferay* 103–7) on January 29. A ruined castle and
a ruined nunnery lie near Datchet, Buckinghamshire, where the
narrator was born. Returning home from a neighboring village
near midnight, he encounters a man in knight's attire near what
appears to be a door to the nunnery. The knight says: "We had
hoped to see you, and your partner is even now expecting you at
her side, to dance a measure with her." A dozen beautiful nuns
line one side of the hall, while eleven knights, whom he joins,
line the other, and they proceed to dance, "most gravely and se-
dately at first, but with more liveliness and merriment soon."
Knights and nuns enjoy "most excellent wine at one end of the
room, from a great silver flagon, to which we would, as occasion
required, betake us, and pledge each other, in some curiously
wrought silver cups." The narrator finds that his partner "was of
such dainty ways and manners, as quite delighted me, the more I
talked with her." The beautiful nun finally announces that they
must soon part, and presses upon him a ring with the explanation: "My father dying, I vowed I would love no man, losing him,
and so became a nun; yet have we one night in the year when
we do dance this measure, which I have done but heavily, till to-
night; but now, since meeting thee—" But the knight who invited him into the hall appears and announces that the narrator is
called for at the door. When the narrator complies, the music
falls silent, all goes dark, and the door closes behind him. When
he returns by daylight, he finds only ruins; his friends speculate
that he may have fallen in with robbers who wished to frighten
everyone away from their lair. The ring bears the inscription:
"None so fair." He tells his listeners: "My wife seemeth to set little store by this ring, and would fain have me melt it to a better
shape and use than thus hanging to my chain; but I keep it
there, as I do tell her, not for any love of it, now, but that, per-
chance, some one wiser, seeing it, may tell the meaning of it;
none doing so yet, to my satisfaction."

---

20. Francis Brinley, born 15 November 1632, died autumn 1719. See Jefferay
142 and GDRI 256.

Mr. Clark[e][21] continues with "The Wrecked Galleon; or, The Second Coming of the Strange Visitor" (*Jefferay* 107–15) on February 5. His tale features a second appearance by the strange nautical visitor with a ring in his left ear only who first appeared in Mr. Jefferay's tale on January 1. Mr. Clarke was lodging in London, and negotiating for a royal charter on behalf of his fellow colonists. As when he visited Mr. Jefferay at his fishing outpost in the Isles of Shoals, the visitor demands tobacco and proceeds to raise a thick cloud of smoke from his pipe. He relates how he and his shipmates were captured by a richly laden Spanish galleon on a voyage from Bristol to the Barbadoes. The rest of his shipmates are set adrift in the captured ship's boats, but he is retained—perhaps for his knowledge of the locality—by his captors. Dismasted by a hurricane, the galleon drifts near a small rocky island. The crew members tow their ship into a harbor on the island, but are lifted with a roar by a great rising of the water and thrown into the sea to drown—all but the narrator, left on the ship. Left with plentiful food and useless wealth, the narrator finds a way to a hidden lake by way of terraced basins. He rides a boat made from the shell of a giant sea-turtle to a grotto, where he encounters a fairy with a single great diamond in her hair, who greets him with this speech: "Strange visitor, thou art welcome, and, after some refreshment and converse on other matters, I will escape thee from this island if that be still thy wish." Tempted to remain with the beautiful fairy, the narrator nevertheless departs, descending the basins in the turtle-shell boat and being picked up at last by a Dutch brig. A Dutch widow ("being still young and very comely") provides shelter for the nautical man and his strange boat, and he proposes to settle with her, if the narrator will accept his chart and go to claim the love of the beautiful fairy. But when the narrator expresses interest only in the chart, the nautical visitor vanishes as mysteriously as he first appeared. The narrator never seeks the turtle-

---

21. John Clark[e], died 20 April 1676. See Jefferay 142 and GDRI 45. For a full modern biography of John Clarke, see Cherry Fletcher Bamberg, FASG, and Judith Crandall Harbold, *John Clark's World* (Rhode Island Genealogical Society, 2018). John Clarke was probably not an ancestor of HPL's uncle Dr. Franklin C. Clark.

shell boat left with the comely young Dutch widow, but keeps the chart, which he shows to his fellow Club members.

To conclude the series of tales, Mr. Vaughan[22] tells "The White Heron of Bedfordshire; or, How a White Feather May Not Show a Coward" (*Jefferay* 116–25) on February 12. This tale was not the experience of the teller, but of his father-in-law, who had served as the king's falconer. As a youth, he seeks determinedly for a mysterious white heron. The urgency of his search is intensified by the fact that he had pledged a feather from the heron to his beloved, so that she might fashion a pen from it. Finally, they admit their love to each other, and she excuses him from his unsuccessful quest, with the agreement that he may make one final attempt. The quest nearly costs him his life: the heron drags him over a cliff as he grasps one of its tail feathers. However, he accomplishes his mission and presents the feather to his beloved, who cuts herself with the feather and writes a message for her beloved in her blood, placing it in a locket. Only when the plume flies out the window and is recovered by the heron does her blood stanch. Having wed his beloved, the father returns to Bedfordshire after many years to finish his days. He sees the white heron one more time, but announces: "I follow him no more, and, giving him peace, only wish the same of him, and that he take not from me my locket, which, since it left my wife's heart, has ever been next to mine."

The diary's descriptions of historical events and of everyday life notwithstanding, readers evidently found the tales of the Seven Club one of the most fascinating parts of *The Journal of William Jefferay, Gentleman*;[23] so much so that Austin followed the very next year with *More Seven Club Tales*. He explained the origin of these further tales as follows:

---

22. William Vaughan, died 1677. See GDRI 211–12.

23. The book concludes with "Jefferay's Dream of True Values" (145–63), which he has written down at the insistence of his wife. Members of various professions seek to have the worth of their lives measured by a mysterious scale and be awarded with gold, silver, or brass medals according to their merit. Some of the results are unexpected: a bishop and a successful merchant each receive only a brass medal. Mr. Jefferay moralizes that steady work in one's own profession, without the objective of either wealth or fame, is the best path to be taken in life.

It was doubtless Mr. Jefferay's intention to have read these tales at the Seven Club, though whether he ever did so is unknown. Evidently those who sent them to him were familiar with the tales already told at the club, and were acquainted with the members. The narrations heretofore published (as a part of Mr. Jefferay's Journal) were so favorably received, that it has been decided to print these later found stories, as a proper sequel. (*More* 3)

The first of the new tales, by Mr. Ray,[24] is entitled "An Indian Legend of Block Island" (*More* 5–16), and is a retelling, in an Indian voice, of the legend of the Palatine Light. An ancient Indian relates to Mr. Ray, upon his coming to Block Island in 1661, the story he had heard from his grandfather, who had heard it from his own grandfather. A great ship is driven into the harbor by a storm, only to find itself trapped when the entrance to the harbor is sealed by the storm. The trapped sailors commence a settlement and before long take Indian maidens as their partners. However, their leader rejects the attentions of the local sachem's daughter. Finally, another storm arrives and unseals the harbor. The settlers propose to return to their native land, but, fearing for the loss of her beloved, the sachem's daughter sets their ship afire. Afterward, a plague takes the lives of all the settlers except the leader, whom the sachem's daughter lovingly nurses to recovery. The leader at last relents and marries the sachem's daughter. The couple loses a daughter, and the mother follows her daughter to the grave. From time to time, the Indians go to the shore when the specter of the burning ship appears. Before his own death, the leader gives his ring to a trusted servitor, charging that it be handed down until it can be turned over to the first Englishman to appear in the locality. So the ring comes to Mr. Ray upon his arrival on Block Island. It bears the arms of the original English settler, which he is unable to identify. Mr. Ray closes with the ancient Indian's description of the sachem's daughter:

> Straight as an arrow, lissome as any fawn, hair black as night, but lustrous, and eyes like stars, yet melting (when turned toward one), teeth of pearl and voice sweet as wood thrush song,

---

24. Simon Ray, born 1636, died 17 March 1737. See GDRI 160.

were only part that he told of her. In our plainer way, she was
beautiful, tender and true; and those of us who believe love best
of all, (as nearest like God who made us), will not pity too much
the one whose heart was hers, e'en tho' his fate at first seemeth
so hard to bear. (*More* 16)

The next tale is Mr. Smith's,[25] entitled "A Nameless Guest
at Narragansett" (*More* 17–33). The narrator's father established his trading post at Narraganasett as early as 1640. While
the narrator is gathering seaweed at the shore to dress a field, a
boat arrives and discharges a gentlemanly visitor, who begs leave
to remain for three months and offers his services as a scribe to
pay for his room and board. When asked to identify himself, he
begs to be known as "The Nameless Guest," and his hosts agree
to his stipulation. He offers to tutor any of the local youth in
Hebrew, Greek, or Latin, but the settlement is too sparse to take
advantage of his offer. A week before his anticipated departure,
a king's ship is sighted, and "The Nameless Guest" goes into hiding in the woods. When the ship sails onward, he reappears and
discloses that he had sided with the Protector during the late
Civil War in England. The very eve before his scheduled departure, two of the king's officers appear at the door to arrest him;
he escapes, shouting out that he intends to follow the Pequot
Path to New London. The officers hasten away to follow him in
their ship, but the very next day he reappears to meet his own
ship and bid farewell to his hosts. In a note appended to the story, Austin speculates whether "The Nameless Guest" might
have been one of the judges who condemned King Charles I to
death in 1649.

Mr. Willett[26] follows with "A Strange Lading at the Kennebec" (*More* 34–45). Although he has no real economic need to
do so, Mr. Willett decides to venture a last trading venture to

---

25. Richard Smith [Jr.], born 1636, died 1692. See GDRI 185. Following his father,
he was a trader at Smith's Castle in Narragansett, Rhode Island. His trading house
at Cocumscussoc (erected by him in 1678 after his father's original trading house
was burned in King Philip's War in 1676) still survives in Wickford, Rhode Island.
26. Thomas Willett, born 1605, died 4 August 1674. See GDRI 426–27. He
was appointed the first English mayor of New York in 1665.

Kennebec, with fine beaver pelts as his principal objective. But he finds even poorer quality pelts in scarce supply. An old Indian finally paddles to his boat and maintains that he will seek no pelts because of the Great Spirit's anger over the large number of beavers killed in previous years. Mr. Willett continues:

> When I pressed him for a method by which I might load my vessel, he would not allow he knew of any, until finally (finding me determined to stay the season out) he did admit there was one speedy and sure way. This could only be, however, by selling my soul to the Spirit of Evil; at which word he fell into such a trembling that I thought he might lose what few teeth were left him. (More 37)

After much persuading, the ancient Indian reluctantly provides directions to the pelts to be provided by the Evil Spirit. Mr. Ray follows the directions and he and his men discover "a pile of beaver skins that might not have their match for beauty anywhere" (More 39). Through seven days, including the Sabbath, they continue to load the miraculously replenished pelts. Soon after setting out to return home they are overtaken by a terrific storm that sends pelts, ship, and all the men except Mr. Ray to the bottom of the sea. Mr. Ray manages to reach home in the ship's boat, which had come loose from the doomed vessel. He concludes his narration with the reflection:

> One thing I learned from this bitter experience; to be ever careful of taking something and giving nothing in exchange. Such may well prove the costliest kind of gift, as you have seen in my own case . . . within man much evil is engendered when once he setteth his mind upon following a short path to wealth. It were much wiser to keep in the old ways (well proved as good) even when toilsome and slow of travel. (More 44)

Mr. Blackstone[27] follows with his tale, entitled "Three Ghostly Appearings at Study Hill" (More 46–59), Study Hill being his own remote home just inside the Plymouth Colony

---

27. William Blackstone, born 1595, died 26 May 1675. See GDRI 21–22. He arrived in America as early as 1623 and was noted as the first English settler of Boston and of Rhode Island.

bounds. One evening about dusk he witnesses "a sudden flaming up of fire, yet not like burning brush; spreading and playing differently and climbing not so high as that." He follows the flame through a mire to "a little pond that was all aflame, though water hath no quality to burn as I had ever been taught" (*More* 50). He hears a sudden wail behind him, and when he turns, he finds the fire extinguished and himself plunged into total darkness. With difficulty he manages to return safely to his home. A second ghostly appearance also involves fire. He has gone on an excursion to visit "Cobbling Rock" (a huge boulder perched precariously on a stone surface) with an Indian guide, and when returning he observes a "dancing light near the ground" toward Scott's Pond. He finds himself on a floating island in the pond when the light suddenly goes out. Instead of diving into the water to attempt to swim to shore—which would surely have led to his death—he waits until the island drifts to shore and then finds his own way home (his Indian guide having declined to follow him to the pond). The final ghostly visitation is by Dr. Caius, his old tutor at Cambridge. They have a short converse, which ends with the spirit of Dr. Caius telling him:

> . . . I am well pleased to see thee placed in so sweet a retiracy for study of nature and books. I am much drawn to thee and this reposeful spot, but time presses, and duty now calls me far away; wherefore I must follow that call, for so I ever taught my lads that they must do. I came to see if thou hadst chosen as wisely as reported to me, and leave thee content in that. (*More* 58)

The spirit of Dr. Caius suddenly disappears. Although Mr. Blackstone was spared another visitation by fire in his lifetime, Mr. Austin noted that his home was burned during King Philip's War in 1676.

Dr. Cranston[28] follows with "A Marvelous Cure at Newport" (*More* 60–72). Late at night, after a long day of work, the doctor is disturbed in his home by a visitor who has broken his leg so severely that it must be amputated—the doctor's first amputation without supervision. He performs the work well, and the man cu-

---

28. John Cranston, born 1626, died 12 March 1680. See GDRI 60.

riously asks to take his severed leg with him, promising to return in a year and to pay the doctor double his customary fee, unless he has succeeded in reattaching his severed limb. He leaves a curious old snuff box as security for the fulfillment of his promise. He returns on the anniversary of his first visit, and, lo, the severed limb has miraculously rejoined itself to his body. He leaves as mysteriously as he first appeared, leaving the snuff box as payment for the services rendered by the doctor. He promises to publish the doctor's skill far and wide. Some speculate that the mysterious visitor has sent a twin brother to deceive the doctor; others, that the doctor has invented the whole tale in an effort to drum up business.

In Mr. Baulstone's[29] tale, "The First Caller to Mine Inn at Portsmouth" (*More* 73–85), we have a third appearance by the nautical man with the ring in his left ear only, who first appeared in Mr. Jefferey's and Mr. Clarke's tales in the first collection. Mr. Baulstone is just opening his first inn in 1638 when the incident occurs. The nautical man mysteriously appears seated next to Mr. Baulstone on his first day of business, accompanied by a heavy bag presumably filled with gold coins. As before, he asks for tobacco and soon sends up large clouds of smoke from his puffing. He tells his host: "I have traveled in this America of yours from the Isles of Shoals to the Carribees, and am lately come from the first, tho' how, thou shalt ne'er guess" (*More* 77). He claims to have arrived so swiftly on a magic boat fashioned from a sea serpent's scale, accompanied by a beautiful mermaid whom he deposits at Cormorant Rock lest she be eaten by the serpent. He boasts that his voice is "sweet and low to women, (who ever delight in my converse)" (*More* 78). (The nautical man has apparently lost none of his way with women since he consorted with the comely young Dutch widow in Mr. Clarke's tale.) The boat has been drawn so swiftly from the Isles of Shoals to Portsmouth by the serpent, whom the nautical man has commanded into service. The visitor refuses all offers of refreshment, but before he retires to his bed he offers to pay for the entertainment of all first night visitors to the inn. Mr. Baulstone's neighbors celebrate the opening of his inn well and late because of

---

29. William Baulstone, born 1600, died 14 March 1678. See GDRI 16.

the generous offer of the nautical man, but when he does not answer summons in the morning, his room is found empty and he himself vanished. The nautical man has the effrontery to leave only a receipt reading: "Rec'd of mine host, Mr. Baulstone, a rare night's enjoyment (seeing all, yet myself unseen). I say received. (Signed) THE STRANGE VISITOR" (*More* 83). Mr. Baulstone offers for examination by the members of the Seven Club the receipt, which bears in one corner "a mark . . . like the Evil One's coat armour" (*More* 85), as also observed by Mr. Clarke on the chart he received. Despite his having been cheated by "The Mysterious Visitor," Mr. Baulstone allows that the added custom generated by the fame of the strange visit has benefitted his business.

Mistress Porter concludes with her tale, "My Husbands and Other Trials" (*More* 86–101). She was born Herodias Long, commonly known as "Horod." Losing her father at the age of ten, she comes to London with her mother. Not yet fourteen, she marries a handsome young apprentice, John Hicks, and they set out to the New World to seek their fortune, living first at Weymouth and then at Newport. But her husband absconds to Manhattan, taking with him most of her estate and their young son. She takes as her second husband George Gardiner, remaining with him for twenty years and bearing multiple children. Having joined the Quakers, she journeys with Mary Stanton to Weymouth to witness for her faith and is rewarded with ten lashes of the knotted cord on her bare back and a jail sentence. Later she returns to witness the martyrdom of Mary Dyer on Boston Common on 1 June 1660. Eventually, she decides to separate from Gardiner:

> Toward the last of it, however, there grew a feeling that an ill considered union had proved but an ill assorted one, the yoke too hard to bear; tho' fault not all of either, as I will freely say.
>
> Upon seeing (or fancying so) he wished no more of me, I resolved not to be left a second time, but e'en leave him; and desired the most honored Assembly that I might have due allowance for my livelihood. (*More* 96)

Just turned forty, she decides to marry a third time, to Mr. Porter,[30] and they go to dwell at Narragansett. He has living a former wife, Margaret, of whom Horod writes:

> I do know this ancient dame as a most worthy woman, and would not have her rest in the belief some would fasten upon her, that this late husband (now mine) did plot with me in putting aside our former mates, to join ourselves. This is so false I would pass it by altogether, had not some assent been made by such as are always ready to believe the worst of their neighbours. (*More* 98–99)

She concludes by expressing a wish for her three living husbands:

> My husbands three (with wives having or had) shall believe this if no more of me: that I wish them such good health and sober happiness as God in his great mercy may vouchsafe them. . . . Ah! Who can tell (of us here) about the last weighing, and how it will go with self, friend or neighbor. Not always as we have deemed it. The Searcher of all things alone doth know, and we may but do our best and leave all judgment to Him. (*More* 99–101)

Analysis of Austin's Seven Club Tales and Their Possible Influence on Lovecraft

The Seven Club tales would certainly have been of interest to Lovecraft. All but three of the tales (Mr. Coddington's, Mr. Smith's, and Mistress Porter's) contain some elements of the supernatural. Seven of the tales involve some kind of token or legacy: rings in the cases of Mr. Brenton's, Mr. Brinley's, and Mr. Ray's tales; a mysterious boat and chart in Mr. Clark's; a locket in Mr. Vaughan's; a snuff box in Mr. Cranston's; and a receipt in Mr. Baulstone's. In the first collection, five of the tales were set in Old England, while only two (Mr. Jefferay's and Mr. Arnold's) were set in North America. The situation is reversed in the second collection, where all the stories are set in New England (except for a small portion of Mistress Porter's tale, set in

---

30. John Porter, died 1674+. He married (1) Margaret Odding and (2) Herodias Gardiner. See GDRI 155.

London, before she and her first husband leave for the New World). Mr. Ray's tale transpires on Block Island (Shoreham, Rhode Island); Mr. Smith's, in Narragansett, Rhode Island; Mr. Willett's, in Kennebec, Maine; Mr. Blackstone's, at his home at Study Hill, Blackstone, Massachusetts; Mr. Cranston's, in Newport, Rhode Island; Mr. Baulstone's, in Portsmouth, Rhode Island; and Mistress Porter's, in London, England, Weymouth, Massachusetts, and Newport, Rhode Island. The strong predominance of Rhode Island settings in the second volume is especially notable. All fourteen narrators were early Rhode Island settlers, and numerous references to them can be found in the works of Samuel G. Arnold, Thomas W. Bicknell, and other Rhode Island historians.

Since John Osborne Austin was himself born and bred in Providence, it is somewhat surprising that he did not choose to set any of his Seven Club tales in Providence. The predominance of southern Rhode Island homes among his own ancestors may account for this omission. We do not know when Lovecraft first read *The Journal of William Jefferay, Gentleman* or *More Seven Club Tales*. We know that the former was a presentation copy inscribed by Austin for Lovecraft's uncle Dr. Clark; so we may presume that the three volumes owned by Lovecraft—if all from Dr. Clark—came to him after his uncle's death in 1915. He did read extensively in Rhode Island history at the Providence Public Library in his early years and claimed to have perused the entire file of the *Providence Gazette and Country-Journal* (1762–95). So it is possible that he read some of Austin's works before he came to possess his own copies of three of them.

During his stay in New York City in 1924–26, Lovecraft carefully made his way through Gertrude Selwyn Kimball's *Providence in Colonial Times* (1912) at the main public library—the book was non-circulating, so he had to read it there. After his return to Providence in 1926, his interest in local history and genealogy was stoked by the enthusiasm of his young friend Wilfred B. Talman. They spent several sessions researching their family histories at the cabinet of the Rhode Island Historical Society. Unlike his uncle Dr. Clark, Lovecraft was never elected a member of the Rhode Island Historical Society. However, if less than an ardent devotee of family history, he remained vitally interested in Rhode Island history. He was delighted in July 1933 when with the help of visiting E. Hoffmann Price and Price's automobile Juggernaut, he was able to visit a number of southern Rhode Island sites he had never been able to see before (*Letters to James F. Morton* 332–33; *IAP* 854).

While we do not have any surviving comment by Lovecraft on Austin's fiction, the appeal of the basic historical framework of *The Journal of William Jefferay, Gentleman* to Lovecraft as a devotee of Rhode Island history is readily apparent. The fact that eleven of the fourteen Seven Club tales involved some elements of the supernatural would also have appealed to him. While settings in England predominated in the first collection, four of the tales in the second collection have Rhode Island settings, while a fifth tale (Mr. Blackstone's) is set in Blackstone, Massachusetts—very close to Rhode Island—and a sixth tale (Mistress Porter's) is set partially in Newport, Rhode Island. Also, the motif of tangible relics of the mysterious events narrated—be they rings (Mr. Brenton, Mr. Brinley, Mr. Ray), receipt (Mr. Baulstone), boat and chart (Mr. Clark), or snuff box and crutches (Mr. Cranston)—would probably also have been a source of fascination for Lovecraft.

That Lovecraft did not exploit his wide historical knowledge of Providence in his early fiction is probably explained by the fact that he regarded Massachusetts Puritan theocracy as the darkest element in New England history. Massachusetts exiled Roger Williams, the founder of Providence, as early as 1636 and engaged in the cruel persecution of Quakers, including the hanging of Mary Dyer in 1660. Perhaps the cycle of persecution may be said to have culminated in the witchcraft persecution in Danvers in 1692. In any case, it is little wonder that Lovecraft saw his home state of Rhode Island as a place of refuge and toleration, while the Massachusetts theocracy engendered for him visions of darkness. Lovecraft had strong psychological motivation to set the secret horrors of early stories like "The Picture in the House" and "The Terrible Old Man" in Massachusetts. Even later, as he developed his fictional landscape, the principal foci of his horrors—Arkham, Innsmouth, Kingsport, Dunwich—

were all situated in Massachusetts.

In Lovecraft's fiction, Rhode Island is often cast as a place of refuge or solace—as when the detective Thomas F. Malone retires to Chepachet in the attempt to recover from the shattering events he has experienced in "The Horror at Red Hook," or when Randolph Carter seeks refuge in memories of his ancestral home in Foster in "The Silver Key." It is possible that thoughts of creating some analogues of Austin's Seven Club tales percolated for some time in Lovecraft's mind. On 7 March 1920, he wrote his friend Rheinhart Kleiner: "I am at present full of various ideas, including a hideous novel to be entitled *The Club of the Seven Dreamers*" (*Letters to Rheinhart Kleiner* 183). S. T. Joshi speculates that Lovecraft may have drawn inspiration for his projected novel (which is nonextant) from Austin's Seven Club tales (*IAP* 360–61).[31]

Lovecraft probably noticed the absence of Providence settings in the Seven Club tales. The use of historical figures in Austin's tales and their solid grounding in local history probably charged his imagination. Why could he not craft his own historical fictions, with settings in his own beloved Providence, neglected by Austin? His reading of Gertrude Selwyn Kimball's *Providence in Colonial Times* in New York City in 1925 may have formed a principal inspiration for his great short novel *The Case of Charles Dexter Ward*, but I am of the opinion that the Seven Club tales of John Osborne Austin may have formed an ancillary inspiration—if not for the Providence setting, at least for the concept of weaving a solid budget of local history into a narration of supernatural events. The discovery of the hidden portrait of Joseph Curwen in the dilapidated house in Olney Court uses the same relic motif used by Austin in several of his

---

31. On 29 November 1933, HPL wrote to his friend Clark Ashton Smith of a dream he had experienced the prior week, involving twelve or thirteen strange, almost identical-appearing men who lived on a hillside street in Providence and visited his home (598 Angell Street) to demonstrate wonders to him (*Dawnward Spire* 484–86). August Derleth used HPL's account of his dream as the basis for his story "The Dark Brotherhood." While the number of the strange men is not seven, the idea of a group of men discussing mysteries is still suggestive of Austin's *The Diary of William Jefferay, Gentleman* and *More Seven Club Tales*. I am indebted to David E. Schultz for this reference.

Seven Club Tales. The idea of resurrecting historical figures from their remains is grotesque—but aligns with Austin's determined effort to recapture the past in the writing of historical fiction.

Because of the lack of any direct comment by Lovecraft, we will probably never know just how important the Seven Club tales of John Osborne Austin were for the writing of the stories that Lovecraft set against historical backgrounds in Providence. Doubtless, Dr. Clark's antiquarian interests also influenced Lovecraft in his use of historical Providence settings. The depth of his reading in other local historians such as William Staples, Samuel G. Arnold, Henry C. Dorr, Sidney S. Rider, James N. Arnold, and Thomas W. Bicknell, while not known exactly, was probably considerable. I think, however, that it is incontrovertible that Austin's Seven Club tales showed that Rhode Island antiquities could provide an ample accommodation for supernatural happenings. Lovecraft probably felt that Austin had neglected Providence in these tales and determined to remedy the deficiency. How magnificently he did so in such tales as "The Shunned House" and "The Haunter of the Dark" and in the short novel *The Case of Charles Dexter Ward* is left for posterity to judge.

Works Cited

Austin, John Osborne. *The Genealogical Dictionary of Rhode Island.* Albany, NY: Joel Munsell's Sons, 1887. [Abbreviated in the text as GDRI. Available at archive.org.]

Kimball, Gertrude Selwyn. *Providence in Colonial Times* (Boston: Houghton Mifflin, 1912).

Lovecraft, H. P. *Dawnward Spire, Lonely Hill: The Letters of H. P. Lovecraft and Clark Ashton Smith.* Ed. David E. Schultz and S. T. Joshi. New York: Hippocampus Press, 2017.

———. *Letters to James F. Morton.* Ed. David E. Schultz and S. T. Joshi. New York: Hippocampus Press, 2011.

———. *Letters to Rheinhart Kleiner.* Ed. S. T. Joshi and David E. Schultz. New York: Hippocampus Press, 2005.

———. *Letters to Wilfred B. Talman and Helen V. and Genevieve Sully.* Ed. David E. Schultz and S. T. Joshi. New York: Hippocampus Press, 2019.

Appendix: Works of Fiction by John Osborne Austin

Note: Lovecraft-owned titles marked with an asterisk (*).

*The Journal of William Jefferay, Gentleman. Providence, RI: Press of E. L. Freeman, 1899 (LL 63). [Abbreviated in the text as Jefferay. Available at hathitrust.org.]

A Modern Love Chase/Peggy Rogers/An Incompetent. Rahway, NJ: The Quinn & Boden Co. Press, n.d. [1916].[32] [Available at hathitrust.org.]

*More Seven Club Tales. Newport, RI: Press of Newport Daily News, 1900 (LL 64). [Abbreviated in the text as More. Available at hathitrust.org.]

*Philip and Philippa: A Genealogical Romance of Today. Newport, RI: Newport Daily News, 1901 (LL 65). [Available at loc.gov.]

A Week's Wooing and Dolph and Dolly. New York: Abbey Press, 1902. [Available at loc.org.]

---

32. This work was privately printed for the author in a "Memorial Edition" of 10 copies. The 10 copies were given to Richard Sisson Austin (son), Rosamond Whitaker Austin (daughter), Rachel Austin (sister), British Museum, Providence Athenaeum, Providence Public Library, Redwood Library (Newport, R.I.), New York Public Library, and Library of Congress. The New York Public Library copy was received on 18 September 1916. The portrait of a young female serves as frontispiece for this book and probably depicts Austin's wife Helen Augusta Whitaker.

The "Extreme Fantasy" of Delirious New York

Andrew Gipe-Lazarou

[The following essay is a condensation of a section of the author's "Marvellous Marblehead: The Architecture of Weird Fiction" (Ph.D. dissertation: National Technical University of Athens, 2020).—Ed.]

Introduction

On 28 February 1925, seismic tremors originating just north of Quebec rippled through the American landmass as far south as Virginia and as far west as the Mississippi. In his apartment at 169 Clinton Street in Brooklyn, Lovecraft's dishes rattled, his pictures skewed, and his chandeliers rocked as the "old brownstone house . . . sway[ed] perceptibly from side to side (*A Means to Freedom* 210). It was the only time in his life that he experienced an earthquake, and its coincidence with his only period of residence outside New England aptly symbolizes the scope and magnitude of his existential conflict with the city of Manhattan. (In the following year, he weird-fictionalized the tremor in his short story "The Call of Cthulhu" as a foreboding force, presaging the protagonist's imminent conflict with otherworldly phenomena.)

Lovecraft's lifelong relationship with New York is a definitive confrontation of creative worldviews—a didactic exhibition of the incompatibility of weird fiction and critical paranoia, both of which find their maximum material expression in the architecture of the city.

Initially, Lovecraft perceived New York as a laboratory of weird fiction—a mythical island where the real and the marvelous are tested in infinite architectural combinations consistent with the cultural continuity of his native Anglo-Colonial narrative. But he was deceived. He experienced the city during a period of urban metamorphosis, at a moment in its history when elements of the real and elements of the marvelous were temporarily coinciding to spatially manifest weird-fictional scenes. In actuality, the elements of *old* New York—of the city's cultural memory—were being systematically eradicated by the PC-dynamics of machine-age Manhattan. As this metamorphosis approached fulfillment, the natural and historical ceased to exist and the fantasies of man dominated the island.

WFM

In 1927, Lovecraft published his great treatise, "Supernatural Horror in Literature," and injected the Weird Fiction Method (WFM) into the bloodstream of speculative fiction. The method, which is an extension of his own creative worldview, is designed "to give the imagination a ground for limitless expansion, & to satisfy aesthetically the sincere & burning curiosity & sense of awe which a sensitive minority of mankind feel toward the alluring & provocative abysses of unplumbed space & unguessed entity which press in upon the known world from unknown infinities" (*Dawnward Spire* 248). It is the "consciously artificial manipulation of the theogonist's and myth-maker's privilege . . . the deliberate exercise of the human instinct for . . . cosmic identification through the weaving of fantastic impressions" (*JFM* 226–27). Its motto is *The Expansion of the Real*.

The WFM is characterized by two simultaneous operations:

1. the composition of elements according to an established cultural narrative—with its rich harvest of creative unevenness and irrational impressions; and
2. "the maintenance of careful realism in every aspect *except* that touching on a given marvel, . . . [which] must be treated impressively and deliberately" ("Notes on Writing Weird Fiction" [*CE* 2.177]) to maximize its emotional impact—to generate a "strong impression of the suspension of natural laws or the presence of unseen worlds or forces close at hand" (*Letters to Wilfred B. Talman* 38).

The WFM builds on the ambiguity of reality, which results from the simultaneity of perception and interpretation, in order to temporarily liberate the interpretive faculty. The rabbit-duck illusion depicts this critical moment of

Image 1

cognitive slippage, when the observer's grasp of reality slackens and he is ostensibly free to *choose* what he perceives (Image 1). WF master Nicholas Roerich, whose work Lovecraft greatly admired, employs this technique in his paintings of oneiric landscapes, which carefully incorporate depictions of the unreal—such as the cloudy visage of a god lumbering across the Himalayas

Image 2

The WFM's quintessential urban expression is the colonial New England town—the mutant progeny of Old England and the New World, which captures the continuous history of its inhabitants (what Lovecraft describes as "the marks of original settlement, slow expansion, and development in channels and directions determin'd by the . . . aspirations and genius of the people") and the quaint irregularity of its geographical location ("the suggestions of hill and dale, river and shore") in a single composition (*SL* 1.287–88).

In his unofficial town planning manifesto, which he drafts in a letter to Frank Belknap Long on 26 January 1924, Lovecraft identifies those towns whose "antiquity & historic linkages" most effectively correspond to the "fixed childhood dream-patterns" shaped by his culture-stream—"Salem, Portsmouth N.H., Newburyport, Newport, Bristol, Exeter N.H., and East-Greenwich R.I. . . . And of course MARBLEHEAD . . . but I cannot talk of that save in rhapsodies" (*SL* 1.289).

The urban narratives of these towns are substantiated by what Lovecraft refers to as the "secondary aestheticism" of colonial homes, which cultivate a profound sense of weirdness with their creative unevenness and responsiveness to the natural terrain. And their impetus for marvelous escape is assumed by vertical landmarks that penetrate the "massed silhouette of blended roofs and chimneys" with their "sharp gables, tall spires, and glittering vanes" (*Letters to Rheinhart Kleiner* 226)—*and* by the commanding presence of natural cycles and unpredictable weather conditions (like lightning storms, fog banks, heavy snows, and full moons) that periodically transform the city into a mystical dreamscape.

PCM

In 1929, surrealist painter Salvador Dali "turn[ed] his attention to the internal mechanism of paranoid phenomena" (Bosquet 61) and formalized the Paranoid Critical Method (PCM)—a "tourism of sanity into the realm of paranoia" (Koolhaas 237) *or* "the reality of the external world used for illustration and proof to serve the reality of our minds" (Dali 216).

Like the WFM, the PCM is "a sequence of two consecutive but discrete operations:

1. the synthetic reproduction of the paranoiac's way of seeing the world in a new light—with its rich harvest of unsuspected correspondences, analogies and patterns; and

2. the compression of these gaseous speculations to a critical point where they achieve the density of fact: the critical part of the method consists of the fabrication of

objectifying 'souvenirs' of the paranoid tourism, of concrete evidence that brings the 'discoveries' of those ex-
cursions back to the rest of mankind" (Koolhaas 238).

The juxtaposition of two historic images provides a basic
demonstration of the PCM's false-fact-making process in action—King Kong atop the Empire State Building, fighting off an
aeronautical assault; and a patriotic rendering of the Palace of
the Soviets, a Neoclassical skyscraper mounted by a giant statue
of Stalin with Soviet aircraft flying overhead (Image 3). The
conceptual associations of Kong's primitive quest and Stalin's
dream of Moscow are automatically drawn out by the scenes'
visual parallels, substantiating a rational basis for the paranoiac's
conclusive false-fact: Stalin dreams to be the king of the jungle
(or King Kong rules Soviet Russia).

Image 3

In 1978, PC protégé Rem Koolhaas presented the PCM as
the basis for machine-age Manhattan's urban ideology in his ret-
roactive manifesto *Delirious New York*. He refers to the process,
which became active between 1890 and 1940, as *Manhattanism*.

Manhattanism's *paranoid* aspect is activated by the city's de-

finitive demographic condition—metropolitan congestion—
which maintains the island in a state of perpetual animation,
expressed as dissociated architectural "episodes" within the
Grid: "In the single block—the largest possible area that can fall
under architectural control—[Manhattan] develops a maximum
unit of urbanistic Ego. Since there is no hope that larger parts of
the island can ever be dominated by a single client or architect,
each intention—each architectural ideology—has to be realized
within the limitations of the block" (Koolhaas 20). Fueled by
"hyper-density" (10) and empowered by emerging technology
(namely, steel construction and the elevator), each episode
maximizes the potential of its block by projecting vertically into
the sky. As a consequence, the building envelope becomes unrelated to the program it contains and the "seepage of symbolism"
(100) between stories is altogether interrupted. This double disconnection (what Koolhaas refers to as "lobotomy" and "schism"
[296]) enables Manhattan's skyscrapers to "devote their exteri-
ors *only* to formalism and their interiors *only* to functionalism"
(296)—realizing the paranoiac fantasy, to maximally disconnect
his mind from the limitations of reality.

Manhattanism's *critical* framework was established in 1811
with the superimposition of the Grid over the whole of Manhattan island. "[The Grid] implies an intellectual program for the
island: in its indifference to topography, to what exists, it claims
superiority of mental construction over reality. The plotting of
its streets and blocks announces that the subjugation, if not
obliteration, of nature is its true ambition. . . . With its imposi-
tion, Manhattan is forever immunized against any (further) totalitarian intervention" (Koolhaas 20).

The Grid is the "urban canvas" onto which the "tourisms of
Western culture" are projected—it is an "archipelago of colossal
souvenirs" (Koolhaas 245), of "Cities within Cities," where each
"island" block celebrates different values, paradoxically reinforc-
ing the unity of the archipelago system. In the three-dimensional
anarchy of the urban archipelago, each Skyscraper—in the absence of real history—develops its own "instantaneous folklore,"
creating a city "where permanent monoliths celebrate metropolitan instability" (296).

Lovecraft was exposed to the history of the Grid in a travel guide titled *Little Old New York* (1910), which was shared with him by his friend Arthur Leeds in August of 1924. The book includes an engraving of a historical house on a rocky outcrop at Second Avenue and 42nd Street (Image 4), with the caption: "Inconvenient situation of many houses after new streets had been opened through the solid rock in order to conform to the established grade" (27). While renting a similar, inconveniently

Image 4

situated house at 84th St. and Broadway in the 1840s, WF master Edgar Allan Poe witnessed the Grid's application, lamenting the loss of Manhattan's "sublime" natural features: "these magnificent places are doomed. The spirit of Improvement has withered them with its acrid breath. Streets are already 'mapped' through them, and they are no longer suburban residences, but 'town-lots.' In some thirty years every noble cliff will be a pier, and the whole island will be densely desecrated by buildings of brick, with portentous facades of brown-stone, or brown-*stonn*, as the Gothamites have it" (Poe 25).

WFM *vs.* PCM

Lovecraft knew of Dali and the surrealists; he rejected them as he rejected New York—as *"extreme fantasy"*:

> I am not a surrealistic enthusiast, for I think the practitioners of the school give their subconscious impressions too much automatic leeway. Not that the impressions are not potentially invaluable, but that they tend to become trivial and meaningless except when more or less guided by some coherent imaginative concept. A thing like Senor Dali's humorously-dubbed Wet Watches tends to become a reduction ad absurdum of the fantastic principle, and to exemplify the aesthetic decadence so manifest in many phases of our moribund and socially transi-

tional era. . . . There is no drawing a line betwixt what is to be called extreme fantasy of a traditional type and what is to be called surrealism. (JFM 404)

The WFM is incompatible with the PCM:

1. where the WFM actively maintains the coherence of an established narrative context, the PCM actively defies it by indiscriminately generating extra-contextual (i.e., metropolitan) correspondences; and

2. where the WFM employs a careful balance between realistic and marvelous elements (as an exercise in creative discipline) to build up and reveal the momentarily unreal, the PCM altogether disregards this balance to unleash the full potential of paranoid thought, surrendering the whole of the creative process to fantasy.

The WFM is a storytelling method with a single, climactic exaggeration designed for maximum emotional impact. The PCM is a joke-telling method that takes seemingly unrelated facts out of their original contexts and creates a "funny" false-fact by unexpected (often ironic) association. (Humor, incidentally, according to Lovecraft, is incompatible with the WFM, because it eases the emotional tension which is necessary for the marvelous reveal to be maximally effective [A Means to Freedom 401f.].)

The WFM is ineffective in conditions of rapid and continual change; the effectiveness of its narrative depends on successfully establishing a stable sense of realism in the conditions that the marvel is designed to transcend. The PCM thrives on a constant supply of unrelated phenomena with which to generate "gaseous speculations" from "unsuspected correspondences, analogies, and patterns" (Koolhaas 238).

The WFM is emotional exploration of subjective reality and unreality (i.e., of what does and doesn't feel real). The PCM is intellectual speculation about objective truth and falsehood (i.e., about what is and isn't factually true).

The methods' incompatibility is materially expressed in the urban domain:

1. where the colonial town cultivates its inherited neoclas-

sical aesthetic, in Manhattan, anything goes (within the confines of the block); and

2. where the "massed silhouette" of the colonial town is penetrated intermittently by church spires and belfries, like the measurement of a slow and steady pulse, in Manhattan, skyscraper fantasies riddle the horizon line like a heart attack (Image 5).

Image 5

Ultimately, both methods are expressions of human nature—as a commitment to the continuity of the past, on the one hand, and as an urge to explore the fantastical possibilities of the future, on the other. To varying degrees, they will always coexist—

together with the seismic friction generated between them. For the metropolitan paranoiac, the colonial town will always be backwards and boring; and, for "antiquarian fantaisistes" (SL 2.229) like Lovecraft, Manhattan will always be too new and too much.

Ground

There are two aspects in particular that complicated Lovecraft's perception of Manhattan and initially led him to believe that its context is a sustainable expression of the WFM: the lingering presence of *old* New York and the city's appearance as a distant vista. "There are really two New-Yorks[:] the increasingly Georgian New-York of the ground, which passengers on the street see—the New-York of Minetta Lane and Fraunces Tavern— and the elfin, heav'n-scaling New-York of the air—the New York which rears Babylonian pinnacles for admiration afar off, and is brother to the thin delicate clouds of vernal dawns" (SL 1.293).

The New York of the ground is a New York of the past, with roots in the Anglo-Colonial tradition. Its first landmark is Minetta Street, a curving, one-way street that begins at the northeast corner of Bleecker Street and the Avenue of the Americas in Greenwich Village. In the mid-1640s, when the Dutch ruled Manhattan Island (the first time, from 1625 to 1664), partially freed landowning slaves formed a community to the northwest of the New Amsterdam settlement, in a marshy valley referred to as "the Negroes farm" (Booth 324). A trout-filled brook called "Manetta" flowed through the land and into the Hudson River (Sanderson 253); and a footpath called the "Negroe's causey" gradually developed along its curving shore (Stokes 76). The "easy going methods of growth" (Stokes 284) that shaped old New York maintained the Minetta curve for well over a century. (At one point it even defined part of the northernmost boundary of New York's city limits.) Then, in the early nineteenth century, the so-called "old carelessness of method" (Stokes 284) was rigidified by the Grid, initiating the conversion of the Minetta brook into the Minetta sewer. But even with the Minetta waters entombed in concrete culverts beneath the Grid (Image 6), the curve that would become modern-day Minetta Street remained—as the superficial shadow of an underground ghost river.

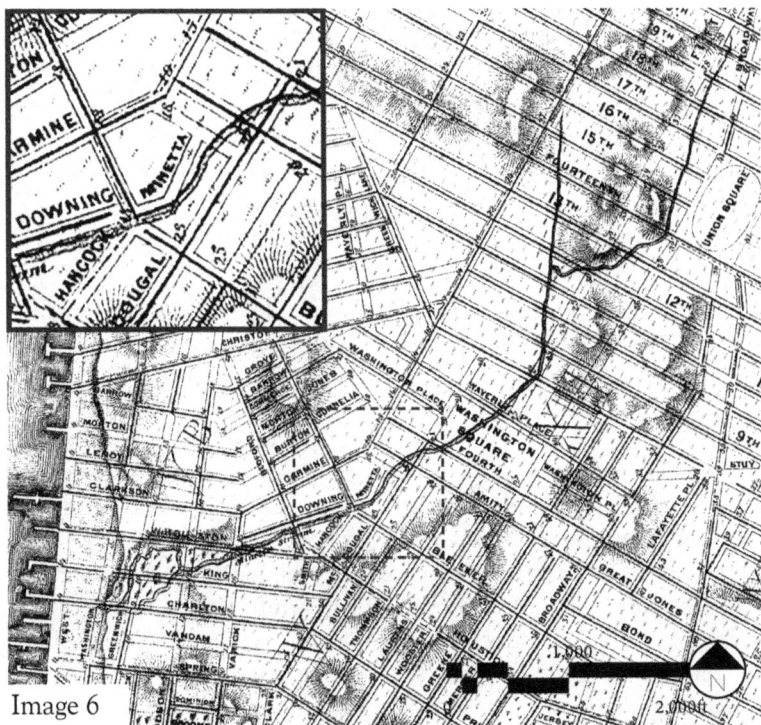

Image 6

Old New York's second weird-fictional landmark is the Fraunces Tavern Block, located adjacent to the Coenties Slip in the financial district of Lower Manhattan. The block is the site of George Washington's great farewell to his officers, which took place on 4 December 1783, in the Long Room of Fraunces Tavern, a week after the British exodus from New York. Despite a number of attempts to demolish and replace it, it was made a permanent landmark in 1900 and survives today as a colossal historical void, surrounded by skyscrapers (Image 7). (Its average number of stories is 4.6, while that of the surrounding buildings is

Image 7

a comparatively ridiculous 32.6.) Referred to by New York preservationists as the "Mecca of American Patriotism" (Davis 40), the block is forever resistant to the dynamics of Manhattanism because it answers to the higher authority of the historical American narrative's most powerful cultural symbol— "WASHINGTON ... the mightiest name on earth" (*The Landmark of Fraunces Tavern* 40).

Lovecraft adopted the block as a temporary escape from machine-age Manhattan. On one occasion, in August of 1924, together with his wife Sonia, he commenced an antiquarian tour of the "New-York of the ground" with an immersive meal in the anachronistic atmosphere of Fraunces Tavern:

> the door was open'd for us with great ceremony by a servitor in periwig and small-cloaths; and we at once proceeded to the oak-panell'd dining hall, where under the beaming eye of our pro-tray'd host (for Saml. Fraunces' painting hangs over the mantel-piece) and in sight of a magnificent white Colonial archway in the corridor adjacent, we partook of a good repast (S.H. fried clams, H.P. spaghetti) in an atmosphere redolent of greater and earlier dinners—General Washington, Alexander Hamilton, Esq., Nathaniel Greene of Rhode-Island, and the like... all of whom I cou'd clearly discern in spirit, with gleaming silver buckles and periwigs new-powder'd ... (*LFF* 148)

Air

The New York of the air is the marvelous expansion of reality "into unsuspected reaches of aether." It is a remote New York— the Manhattan skyline perceived as a distant vista.

Lovecraft describes his experience of viewing the city in the changing light while arriving for the first time, by train from the northeast: "It was a mystical sight in the gold sun of late afternoon; a dream-thing of faint grey, outlined against a sky of faint grey smoke. City and sky were so alike that one could hardly be sure that there was a city—that the fancied towers and pinnacles were not the merest illusions" (*MWM* 84).

The "Cyclopean outlines of New-York" (*MWM* 84) evoke an 'adventurous image of strangeness, magnitude, & complex mystery' (*JFM* 208–9) which Lovecraft perceives as a marvelous departure point from the terrestrial realism of the horizon. From within the city, this effect is imperceptible; the horizon is a compositional anomaly—the primary orientation of the streetscape is vertical (Image 8).

By contrast, in his native New England, what Lovecraft perceives of New York from a distance *is* accessible from within the city—from places like Prospect Terrace in Providence or Old Burial Hill in Marblehead (Image 9), where intra-urban vistas provide the city with a sense of self-awareness by taking advantage of the areas natural topography—topography that, in Manhattan, was deliberately obliterated by the Grid.

Image 8

Image 9

The "New-York of the air" and the "New-York of the ground" are spatially disintegrated; the city can only see itself from a distance. New York *is* a case of urban paranoia—it is a city out of its mind.

Duality

At first glance, Lovecraft thinks he sees the modern triumph of the WFM in Manhattan—a dreamlike city of structures with deep cultural foundations projecting their accumulated historical continuities infinitely skywards:

> The architecture of the future seems design'd to perpetuate this duality of beauty, and none may say what unheard-of-forms may not rise into unsuspected reaches of aether as the decades pass—until the final decadence comes. This flowering of ambitious stone will be utterly original, and it will form America's only genuine and spontaneous contribution to the architecture of the world. With such ecstasies of wild beauties above them, I do not see how New-Yorkers can think sordid, circumscribed thoughts, or remain in the bestial wallow which ingulphs not only them but most of the rest of mankind. (SL 1.293–94)

He briefly considers the potential of its most critical feature—the Manhattan skyscraper (the connective tissue between the "New-York of the air" and the "New-York of the ground")—as an architectural symbol of the WFM. He explores the skyscraper's relationship with the air from the Manhattan periphery, where he perceives the most colossal among them— the "old Woolworth" (tallest building in the world from 1913 to 1930)—as the apex of an otherwordly urban landscape projected vertically into the sky. And he explores the skyscraper's relationship with the ground by descending below the Grid, into the crypt of the American Radiator Building, where he finds a seat of genuine weirdness:

> we repaired to 40th Street to inspect the American Radiator Company's building—the new black & gold Dunsanian skyscraper design'd by the Pawtucket architect [Raymond Hood]— & for the first time explored the interior. The basement is a dream of picturesqueness & spectral charm—crypt under crypt

of massive vaulted masonry . . . terrible arches on Cyclopean columns, black things & haunted niches here & there, & endless stone steps leading down . . . down . . . down . . . to hellish catacombs where sticky, brackish water drips. It is like the vaulted space behind the entrances to some ancient amphitheatre in Rome or Constantinople, or some ghoulish tomb-nightmare not to be imagined saved in visions of nameless drugs of unfathomable Ind. (*LFF* 194–95)

Despite their intense emotional impact, Lovecraft's first impressions of the Manhattan skyscraper gradually subside. In the years to follow, as the city's "exotick strangeness" loses its *"distant mystery"* (*JFM* 224), he comes to realize the skyscraper's colossal presence is not a momentary marvelous release, but a perpetual overbearing delirium (Image 10)—that the Manhattan aesthetic (like the Manhattan narrative) is neither consistent,

Image 10

nor historical—and that the duality of beauty between the ground and the air is too dissociated to reconcile in a single architectural composition.

Syrian

Lovecraft confronts his traumatic experiences of New York's cultural discontinuities by applying the WFM to interpret them as terrifying cosmic anomalies, which take their most authentic form in the city's "roaring slums." While exploring these spaces, he composites their exotic biological and architectural elements, in real time, into weird-fictional scenes—on one occasion during a guided walking tour of Hell's Kitchen in 1922:

Morbid nightmare aisles of odorous Abaddon-labyrinths and Phlegethontic shores—accursed hashish-dreams of endless brick walls bulging and bursting with viscous abominations and star-

ing insanely with bleared, geometrical patterns of windows—
confused rivers of elemental, simian life with half-Nordic faces
twisted and grotesque in the evil flare of bonfires set to signal
the nameless gods of dark stars—sinister pigeon-breeders on the
flat roofs of unclean teocallis, sending out birds of space with
blasphemous messages for the black, elder gods of the cosmic
void—death and menace behind furtive doors—frightened po-
licemen in pairs—fumes of hellish brews concocted in obscene
crypts—49th St.—11th Ave.—47th St.—10th Ave.—9th Ave.
elevated . . . (MWM 256)

Lovecraft's xenophobic reaction to Manhattan metropolitanism
is part of a greater existential conflict that emerges from the
conflict between the protagonists of the Anglo-Colonial narrative and the new natives of delirious New York, who are collec-
tively represented by the *Syrian.*

The sounds in the hall! The faces glimpsed on the stairs! The
mice in the partitions! The fleeting touches of intangible horror
from spheres and cycles outside time . . . once a *Syrian* had the
room next to mine and played eldritch and whining monotones
on a strange bagpipe which made me dream ghoulish and in-
credible things of crypts under Bagdad and limitless corridors of
Eblis beneath the moon-cursed ruins of Istakhar. I never *saw*
this man, and my privilege to imagine him in any shape I chose
lent glamour to his weird pneumatic cacophonies. In my vision
he always wore a turban and long robe of pale figured silk, and
had a right eye plucked out . . . because it had looked upon
something in a tomb at night which no eye may look upon and
live. (MWM 440)

The Syrian, according to Lovecraft, is responsible for the death
of old New York; he is a purveyor of cultural discontinuity who,
by not relinquishing his own traditions, distorts the American
fabric in the direction of his own; he is an agent of the "de-
provincialisation" of America and of its merger with the modern
"world-culture" stream (MWM 453); and he is an existential
threat to its "historic" cultural identity, attacking it at its weak-
est point—the legitimacy of its morally questionable three-
hundred-year dominion—implicitly contending that neither

narrative's claim to the American continent is any more or less authentic than the other.

Lovecraft's reaction to this existential threat is the cultivation of a racist disposition, which is intensified by his inability to functionally adapt to the metropolitan condition. During his New York "exile" (JFM 93), he was unable to find work and is in a constant state of financial crisis (compelling him, at one point, to put his "preservative" antique furniture up for sale); the quality of his living conditions rapidly declined (his landlady refused to properly heat his apartment; he slept on a fold-out couch that he never folded out; and, without a proper stove, he subsisted on canned food and A&P spaghetti cooked over a Sterno); and, in May 1925, his living room was broken into and he was robbed of suits, a suitcase, and his friend's radio set (Tyree 12).

Image 11

Lovecraft's definitive condemnation of the Syrian, and of the delirious metropolitan context that accommodates him, culminates in a WF-survey of the apartment building in which they both reside [Image 11], composed in a letter written to Bernard Austin Dwyer, written on 26 March 1927:

> I conceived the idea that the great brownstone house was a malignly sentient thing—a dead, vampire creature which sucked something out of those within it and implanted in them the seeds of some horrible and immaterial psychic growth. Every closed door seemed to hide some brooding crime—or blasphemy too deep to form a crime in the crude and superficial calendar of earth. I never quite learned the exact topography of that rambling and enormous house. . . . there were wings and corridors I never traversed; doors to rear and abutting halls and stairways that I never opened. I know there were rooms above ground without windows, and was at liberty to guess what might lie below ground. There lay a pall of darkness and secrecy upon that house—it subtly discouraged from first to last one's inclination

to speak aloud, and at times one felt a faint miasmal tangibility in the circumambient air. The great high rooms had something of the mausolean in their crumbling stateliness, and in the halls at night one always had to be sure the great, white flamboyant Corinthian pilasters never moved just the least bit. Something unwholesome—something furtive—something vast lying subterranely in obnoxious slumber—that was the soul of [169] Clinton St. at the edge of Red Hook. (MWM 441)

Lovecraft perceives the "vampiric" brownstone house as an architectural metaphor for the effect of the Syrian on the Anglo-Colonial legacy. The presence of its mysterious program, which occupies hidden "windowless" and "subterranean" spaces, is ultimately responsible for the "loathsome and insidious decay" of "reliques of former splendour and beauty" (e.g., the "crumbling stateliness" of "flamboyant Corinthian pilasters"). He implicitly condemns the diabolical dynamics of Manhattanism—rejecting the notion of "lobotomy" and "schism" that accommodate the Syrian's cultural disconnection from his surroundings. He advocates the honest façade (whereby the exterior makes certain revelations about the interior that the interior corroborates) and the seepage of program between floors (Koolhaas 100), which substantiate the composition of a culturally coherent architectural narrative.

Lovecraft ultimately rearchitects his criticism of Manhattanism at the scale of a city, in "The Horror at Red Hook" (1925), implicating the Syrian in the urban design of "a horror beyond all human conception—a horror of houses and blocks and cities leprous and cancerous with evil dragged from elder worlds" (CF 1.482).

Red Hook is a maze of hybrid squalor near the ancient waterfront opposite Governor's Island, with dirty highways climbing the hill from the wharves to that higher ground where the decayed lengths of Clinton and Court Streets lead off toward the Borough Hall. Its houses are mostly brick, dating from the first quarter to the middle of the nineteenth century, and some of the obscurer alleys and byways have that alluring antique flavour ... (CF 1.483–84)

He portrays the area's past as beautiful and pure—a testament to the qualities of the three-hundred-year legacy of the Anglo-Colonial narrative:

> Here long ago a brighter picture dwelt, with clear-eyed mariners on the lower streets and homes of taste and substance where the larger houses line the hill. One can trace the relics of this former happiness in the trim shapes of the buildings, the occasional graceful churches, and the evidences of original art and background in bits of detail here and there—a worn flight of steps, a battered doorway, a wormy pair of decorative columns or pilasters, or a fragment of once green space with bent and rusted iron railing. The houses are generally in solid blocks, and now and then a many-windowed cupola arises to tell of days when the households of captains and ship-owners watched the sea. (CF 1.484)

By 1925, however, in this previously-peaceful and serene colonial landscape, "it is a babel of sound and filth." Its population has become metropolitan—a "hopeless tangle and enigma; Syrian, Spanish, Italian, and negro elements" occupying a mysterious network of "squalid brick houses" connected by vast expanses of "subterranean channels and tunnels" (CF 1.503). The Syrian's Red Hook is a hidden city within a city. Its secret "public" entrances are blasphemously concealed within the architectural icons of the past (in a "Georgian villa" [CF 1.482] and an "old Dutch church" [CF 1.502]) that have been lobotomized by its metropolitan inhabitants' sacrilegious program.

And, at its epicenter, is a gateway to hell—a luminous crypt with "titan arcades" and "avenues of limitless night [that seem] to radiate in every direction, till one might fancy that here lay the root of a contagion destined to sicken and swallow cities, and engulf nations in the foetor of hybrid pestilence" (CF 1.499). After an extensive investigation of "the polyglot abyss of New York's underworld," the story's protagonist—a "police detective named Thomas F. Malone" (CF 1.481) (Lovecraft's fictional surrogate)—eventually discovers the crypt (and the truth about the Syrian's anti-city) and is nearly driven insane.

Lovecraft prescribes the same treatment for his protagonist's metropolitan trauma as the treatment that he eventually applies

to himself—the architecture of old New England—sending him
to "psychologically convalesce" in the "quaint hamlet of wooden
colonial houses" (CF 1.481) of Chepachet in northwestern
Rhode Island.

Decay

Lovecraft considered himself corpselike when he left New England to live in New York in 1924. But he quickly realizes the
consequences of severing his spirit from its geographical origins
(MWM 440): that he cannot survive life after death without the
elements of his native Anglo-Colonial culture-stream. In order
to self-preserve, therefore, he surrounds his corpse with traces of
New England; he uses cultural artifacts (as Dr. Muñoz, the protagonist of Lovecraft's homonymous short story, uses *cool air*) as
preservatives to keep himself alive while living in Manhattan. In
his own living space, he manages the requisition and administration of old-world artifacts like a seasoned curator:

> I could not live anywhere without my own household objects
> around me—the furniture my childhood knew, the books my
> ancestors read, and the pictures my mother and grandmother
> and aunt painted. The presence of all these things at the edge of
> Red Hook was really almost humorous [. . .] and visitors not in-
> frequently commented on the virtual transition from one world
> to another implied in the simple act of stepping within my door.
> Outside—Red Hook. Inside, Providence, R.I.! (MWM 440)

Outside, in the urban territory, Lovecraft requisitions the necessary preservatives from what remains of old New York. His preferred scouting technique is the twilight perambulation, during
which he casually disregards the logic of the Grid and weaves his
own labyrinthine path through the oldest areas of the city, taking special care to incorporate key WF-plot points (such as the
"Minettas" and Fraunces Tavern). He meticulously documents
and describes the spaces he encounters and the artifacts they
contain (like Dr. Muñoz documenting his regimen of preservatives), desperate to buy himself more time.

But, as Manhattanism accelerates the deterioration of old
New York (and the breakdown of the "cooling" mechanism

which is keeping him alive), Lovecraft's spiritual condition worsens. Throughout his life, he witnesses the dynamics of this urban decay firsthand. On one occasion, he notices "with horror the replacement of a fine colonial row [on Vandewater St.] by a damnable new garage, (other excellent colonials have vanished in Greenwich, at Barrow & Hudson Sts.)" and the demolition of "the old Harpers publishing house" (*LFF* 345); on another occasion, he observes that

> the quaintness of Greenwich-Village is rapidly passing. Whole blocks of colonial houses have come down since I knew the place; & now the more placid but less ancient Chelsea-Village to the north of it is menaced. Famous "London Terrace" in West 23rd St.—where a friend of mine has lived all his life—is to come down shortly to make room for a wretched apartment skyscraper. (*Letters to Elizabeth Toldridge* 56)

Eventually, Lovecraft's preservative "cooling" mechanism breaks down completely and the metropolitan delirium of *new* New York prevails. He declares his final verdict—"old New York is dead" (*SL* 2.45).

"He"

In the early morning of 11 August 1925, after a twilight walkabout through old New York, Lovecraft departed the island for the "nearest New-England substitute"—Elizabeth, New Jersey, across the Newark Bay. Upon arrival "in the central district of the village" at 7 A.M., he bought a "dime composition book," sat in Scott Park ("pleasantly intoxicated by the wealth of delicate un-metropolitan greenery & the yellow & white colonialism of the gambrel-roofed Scott house" [*LFF* 346]), and transmuted his gradual disillusionment with Manhattan into a weird tale— "a hellish midnight tale—a tale of cryptical horrors among tangles of antediluvian alleys in Greenwich Village . . . & the abiding terror of him who comes to New-York as to a faery flower of stone & marble, yet finds only a verminous corpse—a dead city of squinting alienage with nothing in common either with its own past or with the background of America in general. I named it 'He'" (*LFF* 346).

The story's narrative begins when an unnamed protagonist, "on a sleepless night's walk" in Greenwich Village, meets a mysterious old man, who, responding to the protagonist's evident interest in the city's antiquarian details, invites the "obvious newcomer" on a guided tour. The protagonist follows, driven by his "quest for antique beauty and mystery," which is "all [he] has to keep [his] soul alive" (CF 1.509).

As he advances along his route, into a "maze of unknown antiquity," its architectural details—"tottering Ionic columns and fluted pilasters and urn-headed iron fence-posts and flaring-lintelled windows and decorative fanlights"—appear to "grow quainter and stranger" (CF 1.509–10), and the impression that he is walking into the past begins to crystallize into an authentic human mood. As the day breaks, the protagonist arrives at his destination (the old man's private estate), primed by the mysterious route for the city's marvelous reveal.

The soul of Old New York presents itself to the unnamed protagonist. It appears as an architecture (inspired by the Van Nest Mansion on Bleecker Street [Joshi and Schultz 108]) (Image 12)— constructed c. 1744 and razed for new development c. 1864) and as a man, both possessed by the same spirit: the spirit of the eighteenth century, the golden age of the Anglo-Colonial narrative.

Image 12

"Reflecting upon better times," the spirit of old New York maintains the "dress and manners" of its pre-Revolutionary colonial ancestry; it occupies a rural seat on Manhattan Island, "swallowed though it was by two towns, first Greenwich, which built up hither after 1800, then New-York, which joined on near 1830"; *and* it wields ancient wisdom, which it once requisitioned, together with ownership of the land, from "sartain half-breed red Indians once encamped upon this hill" (CF 1.512).

It explains to the protagonist that, since its inception (with the colonization of the American continent), it has been suspicious of Manhattan Island's *metropolitan* destiny, having already detected the ambitions of the Grid in the heart of western man: "there appeared to reside some very remarkable qualities in the will of mankind; qualities having a little-suspected dominance not only over the acts of one's self and of others, but over every variety of force and substance in Nature, and over many elements and dimensions deemed more universal than Nature herself" (CF 1.512).

And, finally, it resolves to show the protagonist what he desires to see: the terrifying consummation of Manhattanism as a time-defying sequence of vistas.

> My host now took my hand to draw me to one of the two windows on the long side of the malodorous room. [. . .] Once at the window, the man drew apart the yellow silk curtains and directed my stare into the blackness outside. For a moment I saw nothing save a myriad of tiny dancing lights, far, far before me. Then, as if in response to an insidious motion of my host's hand, a flash of heat-lightning played over the scene, and I looked out upon a sea of luxuriant foliage—foliage unpolluted, and not the sea of roofs to be expected by any normal mind. On my right the Hudson glittered wickedly, and in the distance ahead I saw the unhealthy shimmer of a vast salt marsh constellated with nervous fireflies. (CF 1.513–14)

The first vista presents the continent's pristine natural landscape (as it was prior to colonization)—a wellspring of weird, natural design parameters waiting to be engaged by the Anglo-Colonial narrative.

> Again the lightning flashed—but this time upon a scene not wholly strange. It was Greenwich, the Greenwich that used to be, with here and there a roof or row of houses as we see it now, yet with lovely green lanes and fields and bits of grassy common. The marsh still glittered beyond, but in the farther distance I saw the steeples of what was then all of New York; Trinity and St. Paul's and the Brick Church dominating their sisters, and a faint haze of wood smoke hovering over the whole. (CF 1.514)

The second vista presents the golden age of Old New York—
historical Greenwich in harmony with the land and, in the distance,
Lower Manhattan and the imminent origins of *new* New York.

> . . . he gestured anew; bringing to the sky a flash more blinding
> than either which had come before. For full three seconds I could
> glimpse that pandaemoniac sight, and in those seconds I saw a
> vista which will ever afterward torment me in dreams. I saw the
> heavens verminous with strange flying things, and beneath
> them a hellish black city of giant stone terraces with impious
> pyramids flung savagely to the moon, and devil-lights burning
> from unnumbered windows. And swarming loathsomely on aer-
> ial galleries I saw the yellow, squint-eyed people of that city,
> robed horribly in orange and red, and dancing insanely to the
> pounding of fevered kettle-drums, the clatter of obscene crotale,
> and the maniacal moaning of muted horns whose ceaseless dirg-
> es rose and fell undulantly like the waves of an unhallowed
> ocean of bitumen.
>
> I saw this vista, I say, and heard as with the mind's ear the
> blasphemous domdaniel of cacophony which companioned it. It
> was the shrieking fulfilment of all the horror which that corpse-
> city had ever stirred in my soul, and forgetting every injunction
> to silence I screamed and screamed and screamed as my nerves
> gave way and the walls quivered about me. (*CF* 1.514–15)

The third and final vista presents the total triumph of the modern metropolis (Image 13), the ultimate denouement of Manhattanism; it presents the PCM operating beyond its full
capacity—turbocharged—to effect a state of perpetual fantasy in
its paranoiac inhabitants and their architecture. The city has finally succeeded in totally denying its connection with nature
and history, and has architected its delirium into an alternate
reality. In this alternate reality, man inhabits Manhattan's *frontier in the sky* ("with strange flying things" and "on aerial galleries")—totally denying the natural foundations and historical
experience which elevate and stabilize him.

In the context of the WFM, it is a terrifying marvel, an alien
dreamscape "out of space, out of time" (*JFM* 209 [quoting
Poe]). Discarded and denied by the metropolis of the future, the
soul of Old New York submits to decay, instantaneously expos-

ing its *true* form—"musk-reeking," "wormy," "sagging," "battered," "rickety," and "ragged." The story here exposes the gruesome reality of the hyper-consumption of PC-activity from the perspective of the material-being-consumed; it "survives" the PCM's constant recycling like a living corpse, as a shell of its former self. Its superficial significance (i.e., what the paranoiac interprets as its significance), represented by the outward appearance of the old man's private estate, *remains*, but its soul (i.e., its cultural significance—its connection with the sociohistorical dynamics that produced it), represented by the estate's *true* form, gradually decays and ultimately collapses.

Image 13

Now swift and splintering blows assailed the sickly panels, and I saw the gleam of a tomahawk as it cleft the rending wood. I did not move, for I could not; but watched dazedly as the door fell in pieces to admit a colossal, shapeless influx of inky substance starred with shining, malevolent eyes. It poured thickly, like a flood of oil bursting a rotten bulkhead, overturned a chair as it spread, and finally flowed under the table and across the room to where the blackened head with the eyes still glared at me. Around that head it closed, totally swallowing it up, and in another moment it had begun to recede; bearing away its invisible burden without touching me, and flowing out of that black doorway and down the unseen stairs . . . (CF 1.516)

Compelled by the native American spirit (itself relegated to oblivion by the Anglo-Colonial narrative), the soul of Old New York joins the "colossal, shapeless influx" of forsaken history that lurks beneath the modern city. As the protagonist returns to the present time, his body bloodied and broken by the revelation of the city's impending future, he resolves to leave New York and return to the living past—"to the pure New England lanes up which fragrant sea-winds sweep at evening" (CF 1.517).

Alive!

. . . all at once there came a sight which presaged a return to the world of reality—an old-fashion'd wall of tumbled stone betwixt rolling meadows! Memory! Broken threads! But see! A little white farmhouse amidst green hills! A village steeple beyond a distant crest! A square wooden Georgian building on an eminence! Who am I? What am I? Where am I? I—a corpse—once lived, and here are the signs of a resurrection! . . . look! The old familiar billboards! Packer's Tar Soap! Gorton's Codfish! GOD, I AM ALIVE!" (SL 2.45–46)

Lovecraft's New York story has a surprise ending. In mid-April of 1926 he returned to New England—wellspring of weirdness and reservoir of "authentic" American culture—and reunited his spirit with its cultural roots. The revivifying force that he left New England to seek in New York had been in New England all along: "In New York my mental processes were virtually atrophied for want of contact with the impressions which form their exclusive nourishment . . .the return home liberated & resuscitated my faculties, such as they are" (*Dawnward Spire* 146).

Lovecraft's rejection of New York is a definitive moment for the WFM: by forced exposure to the incompatible PC-delirium of Manhattan, it achieves greater resolution. And the effect of this pronounced maturation is no more evident than in the subsequent life and work of the WF master himself.

Works Cited

Bosquet, Alain. *Conversations with Dali*. New York: E. P. Dutton, 1969.

Booth, Mary L. *History of the City of New York*. New York: W. R. C. Clark & Meeker, 1859.

Dali, Salvador. *The Collected Writings of Salvador Dali*. Edited by Haim Finkelstein. Cambridge: Cambridge University Press, 1998.

Davis, William, and J. Esther Singleton, ed. "Fraunces Tavern." In *Historic Buildings of America as Seen and Described by Famous Writers*. New York: Dodd, Mead, 1906.

Joshi, S. T., and David E. Schultz. *An H. P. Lovecraft Encyclopedia*. Westport, CT: Greenwood Press, 2001.

Koolhaas, Rem. *Delirious New York*. New York: Montacelli Press, 1978.

The Landmark of Fraunces Tavern: A Restrospect. New York: Women's Auxiliary, 1901.

Little Old New York. New York: Oxford Publication Co., 1910.

Lovecraft, H. P. *Letters to Family and Family Friends*. Edited by S. T. Joshi and David E. Schultz. New York: Hippocampus Press, 2020. [Abbreviated in the text as *LFF*.]

———. *Letters to James F. Morton*. Edited by David E. Schultz and S. T. Joshi. New York: Hippocampus Press, 2011. [Abbreviated in the text as *JFM*.]

———. *Letters to Maurice W. Moe and Others*. Edited by David E. Schultz and S. T. Joshi. New York: Hippocampus Press, 2018. [Abbreviated in the text as *MWM*.]

———. *Letters to Rheinhart Kleiner*. Edited by S. T. Joshi and David E. Schultz. New York: Hippocampus Press, 2005.

———. *Letters to Wilfred B. Talman and Helen V. and Genevieve Sully*. Ed. David E. Schultz and S. T. Joshi. New York: Hippocampus Press, 2019.

————, and Robert E. Howard. *A Means to Freedom: The Letters of H. P. Lovecraft and Robert E. Howard.* Edited by S. T. Joshi, David E. Schultz, and Rusty Burke. New York: Hippocampus Press, 2009. 2 vols.

————, and Clark Ashton Smith. *Dawnward Spire, Lonely Hill: The Letters of H. P. Lovecraft and Clark Ashton Smith.* Edited by David E. Schultz and S. T. Joshi. New York: Hippocampus Press, 2017.

Poe, Edgar Allan. *Doings of Gotham.* Edited by Jacob E. Spannuth. Pottsville, PA: Jacoib E. Spannuth, 1929.

Sanderson, Eric. *Mannahatta: A Natural History of New York City.* New York: Abrams, 2009.

Stokes, I. N. Phelps. *The Iconography of Manhattan.* Vol. 6. New York: Robert H. Dodd, 1928.

Tyree, J. M. "Lovecraft at the Automat." *New England Review* 29, No. 1 (2008): 137–50.

Images

1. *Welche Thiere Gleichen einander am moisten?* ('Which animals are most like each other?'). Drawing, from the 23 October 1892 issue of *Fliegende Blatter* magazine. Wikimedia Commons. en.wikipedia.org/wiki/File:Kaninchen_und_Ente.svg (Accessed 3 April 2020).

2. *Kalki Avatar.* Paintings by Nicholas Roerich, 1932. Public domain. www.wikiart.org/en/nicholas-roerich/kalki-avatar-1932/ (Accessed 3 April 2020).

3. Screenshot from *King Kong.* Directed by Merian C. Cooper and Ernest B. Schoedsack. Radio Pictures, 1933; and *Project for the Palace of Soviets, Moscow, 1934.* Architectural perspective, by Boris M. Iofan. Berlin: Collection of the Tchoban Foundation. www.e-flux.com/announcements/289578/building-a-new-new-world/ (Accessed 18 April 2020). archive.org/details/littleoldnewyork01poug/page/26/mode/2up

4. *Second Avenue Near 42d Street.* Engraving, from *Little old New York.* New York: Oxford Publishing Company, 1910. p.27. (Accessed 31 May 2020).

5. *Abbot Hall from Crocker's Park, Marblehead.* Photograph (top), c.1900, by Detroit Publishing Co. The Library of Congress.

www.loc.gov/item/2016801222/ (Accessed 30 May 2020); and *New York Skyline from Brooklyn*. Photograph (bottom), c.1931, by Irving Underhill. The Library of Congress. www.loc.gov/item/00650351/ (Accessed 30 May 2020).

6. *Sanitary and Topographical Map of the City and Island of New York (1865)*. Map, by Egbert Viele, published in 1874. Wikimedia Commons. commons.wikimedia.org/wiki/File: Viele_Map_1865.jpg (Accessed 24 April 2020).

7. *Perspective view of Fraunces Tavern Block, Corner of Pearl and Broad Streets, View Taken Looking East*. Photograph (1), c.1970, taken during the Historic American Buildings Survey. The Library of Congress. www.loc.gov/resource/hhh.ny0975. photos/?sp=1 (Accessed 28 April 2020).

8. *Broad Street looking toward Wall Street, Manhattan*. Photograph, 1936, by Berenice Abbott. Wikimedia Commons. commons.wikimedia.org/wiki/File:Broad_Street_looking_ toward_Wall_Street,_Manhattan._(3110607948).jpg (Accessed 31 May 2020).

9. *Prospect Terrace, Providence, R.I.* Photograph (top), undated. Digital Commonwealth. www.digitalcommonwealth.org/ search/ commonwealth-oai:cf95nf56q (Accessed 31 May 2020); and *Marblehead, Orne Street, Burying Hill*. Photograph (bottom), c.1900, by Frank Cousins. Digital Commonwealth. www.digitalcommonwealth.org/search/commonwealth:2b8 8r202f (Accessed 31 May 2020).

10. *40th Street between Fifth and Sixth Avenues*. Photograph of the American Radiator Building with the Empire State Building beyond, 1935. Wikimedia Commons. commons.wikimedia. org/wiki/File:40th_Street_between_Fifth_and_Sixth_Avenues, Manhattan_(NYPL_b13668355-482659).tiff (Accessed 31 May 2020).

11. 169 Clinton

12. *Sir Peter Warren's House*. Engraving, undated (likely c.1850). The New York Public Library. digitalcollections. nypl.org/items/510d47da-264c-a3d9-e040-e00a18064a99 (Accessed 19 May 2020).

13. Screenshots from *Metropolis*. Directed by Fritz Lang. Universum Film A.G., 1927.

An Arctic Mystery:
The Lovecraftian North Pole

Edward Guimont

Tucked away in a footnote of *Lovecraftian Voyages*, Kenneth W. Faig, Jr. remarks how "Strangely, one locale which seems to have eluded the attention of most Mythos writers is the Arctic." In Faig's view, even Lovecraft had only written one story set in the Arctic, "Polaris" (*Voyages* 256n174). In his article "Lovecraft and the Polar Myth," John Navroth spends a little more than one out of nine total pages on the Arctic, with the balance on the Antarctic (190–91). A cursory glance of indices seems to confirm this boreal paucity. In the index to the series of four Hippocampus Press Collected Fiction volumes, "Arctic" only appears twice, both in "The Horror in the Museum" (CF 4.669). S. T. Joshi's *An Index to the Selected Letters of H. P. Lovecraft* is more mixed; it contains entries for Roald Amundsen, Alaska, "Arctic and Antarctic Regions" (most of which are for the latter), Greenland, Henry Hudson, Iceland, Robert Peary, "Polaris," "Ross's Expeditions," and Scandinavia, but lacks numerous other obvious Arctic entries.

This *apparent* lack of Arctic interest in Lovecraft's writing, both fiction and nonfiction, is surprising for several reasons. First and foremost is his well-established interest in Antarctic exploration, and the fact that his Antarctic novella is perhaps his most influential work. But it is also surprising given the fact that Lovecraft grew up in the golden age of Arctic exploration, particularly by Americans, and news of such expeditions was widespread at the time. In an 25 October 1929 letter to Elizabeth Toldridge, Lovecraft even remembers how he had an early interest in lost Arctic as well as Antarctic civilizations (*ET* 113).

Even if he had not had an interest in the antipodes and exploration, Lovecraft would not have been able to escape it. My goal in this article is therefore fourfold. First, I will point out where the Arctic actually was present in Lovecraft's fiction. Second, I will give a brief overview to the history of Arctic exploration in Lovecraft's lifetime. This will include examples of specific cases from that history which clearly played into Lovecraft's fiction. Third, I will look at what Arctic-set fiction Lovecraft himself read. Finally, I will show how the Arctic has continued to be developed in the fiction that was in turn inspired by Lovecraft.

The Arctic in Lovecraft

The Arctic made its debut in Lovecraft's fiction extremely early, in his 1902 juvenile short story "The Mysterious Ship." The twelve-year-old Lovecraft wrote that

> It is necessary to relate a geographical Fact:—At the North Pole there is supposed to exist a vast continent composed of volcanic soil, a portion is open to travellers and explorers but it is barren and unfruitful. and thus absolutely Impassable. It is called "No-Mans Land."

Later in the story, a pirate submarine journeys to and from No-Mans Land (CF 3.392–93).

The Arctic next appears in his fiction in 1918, in what would be a bumper year for Lovecraftian Arcticana. It appears in two of his poems from that year. "Nemesis" references an age when "Man, yet untainted and happy, dwelt in bliss on the far Arctic isle" (AT 47), while "Astrophobos" references "Gleaming nigh the Arctic car" (AT 48). But more substantially, 1918 was also the year of "Polaris," the only story of Lovecraft's set entirely in the Arctic (even if not the only one with Arctic elements, as Faig claimed). The immediate inspiration for "Polaris" was a dream Lovecraft had in May 1918, and more broadly his appreciation for Edgar Allan Poe—*not* Lord Dunsany, whose influence is often, and incorrectly, read into the story (MWM 70; Joshi, "On 'Polaris'"). Neither the dream nor the Poe stories had Arctic themes, so its setting is particularly indicative that the Arctic was on Lovecraft's mind in 1918.

In "Polaris," the narrator ruminates on the titular "Pole Star" (CF 1.65)[1] in the city of Olathoë in the kingdom of Lomar, under threat from the advance of the "Inutos" (CF 1.67). The narrator's reflections of the past victories of Lomar include not only preserving "the traditions of their ancestors [when] forced to move southward from Zobna before the advance of the great ice-sheet" but also their defeat of the monstrous Gnophkehs (CF 1.68), notable as Lin Carter later integrated them into Clark Ashton Smith's Hyperborean Cycle. The story ends with the narrator dreaming of a far future, presumably our present, when where there is no Lomar and no Arctic population save the "Esquimaux" (CF 1.69–70).[2]

While "Polaris" has been seen as a tale generally overlooked by Lovecraftian scholarship (Vaughan 26), the saga of Arctic Lomar and its war against the Inutos introduced in "Polaris" were referenced by Lovecraft in a number of later stories, spanning tales assigned to both the Cthulhu Mythos and the Dream Cycle. In *The Dream-Quest of Unknown Kadath* (1926–27), Randolph Carter is told of the struggle (CF 2.103). In "The Mound" (1929), (loosely) collaborated with Zealia Bishop, Lovecraft notes that the cult of Clark Ashton Smith's Tsathoggua

> flourished until it almost rivalled the ancient cults of Yig and Tulu, and one branch of the race even took it to the outer

1. Given the 26,000-year cycle of the Earth's axial precession as noted in the story itself, and assuming the "dream" of the narrator is set the next time Polaris is the Pole Star as implied by the Pole Star's message itself, "Polaris" therefore ought to be dated to c. 24,000 B.C.E.—a rare general dating for HPL's mystical or distant-past works.

2. Given the belief that "Polaris" was motivated by HPL's feelings of powerlessness from being unable to enlist in World War I, and considering his fears of Japan later in life, the destruction of Lomar by the invasion of "squat yellow foes" from what would now be Asia possible reflects HPL's fear of a war that would destroy Western civilization and pave the way for Asian dominance in the future (perhaps also reflected by the sixth millennium dominance of the "cruel empire of Tsan-Chan" in "The Shadow out of Time" [CF 3.398]). His thoughts on a potential war between Japan and the Western countries can be seen in his 26 February 1932 letter to Elizabeth Toldridge (*Letters to Elizabeth Toldridge* 201) and April 1932 letter to James F. Morton (*Letters to James F. Morton* 297–98).

world, where the smallest of the images eventually found a shrine at Olathoë, in the land of Lomar near the earth's north pole. It was rumoured that this outer-world cult survived even after the great ice-sheet and the hairy Gnophkehs destroyed Lomar. (CF 4.215)

In *At the Mountains of Madness* (1931), as Dyer gazes upon the Elder Things' city, he thinks of "the daemoniac plateau of Leng, of the Mi-Go, or Abominable Snow-Men of the Himalayas, of the Pnakotic Manuscripts with their pre-human implications . . . of the Hyperborean legends of formless Tsathoggua" (CF 3.72). Shortly thereafter, Dyer thinks that in contrast to the extreme age of the city, "Olathoë in the land of Lomar are recent things of today" (CF 3.75). Later, in reading the carved history of the Elder Things and their ultimate decline, Dyer observes how the "ultimate blow, of course, was the coming of the great cold which once held most of the earth in thrall, and which has never departed from the ill-fated poles—the great cold that, at the world's other extremity, put an end to the fabled lands of Lomar and Hyperborea" (CF 3.111–12).

As a geologist, Dyer can perhaps be forgiven for not knowing the history of Lomar's destruction from a race war rather than cold. But he ought to have known that the migration of the Inutos from the west (presumably prior to that of the "Esquimaux") would probably be over the Bering land bridge linking Siberia and Alaska, which is represented in an Elder Thing map of world, along with an eastern land bridge linking Europe to America via Greenland (CF 3.106). The use of the Bering land bridge by Lovecraft is notable as, while it was first hypothesized in the 1890s, it was not fully accepted by scientists until the 1940s (Fagan 102–11). Lovecraft's scientific instincts bore fruit in making him ahead of the curve. Less so his use of the Euro-American ice bridge, which was a valid theory in the early twentieth century but has been widely discredited in the modern age, and remains the provenance of white supremacists who use it to argue that so-called "Solutreans" from Europe were the true "native" Americans (Eren et al.).

The migration of the Inutos is also referenced in "The Shadow out of Time" (1934–35). One of his fellow time-displaced people whom Peaslee speaks to is "that of a king of Lomar who had ruled that terrible polar land 100,000 years before the squat, yellow Inutos came from the west to engulf it" (CF 3.398). Indeed, the Pnakotic Manuscripts first mentioned in "Polaris" are a major plot point in "The Shadow out of Time" (CF 3.390). The Manuscripts may be the most influential legacy of "Polaris," not only in and of themselves but in the fact that they are the first of the many fictional tomes Lovecraft invented for his fiction. As such, one of the central pillars of the "Lovecraftian" genre stemmed from his sole specifically-Arctic tale.

After "Polaris," Arctic settings next appear in the second portion of his 1926 classic "The Call of Cthulhu," first when the character of Professor William Channing Webb recounts his 1860 "tour of Greenland and Iceland in search of some Runic inscriptions which he failed to unearth; and whilst high up on the West Greenland coast had encountered a singular tribe or cult of degenerate Esquimaux whose religion, a curious form of devil-worship, chilled him with its deliberate bloodthirstiness and repulsiveness" (CF 2.32–33). The climax of that story involves a Norwegian crew's encounter with R'lyeh and a trip to Oslo by protagonist Francis Wayland Thurston (CF 2.45–50).

In his 1930 novella "The Whisperer in Darkness," Lovecraft based the Mi-Go aliens on the "Abominable Snow-Men" of the Himalayas (CF 2.473). In a 18 November 1936 letter to Fritz Leiber, Lovecraft affirmed his belief that the Abominable Snowman was a piece of authentic Nepalese folklore (SL 5.355). This makes it all the more interesting that Lovecraft adapted it for his writing, given that in a 28 September 1935 letter to E. Hoffmann Price, he stated his unwillingness to use established legends (SL 5.197).

The remaining Arctic mentions in Lovecraft's fiction, outside the above-mentioned "Polaris" echoes, are from lesser-known collaborations. Lovecraft's 1932 collaboration with Hazel Heald, "The Horror in the Museum," contains the most Arctic references outside of "Polaris," despite being set in the modern-day "Rogers' Museum" in London. The protagonist, Stephen Jones, plies Rogers with whiskey to get him to share "wild enough stories" about trips to Alaska and Tibet and reading the Pnakotic Manuscripts (CF

4.372). This leads to Rogers eventually showing Jones the titular
horror locked in his museum, which he located from reading the
eighth fragment of the Pnakotic Manuscripts, and learning
about the

> things in the north before the land of Lomar—before mankind
> existed—and this was one of them. It took us all the way to
> Alaska, and up the Noatak from Fort Morton, but the thing was
> there as we knew it would be. Great Cyclopean ruins, acres of
> them. There was less left than we had hoped for, but after three
> million years what could one expect? And weren't the Esquimau
> legends all in the right direction? We couldn't get one of the
> beggars to go with us, and had to sledge all the way back to
> Nome for Americans. (CF 4.377)

Despite this, Rogers manages to get the object back to London
from Nome, although "They must have told queer tales around
Nome later on; though I doubt if they ever went back to those ruins, even for the ivory throne" (CF 4.377–78). However, Jones is
dismissive of the story about "the wildly carved chamber with the
cryptic throne which the fellow had claimed was part of a three-
million-year-old ruin in the shunned and inaccessible solitudes
of the Arctic. Perhaps Rogers had been to Alaska, but that picture was certainly nothing but stage scenery" (CF 4.387). Driv-
en by this (obviously misplaced) sense of skepticism, Jones
wanders around the museum on his own, where he notes one
image "suggested the sharp horn of Gnoph-keh, the hairy myth-
thing of the Greenland ice, that walked sometimes on two legs,
sometimes on four, and sometimes on six" (CF 4.388). At the
end of the story, Rogers' assistant Orabona identifies the "shapeless, colossal god . . . supposed to have come from outer space,
and to have lived in the Arctic three million years ago" as a being named Rhan-Tegoth (CF 4.400). "The Horror in the Museum" therefore establishes an indigenous (so to speak) Mythos
deity in Arctic North America preceding human settlement
there, adding another layer of complexity to the history of the
Lomar saga introduced in "Polaris."

The remaining Arctic references are much more minor in
comparison. In his 1935 collaboration with R. H. Barlow, "'Till

A' the Seas,'" it is said of the final remnants of the human race in the distant future that "none had ever seen the tiny, fabled spots of ice left close to the planet's poles—if such indeed remained. Even had they existed and been known to man, none could have reached them across the trackless and formidable deserts" (CF 4.493)—a coverage of both poles as brief as the ice still covering them, but a prescient call in our age of global warming. And to end by going beyond the earth to a world where global warming has triumphed, Lovecraft mentions the north pole of Venus as having formations of grayish clay in his 1936 collaboration with Kenneth Sterling, "In the Walls of Eryx" (CF 4.569).

With the overview of Lovecraft's use of Arctic fiction complete, it is now time to turn to the events related to Arctic exploration that happened during his life, and which could have served as an influence for those stories.

Contemporary Arctic Exploration

In the second half of the nineteenth century, one of the defining Arctic expeditions was the British voyage led by Sir John Franklin and Francis Crozier to locate the Northwest Passage. The Franklin expedition left Britain in 1845 on two ships, *Erebus* and *Terror*, and by 1848 the first attempt at "rescuing" the expedition was undertaken by the British Admiralty. By 1854, the British explorer John Rae acquired both oral testimony and recovered artifacts from local Inuit appearing to confirm that the expedition's crew had died in terrible conditions, including resorting to cannibalism. However, efforts to locate the ships and the crew's remains continued for decades. From 1848 to 1880, almost every British or American expedition to the Arctic was in some way associated with either rescuing or discovering the fate of the Franklin expedition. One of these, the 1871 expedition of Charles Hall and George Tyson made a voyage on a ship aptly named *Polaris* (Wilkinson 164–65). The at times romanticized question of the Franklin expedition's fate continued to dominate Arctic exploration, up until the discovery of *Erebus* in 2014 and *Terror* in 2016.

Although Lovecraft does not directly cite the Franklin expedition in any fiction (or, as far as I can tell, in his personal letters), there are slight connections to his life. During the War of 1812, *Terror* was stationed on Block Island off the southern coast of Rhode Island; Lovecraft was descended from two of the founding settlers of the island, John Rathbone and Tristram Dodge (Faig, *Unknown* 36nn416, 418). During the war, from its base on Block Island *Terror* participated in the bombardment of Stonington, Connecticut, where Lovecraft's ancestor James Babcock had lived (Palmer 28–37; Faig, *Unknown* 38n880).[3] More directly, *Erebus* and *Terror* were both part of the 1839–43 expedition of James Clark Ross to Antarctica, during which two Antarctic mountains were named after the ships. Mounts Erebus and Terror both appear in *At the Mountains of Madness*, near where the Miskatonic base camp is established (CF 3.18). The Franklin expedition loss also indirectly led to other developments in American Arctic interests that had an impact on Lovecraft.

In 1850, the Massachusetts merchant Henry Grinnell organized an American expedition to attempt to rescue Franklin. This was the first time major public attention in the U.S. was focused on the Arctic and its exploration (Robinson, *Crucible* 25–29). The sudden American interest in the Arctic was so intense that Elisha Kent Kane's 1857 Arctic expedition was a rare point of national unification in a United States rushing toward the Civil War (Robinson, *Crucible* 31–54). Following the end of the Civil War and the closing of the Western frontier, Arctic exploration offered not only a way to help unify the postwar states, but also an alternative frontier where manliness could be proven away from corrupting civilization (Robinson, *Crucible* 107–32). For Lovecraft, the pro-Confederate Yankee, the ability of Arctic exploration to ameliorate ante- and postbellum divides must have had some type of appeal.

A number of these expeditions, particular the one led by Evelyn Briggs Baldwin in 1898, led to debates on whether Norwegians or Eskimos were more prepared for survival in the Arctic—both culturally and biologically—a racial argument that would have ob-

---

3. I have written more in-depth about HPL's connections to Block Island elsewhere (Guimont).

vious interest to Lovecraft (Capelotti, *Greatest* 163–68; Bloom 83–109). The Norwegian/Eskimo dichotomy would also emerge another way through Arctic exploration. In 1910–12, Canadian anthropologist Vilhjálmur Stefánsson led an expedition to Victoria Island, where he encountered what became known as "Blond Eskimos"—groups who while culturally indiscernible from their neighbors appeared to Stefánsson to be of partial (or in some cases full) European descent. Stefánsson believed these Blond Eskimos to be the descendants of the lost Viking settlers of Norse Greenland (Stefánsson, *Life* 190–204; Robinson, *Lost* 162–74). The search for the lost Norse Greenland settlements will be discussed further below. But the broader Blond Eskimo claim, I believe, helped inform Lovecraft's Inuto/Lomar racial categorization of the Arctic in "Polaris."

Beyond general national interests and racial debates, the expeditions of Kane and Isaac Israel Hayes are notable for one other reason. Both explorers were strongly supported by the Masons, and in the aftermath of Kane's expedition spirit mediums claimed to be in contact with Franklin (Robinson, *Crucible* 49, 54, 60). Baldwin himself was a Freemason and called his camp on Greely Island in northern Russia "Kane Lodge," in an attempt to attract the support of Freemasons (Capelotti, *Greatest* 287). The combination of secret societies and psychic powers unleashed by American exploration of the Arctic has an obvious Lovecraftian appeal.[4]

On the decades to either side of Lovecraft's birth, American newspapers and fiction periodicals alike focused on a different search for lost beings in the Arctic: the wave of supposed sightings of mammoths and mastodons in Alaska. The trend peaked in 1899 with the publishing of Henry Tukeman's story "The Killing of the Mammoth," widely believed to be nonfiction at the time despite being an explicitly fictional work published in a

---

4. In August 1930, a Soviet expedition visited Baldwin's former base camp on Alger Island, finding the site apparently looted and disturbed. The explorers registered their displeasure and lobbied the Soviet government to protect it as an historical site (Capelotti, *Greatest* 548). Occurring just before HPL wrote *At the Mountains of Madness*, this event could have helped inspire Danforth and Dyer's discovery of Lake's camp, destroyed by the reanimated Elder Things.

fiction magazine. Jennifer Schell has argued that these accounts drew heavily from the Gothic literature at the time, including Edgar Allan Poe's *The Narrative of Arthur Gordon Pym of Nantucket* (1838), itself an influence on Lovecraft. A number of the mammoth accounts were also written by New Englanders. Although mammoths do not appear in Lovecraft's written fiction—Dyer even notes the absence of their remains in the Antarctic (*CF* 3.33–34)—as a child Lovecraft would have been in an environment where New Englanders were drawing from the same pools of inspiration he would later use to write about fantastic creatures out of time in the frozen Arctic (Schell 175–88; Stefánsson, *Life* 418–19). Indeed, Lovecraft at least had one story idea inspired by a famous discovery of a mammoth (albeit a quite dead one). He wrote this idea early in the 1919 section of his commonplace nook, in entry 31: "Prehistoric man preserved in Siberian ice. (See Winchell—Walks and Talks in the Geological field—p. 156 et seq.)" (*CE* 5.221). The inspiration in question is a passage on the 1799 discovery of the "Adams mammoth," the first mostly preserved woolly mammoth carcass, in Siberia (Winchell 156).

Arctic exploration did not only include searches for the ancient, however. As with the Scramble for Africa several decades earlier and the Space Race several decades later, Arctic exploration at the turn of the twentieth century would not only rely on the cutting-edge of technological development, but also spur new technological innovation (Bloom 15–82). Submarines were one such invention. The first submarine to travel under and surface through ice was *Protector*, built by Simon Lake in Bridgeport, Connecticut, in 1902 and taken for its test dives under the ice outside of Newport, Rhode Island, in early 1903 (Lake 212–14; McLaren 105).[5] Although the successful surfacing of *Protector* beneath the ice was early 1903, it is tempting that the news

5. I had intended to do further research on the details of the early Rhode Island submarine ice testing at the Submarine Force Library and Archives in Groton, Connecticut; however, this proved impossible due to the 2020 coronavirus pandemic. At a future point, I intend to carry out that archival research, which may lead to a revision of how likely it is that a young HPL would have known about Lake's test-dives.

of its construction and planned operations may have influenced
the sub-Arctic submarine in Lovecraft's "The Mysterious Ship"
mentioned above. In 1913, the Australian Sir George Hubert
Wilkins first envisioned using a submarine to cross under the
Arctic ice, a call that Robert Peary publicly made in 1919. In
1930, Wilkins purchased the U.S. Navy submarine *O-12*, re-
naming it *Nautilus* after Jules Verne's submarine and hiring Lake
to redesign it for journeying under the Arctic ice. On 31 August
1931, *Nautilus* attempted to submerge beneath the ice at the
Norwegian island of Spitsbergen, but had abort due to damage.
The first successful operation under the Arctic ice pack was by
the Soviet submarine *Red Guard,* in the year of Lovecraft's death
(Stefánsson, "History" 3–14; McLaren 105–6).

Wilkins's 1930 attempt to use a submarine to cross under the
Arctic stemmed from his previous expeditions in the other dimension. In 1927, Wilkins became the first person to land on
the Arctic ice and take off again in an airplane. He followed this
with his 15 April 1928 flight from Alaska to Spitsbergen, becoming the first person to fly *over* the Arctic in an airplane, gathering
valuable meteorological and navigational data along the way
(Wilkins 325–31; Stefánsson, "History" 3–4, 11–13). These
flights happened years before the first landing by, let alone scientific benefits from, a plane in Antarctica, and bring to mind the
four large, modified Dornier airplanes used by the Miskatonic expedition to traverse the Antarctic in *At the Mountains of Madness*
(*CF* 3.14). However, decades prior to Wilkins's successful airplane flight, there were attempts to cross the Arctic with less ad-
vanced aerial vehicles, and with less success—in particular, the
attempts by Salomon August Andrée and Walter Wellman to
reach the North Pole by airships.

The Fate of Andrée

In 1783, immediately after the Montgolfier brothers first successfully flew in their balloon, an engineer proposed to the
French naval minister the use of the new technology for flying to
the North Pole (Sollinger 21). While the French government
passed for the time being, the balloon as a method of exploring
the air continued to be developed in both reality and fiction. In

1844, Edgar Allan Poe published "The Balloon-Hoax" about a fictional transatlantic crossing by balloon. In turn, Poe aficionado Jules Verne published *Five Weeks in a Balloon* in 1863, describing an aerial expedition across central Africa. Poe and Verne were admired by young Lovecraft, but their works also influenced American journalist Walter Wellman (Capelotti, *Airship* 12–14, 173). Between 1894 and 1909, Wellman carried out four expeditions to the Arctic. His third expedition in 1907 was his first attempt to reach the North Pole—and his first with an airship, as well as the first time a motorized airship was used in the Arctic. Wellman built three wireless stations at his Arctic launch base to send news back to the rest of Europe and the U.S. His airship *America* also contained experimental carburetors, navigation equipment, and maneuverability-enhancing designs. Wellman's expeditions, particularly the 1907 one, were extensively covered by American media, including the *Providence Journal* (Capelotti, *Airship* 47–94; Robinson, *Crucible* 107–18). The use of modified experimental aircraft and wireless reporting pioneered by Wellman would later be used by Lovecraft's Miskatonic expedition (CF 3.15).

While Wellman's 1907 expedition was the first to use a motorized airship in the Arctic, it was not the first time an airship of any type had been used. That distinction belonged to another fan of Poe and Verne, the Swedish engineer Salomon August Andrée (Sollinger 202–4, 371). At the time, Sweden and Norway were politically united through a joint monarchy. While Norway was the subordinate power in the union, it had gained respect for being the acknowledged leader in Arctic exploration. It was important for Swedes to catch up to the Norwegians in that realm, and for Andrée, the use of balloons offered a novel way to do so. Andrée first proposed an Arctic balloon expedition in 1893 and made his first attempt in 1896. This failed from the start due to bad wind conditions at the launch site. However, Andrée tried again the next year, and on July 11 was able to take off from the Norwegian Svalbard archipelago in his hydrogen-filled balloon with two other crewmembers, Nils Strindberg and Knut Frænkel. They were never seen alive again. By July 14, the balloon had crashed onto Arctic pack ice. The three

aeronauts hiked south toward Kvitøya, the uninhabited east-
ernmost island in Svalbard. Andrée and his crew reached
Kvitøya on 2 October 1897; within several days, all had died
(Capelotti, *Airship* 19–46; Robinson, *Crucible* 114–15).

On 6 August 1930, the remains of the three men were acci-
dentally found by the crew of the Norwegian *Bratvaag* expedition, who were engaged in monitoring the glacial ice around
Svalbard. Andrée's remains included his diary and a gun, and his
pelvis had been torn apart by a polar bear and was located several meters away. Strindberg's remains were found in a cairn, also disturbed by polar bears with his skull separated (Putnam,
202–5; Wilkinson 177–80). *Bratvaag* left Kvitøya on August 7
with not only the remains of Andrée and Strindberg, but what
was later realized to be the bones of a polar bear the explorers
killed and butchered for food. *Bratvaag* encountered the Norwegian sealing ship *Ternigen* on August 8; as *Bratvaag* only had a
receiving radio and not a transmitting one, the crew asked *Ternigen* to announce their discovery of the Andrée expedition upon returning to port (Putnam 205–6; Wilkinson 180–81).
Ternigen reached its port of Tromsø on August 22, and news
started to explode worldwide on August 23 (Putnam 207). On
September 1, *Bratvaag* reached Tromsø, and the remains of Andrée and Strindberg were placed in Tromsø Cathedral; the same
day, journalists who had gone out looking for *Bratvaag* arrived
on Kvitøya and found the remains of Frænkel, along with the
logbook and 200 undeveloped photographs taken by Strindberg,
which were then processed to show a photographic account of
the final months of the expedition (Putnam 214–15; Wilkinson,
183–84). It was the combination of Strindberg's photographs
and log and Andrée's diary that allowed for such an accurate re-
construction of the voyage. On 5 October 1930, the remains of
the explorers were returned to Stockholm, praised by King Gus-
tav V, put in state, and finally cremated on October 9 (Putnam
219–21; Wilkinson 184–85).

I mention the above dates for the events surrounding the
discovery of the Andrée expedition remains because it illustrates
how, from late August to early October 1930, there was a steady
stream of highly publicized news about the discovery of a famous

Arctic expedition, which had been equipped with cutting-edge technology but still fell prey to tragedy. In their final days, the expedition had killed and carved up a large polar creature; after their death, their remains had been consumed by members of that creature's same species. The parallels to Lake's camp from *At the Mountains of Madness*—dissecting an Elder Thing, only for the revived creatures to eat Lake and his teammates (CF 3.62)—are evident. And while *At the Mountains of Madness* was written in February/March 1931, with plenty of time for Lovecraft to have digested the news around the Andrée discovery, the connections are even more explicit. It was as early as 18 November 1930—barely a month after the return of the explorers' remains to Stockholm—where Lovecraft first related his idea for an Antarctic novel to Clark Ashton Smith (*SL* 3.218). Even more direct evidence can be found in entry 184 from Lovecraft's commonplace book. Located near the end of the 1930 section, it reads: "Expedition lost in Antarctic or other weird place. Skeletons and effects found years later. Camera films used but undeveloped. Finders develop—and find strange horror" (CE 5.230; entry 184). The late 1930 idea of a lost Antarctic expedition with "strange horrors" was clearly the ur-concept for *At the Mountains of Madness*; just as clearly, a late 1930 idea for a lost polar expedition with skeletons and effects, including undeveloped camera film, has to draw from the Andrée discovery.

Between the Smith letter and the commonplace book entry, it cannot be doubted that the genesis of the Miskatonic Antarctic Expedition of 1930 was the Andrée Arctic balloon expedition of 1897—or more precisely, the discovery of the latter's demise. The Miskatonic expedition and its fate clearly drew inspiration from the Arctic aerial explorers of the fin de siècle. But what of the fate of the Elder Thing civilization discovered by the Miskatonic explorers, and its decline deciphered by Dyer and Danforth? The collapse of the Elder Thing's colonial civilization at the hands—or pseudopods—of an inferior race may have its origins in Lovecraft's perception of a Transatlantic settlement much closer to home.

In Search of Norse Greenland

The period of the 1830s–1890s was one where New Englanders were particularly fascinated by the culture of the ancient Norsemen. This interest was twofold. The first avenue of interest was in the belief that the Scandinavians of a millennium ago and the New Englanders of the nineteenth century had similar worldviews and folk traditions stemming from their austere lives in hardscrabble climes. The second, more popular basis for the Novanglian interest in the Norse was the belief that New England, and specifically the Narragansett region of Rhode Island, had been the Vinland established by Leif Erikson. To this extent, a large number of local landmarks and oddities were repurposed as supposed Viking artifacts. A colonial windmill became the Viking-built Newport Tower; an armored skeleton found in 1832 became a Viking warrior slain by Native Americans; various rocks were suddenly realized to have Viking runes inscribed upon them (Falnes 211–42; Goudsward 21–73, 115–78). It was no coincidence that Henry Wheaton, a Providence lawyer and Brown graduate, was not only the first New England writer to discuss the Norse seriously, but also the first U.S. ambassador to Denmark (Falnes 214–15).

In the 1890s, the idea that Norse had established Vinland in the approximate region of Rhode Island did not fade in New England, but took on a national characteristic. In particular, it was adopted by the Scandinavian settlers of the Midwest, who saw it as a way to bridge the aforementioned Norwegian-Swedish political divide. The English-speaking residents of the United States saw the Norse not only as proto-Protestants, but originators of American democracy and republicanism. As a result, a northern European and implicitly Protestant Leif Erikson could be used as a symbolic discoverer of America, instead of the Catholic and southern European Columbus (Kolodny 213–55; Mathiesen 113–14). The racial undertones of course extended beyond WASP prejudice against southern Europeans.[6] The con-

---

6. For a Mythos example of this, see *The Ballad of Black Tom*, in which Norwegian immigrants are the originators of the mob attacking Robert Suydam's multiracial Red Hook cult (LaValle 115).

flict between the Vinland colonists and Natives was a highlight of these narratives, ignoring that the Norse sagas themselves claim that Vinland was abandoned because of the continuous Native attacks that could not be halted (Kolodny 44–102). Meanwhile, not only did Scandinavian immigrants in the Midwest widely ignore the indigenous Native Americans, they typically described the existing settlers of European descent as the "Native Americans" (Mathiesen 67–72, 117–19).

It might be expected, and is sometimes stated as fact, that Lovecraft was a supporter of the romantic belief that Rhode Island had been the Vinland colony of old. The racial aspects seem like something that would appeal to him. He certainly knew of the claims; take for example his 23 April 1935 response to August Derleth (who from his Wisconsin residence had no doubt asked due to his awareness of the local Scandinavian settler beliefs):

> Icelandic sagas? Yes, indeed, I'm intensely interested in anything about them! You are doubtless aware that R.I. persistently claims to be the "Vineland" of the Sagas, & that local historical sharks are called upon to prove that the hieroglyphs on this or that rock along Narragansett Bay are *not* the ruins of Leif Ericson, Thorfinn, or some other pre-Columbian son of Scandinavia! (*Essential Solitude* 693)

The tone of his letter makes clear Lovecraft's general skepticism of such claims. But he outright opposed at least one central concept of the "New England Vinland" claim. In multiple letters, he rejected the assertion that the Newport Tower is anything other than a seventeenth-century colonial windmill (*Dawnward Spire* 378; *SL* 5.24, 175; *Essential Solitude* 2.695). I myself almost fell into the trap of a similar assumption of Lovecraft's endorsement of the Vinland claims when reading "The Mysterious Ship," with its mention of an island called No-Mans Land. The real Nomans Land is an island in Massachusetts several miles southwest of Martha's Vineyard. Nomans Land is most famous now for the pseudohistorical claims that Vikings landed there and left runes inscribed on a boulder. My initial assumption was that the twelve-year-old Lovecraft was inspired to use No-Mans

Land as a name from the alleged Viking connections to the real Nomans Land. However, the first claim that Nomans Land was Vinland was made only in 1923, with the supposed runestone being discovered there three years later (Fales 241; Goudsward 164–69).

Ultimately, the actual Vinland site would be discovered much further north. In 1960, the Norwegian couple Anne Stine and Helge Ingstad discovered the thousand-year-old remains of a Viking settlement at L'Anse aux Meadows in Newfoundland. But the lure of pseudohistorical romance remains strong. Even after the discovery, and against all historical evidence, Helge Ingstad still considered the Newport Tower to potentially be a true remnant of Norse explorers, although he rejected all other supposed evidence from the Narragansett region (169–70).[7] But although the evidence of brief Norse exploration on the North American mainland was only verified in 1960, the remains of a much longer Norse settlement in North America had been known for centuries: the Norse colony in the western shore of Greenland. Established around the same time as the L'Anse aux Meadows base, the Greenland colonies lasted centuries longer, with a much higher population (approximately 5000, versus under 100). The final record of the Norse settlements known in Europe were from the Hvalsey Church in 1408, mentioning that a man named Kolbein had been burned for witchcraft a few years earlier (McGovern 327). The realization that the Norse had vanished from Greenland was slow coming to the rest of Europe, and not fully evident until 1721. In that year, the Norwegian missionary Hans Egede traveled to Greenland, hoping to convert the Norse to Lutheranism—instead finding no settlers at all (McGovern 327–28).

This set off a series of theories about what exactly the fate of

---

7. Even this view had a measure of scientific basis. In 1930, Poul Nørlund and Aage Roussell excavated the town of Sandnæs in the Western Settlement of Greenland. They discovered a piece of anthracite coal, a type not found in Greenland or Scandinavia, and so unlikely to come from Europe. The only place on the East Coast of North America where anthracite is found is Rhode Island. Ingstad therefore believed the Norse settlers visited Rhode Island and might have built the Newport Tower (163–66).

the Norse settlers had been. The initial theory from Egede had been that the Norse had been massacred by the local Inuit. This was combined with early modern geography beliefs that Greenland was linked with Karelia, and the Inuits were therefore a wave of Karelian invaders descending across the North Pole to wipe out the Norse (Ingstad 289; McGovern 328). In 1924, physical anthropologist F. C. C. Hansen excavated remains leading him to believe the final Norse had "degenerated" due to malnutrition, disease, or inbreeding into feeble stock, thus explaining their ultimate demise. This idea was common for several decades but refuted by Knud Fischer-Møller in 1942 (Ingstad 306–9; McGovern 328–29). Norwegian Arctic explorer Fridtjof Nansen proposed that the Norse intermarried with the Inuit, or that they simply lost their civilization and degenerated into barbarism (Ingstad 314–19).

In these various theories of the fate of the Norse settlers of Greenland that were popular in the early twentieth century, we can find parallels to Lovecraftian plotlines. The massacre of the settlements by Inuits invading south can be seen in the Inuto invasion from "Polaris." The various "degeneration" proposals can be seen in the decline of the Elder Thing civilization from *At the Mountains of Madness*. Indeed, the shoggoth uprising in the latter can be seen as combining the two proposals for what happened to the Norse Greenlanders. It therefore seems likely that for Lovecraft, the excavations of Norse settlements—as with the discovery of the remains of Arctic explorers—were real-world events that served as inspiration for his own polar tales. But for someone who was such an avid reader, what were Lovecraft's written influences?

Lovecraft's Fictional Arctic Influences

Perhaps the best place to start looking at the Arctic-themed works Lovecraft read is his essay "Supernatural Horror in Literature," written in the span of 1925–27 and revised later. It references Mary Shelley's *Frankenstein* (1818; CE 2.94), Arthur Conan Doyle's "The Captain of the 'Pole-Star'" (1883; CE 2.113), Matthew Phipps Shiel's *The Purple Cloud* (1901) and "The House of Sounds" (1911; CE 2.112), Algernon Blackwood's *The Wendigo* (1910; CE 2.120–21), and John Buchan's "Skule Skerry" (1928; CE 2.112). Of these, several are worth looking into more deeply.

Frankenstein, while famously about a mad scientist creating life (and as such a possible inspiration for "Herbert West— Reanimator"), has a framing story where an icebound Arctic explorer encounters both Frankenstein and his monster. While the frame is widely interpreted as being inspired by John Barrow, who organized Arctic exploration for the British Admiralty in the immediate post-Napoleonic period, Shelley was more likely inspired by the 1815 proposal by the whaler William Scoresby to reach the North Pole by sledge (Cavell 295–307). Lovecraft owned a mid-1800s edition of *Frankenstein* (LL 141). A copy of Buchan's 1928 collection *The Rungates Club,* containing "Skule Skerry," was given to Lovecraft by Derleth (LL 42). Lovecraft included a summary of "Skule Skerry" in a list of "Weird Story Plots" he sent to R. H. Barlow (CE 2.166). In 1929, Shiel released a dramatically revised version of *The Purple Cloud,* a copy of which was given to Lovecraft by Richard Ely Morse. Joshi notes that the Arctic expedition in the early chapters of the 1901 *Purple Cloud* could have served as an inspiration for the early portions of *At the Mountains of Madness* (LL 142). In 1936, Derleth gave Lovecraft a copy of Blackwood's *The Lost Valley and Other Stories,* which contained "The Wendigo." However, Lovecraft had already read it by then, with Joshi suggesting it as an influence on "The Dunwich Horror" (LL 37).

In addition to the stories mentioned in "Supernatural Horror," A. Merritt's "The People of the Pit" (1918), which features an underground city in an uncharted mountain in the Yukon populated by antediluvian beings, seems a possible basis for the Elder Thing city in *At the Mountains of Madness* and the Alaskan ruins of "The Horror in the Museum." One of the most popular authors of Yukon-set fiction in the early twentieth century was Jack London; however, the only London book Lovecraft owned was *The Star Rover* (1915), which had no Arctic connection (LL 103).[8] Nonfictionally, as mentioned above, Lovecraft owned Al-

---

8. However, *The Star Rover* has similarities to HPL and E. Hoffmann Price's "Through the Gates of the Silver Key" (1932–33), a potential influence that

exander Winchell's *Walks and Talks in the Geological Field* (1886; LL 168). In addition to its segment on frozen mammoths in Siberia, Winchell's book includes a chapter on the ice age (270–75). Notably, the advance of the glaciers is described as an "invasion" caused by "certain astronomical changes" (271), while it is the fall of increased snow that is blamed for the extinction of the mammoths (274–75), phrasings that potentially point to influences on both the invasion of the Inutos in "Polaris" and the decline of the Elder Things in *At the Mountains of Madness*. The Antarctic landscape and Elder Things' city were also influenced by the paintings of the Himalayas and Tibetan cities done by the Russian artist Nicholas Roerich, which Lovecraft saw in Manhattan in 1930; they are mentioned by both Dyer and Lake in the story itself (*CF* 3.18, 28; Indick).

Of all the above works, "The Wendigo" is perhaps the most important in the development of Arctic Mythos lore—not due to its influence on Lovecraft himself, however, but on those who came after him, starting with Derleth. It is here that we turn to the final segment: how subsequent Mythos authors and pastiche writers incorporated Lovecraftian works into the Arctic.

The Arctic in Lovecraftian Pastiches

The use of the Arctic in Lovecraftian pastiches predates Lovecraft's death, with Derleth's "The Thing That Walked on the Wind" (1933) and its sequel/rewrite, "The Snow Thing"—which would only be published in 1941 under the title "Ithaqua," the name of its central deity. Although preceded by a year by Lovecraft and Heald's "The Horror in the Museum" and its Rhan-Tegoth, Derleth's "Ithaqua" draws indirectly from Algonquin belief in the wendigo entity, as mediated through Blackwood's "The Wendigo." I have elsewhere explored "Ithaqua" in depth, so will not discuss it at length here.[9] It is worth noting, however, that "Ithaqua" has proved to be far more influential in Arctic Mythos pastiches than either "Polaris" or

---

does not seem to have been widely commented on.

9. See my article "An Historical and Environmental Reading of August Derleth's 'Ithaqua,'" *Dead Reckonings* No. 27 (Spring 2020): 71–81.

"The Horror at the Museum," with Robert M. Price compiling a number of them into his 2006 anthology *The Ithaqua Cycle*. Brian Lumley also wrote a number of pastiches with Ithaqua as primary antagonist, most notably his 1978 novel *Spawn of the Winds*, set entirely on Ithaqua's homeworld Borea, populated by those abducted by Ithaqua from across the Earth's Arctic regions (Lumley 42–43).

Appropriately in light of the story's influence, Derleth followed "Ithaqua" with "Beyond the Threshold" (1941). This story was meant to portray the shift in the Mythos' stewardship to Derleth from Lovecraft, with both represented as characters within the story (Price 80). In it, Lovecraft is represented by the character Josiah Alwyn, an explorer who has visited "remote corners of the world" including "Tibet, Mongolia, [and] the Arctic regions" (Derleth, "Beyond" 81). In death if not life, Derleth granted a career of polar exploration to Lovecraft. In addition to his Ithaqua stories, Derleth also wrote "The Black Island" (1952), which briefly mentioned the existence of a Cthulhu cult among the Tlingit and Haida peoples of southeastern Alaska (*Trail* 179). In 1976, Richard L. Tierney expounded on Derleth's inference to explore more fully how aspects of those cultures could be integrated into Mythos stories. The same year, Michael Crichton published his novel *Eaters of the Dead*, in which Vikings combat relict Neanderthals; in the list of works cited at the end, Crichton includes a supposed 1934 edition of the *Necronomicon* edited by Lovecraft, tipping his hat to one of the story's influences (269).[10]

But paradoxically, it is outside of both direct Lovecraftian pastiches and the written medium that the influence of the Lovecraftian Arctic is most pronounced. The most notable example is the 1951 film *The Thing from Another World*, based on John W. Campbell's 1938 novella "Who Goes There?" (itself widely seen as owing a large debt to *At the Mountains of Mad-*

---

10. A central premise of *Eaters of the Dead* is that the Grendel of *Beowulf* was a misremembered Neanderthal (Crichton 259–66). HPL himself had similar musing on whether fairy and gnome legends were based on ancient interactions with Neanderthals; see his 1932 letter to Wilfred B. Talman later collected as the essay "Some Backgrounds of Fairyland" (*CE* 3.323–27).

ness) but relocated to the Arctic, with the body of an alien found near an ancient flying saucer frozen in glacial ice. The 1951 movie was remade in 1982 as the more popular (and Ant-arctic-set) *The Thing* by Lovecraft aficionado John Carpenter. *The Thing* in turn inspired the 1993 *The X-Files* episode "Ice," again set in Alaska and in which a research base crew is gradual-ly infected by an ancient alien parasite found in the ice. *The X-Files* would again return to the North Pole with its 1995 episode "End Game," featuring a submarine encountering an alien craft under the Arctic ice pack, a plot that *Doctor Who* would revisit in its 2013 episode "Cold War."[11]

In terms of an American long-running sci-fi television fran-chise, the 2003 *Star Trek: Enterprise* episode "Regeneration" is a fine piece of Lovecraftian Arcticana. In the year 2153, Starfleet scientists find the remains of a Borg ship that had traveled from the twenty-fourth century into the twenty-first. Two Borg drones are found frozen in the ice and, when thawed out in the lab, wake and begin assimilating the science team. The use of Borgs as stand-in shoggoths is a good fit, and their convoluted time travel origins are also reflective of "The Shadow out of Time." Even given the fact that Lovecraft's friend Robert Bloch wrote for the original se-ries, "Regeneration" is one of the most Lovecraftian episodes of any *Star Trek* series. That being said, it is also fairly optimistic, given it depicts an Arctic Circle in 2153 still cold enough to freeze drones for decades (and polar bears still existing in the wild).

But the most vivid works incorporating Lovecraftian horror and the Arctic have to be Dan Simmons's 2007 novel *The Ter-ror* and its 2018 TV miniseries adaptation of the same title. *The Terror* tells the demise of the Franklin expedition, while adding a supernatural element in the form of the Tuunbaq, an entity stalking the crew and feeding off their fear.[12] The British sailors

---

11. *Doctor Who* had previously properly homaged "Who Goes There?" in its 1976 serial *The Seeds of Doom*.

12. In the novel, the Tuunbaq is described as resembling a polar bear with a "long, impossible snout" (Simmons 680). In the TV adaptation, however, its appearance—much larger and with a rounded snout—brings to mind a similar creature killed by the character Dirk Peters in *The Narrative of Arthur Gordon Pym* (Poe 159), suggesting a possible additional influence on the TV adapta-

are aided in survival by Lady Silence, an Inuit described by the crew as an "Esquimaux witch" (Simmons 8). Of course, survival is impossible for those preordained by history to die, and near their end a group of mutineers engages in the sort of ritual cannibalism that makes the Elder Things' feast of Lake's camp seem tame. At the end of the novel, a history of the Tuunbaq and its relations with the Inuit is given to Captain Crozier. Created by the goddess Sedna as a servitor, the Tuunbaq instead rebels and launches a multi-millennia war against its divine creator, before being defeated. Sedna exiles the Tuunbaq to the Arctic instead of the Antarctic, because only there are there shamans who can contain it. The Inuit create their *sixam ieua* shamans by breeding clairvoyants with one another, enabling long bloodlines of psychic priests dedicated to the service of the Tuunbaq. However, the Tuunbaq is unable to be controlled, depopulating the Arctic and making the surviving Inuit vulnerable to the invasion of white explorers, and later settlers (Simmons 701–12). In both novel and TV, Crozier ends the story going native, abandoning his identity and his past to live among the Inuit, not wanting the forbidden knowledge of the expedition to reach the outside world.

This account has some obvious similarities with the narratives of not only "Polaris" and *At the Mountains of Madness*, but also "The Call of Cthulhu." There are also obvious superficial similarities with Derleth's Ithaqua, particularly in the TV version where the Tuunbaq is associated with the sounds of the Arctic wind in several scenes. However, there is also a major difference. The *sixam ieua* use their "forward-thoughts" to see that the Tuunbaq will eventually die as a result of eating the poisoned souls of the Franklin crew, but this will signal the start of the End Times—the loss of Inuit culture, and the environmental devastation of global warming (Simmons 710).[13] The TV series takes an even more direct route, with the Tunnbaq being *literally* poisoned from eating sickened crewmembers and finally killed in a direct attack by Crozier. Whether by poisoned souls

tion.

13. *The Ballad of Black Tom* takes the opposite route: the melting of Arctic ice due to global warming there is a symptom of the arrival of the era of Cthulhu (LaValle 147–48).

or poisoned bodies, the Tuunbaq is defeated by human action—an outcome that, outside of Dr. Armitage's confrontation with the Dunwich Horror, one does not typically find in Lovecraft's world. Ultimately, however, the titular fear of *The Terror* is not of the Tuunbaq, but of the endless Arctic wastes and the maladies, both physical and spiritual, that await those mere mortals who believe that anything other than death can result from a vain attempt to cross it. It is the environment itself, deadly through its simple indifference to human life, that is the real eldritch horror of *The Terror*, and the real reason it is supreme above any other work of Lovecraftian Arcticana, and unlikely to be surpassed any time soon.

Conclusion

To the above list recounting Lovecraftian Arcticana, I will add one other unlikely entry, the 2013 film *Man of Steel*. This reimagining of Superman's origin transforms his Arctic Fortress of Solitude into an ancient scout ship from the planet Krypton which crashed into the north of Canada's Ellesmere Island, remaining buried under the Arctic glacial ice until discovered by NATO forces initially believing it to be a Soviet submarine. This plot point is a faint echo of a relatively unknown event from the Cold War: a report that, in 1952, NATO forces uncovered "an abandoned silvery disc" deep inside a coal mine on Spitsbergen, which was then sent to the United States for analysis. While the report was true, the event was not. The report was a deliberate piece of misinformation spread by the U.S. government (incidentally the year after *The Thing from Another World*, with its similar plot) to help cover up the CIA's monitoring of a nearby Soviet research station at Yakutsk. The CIA suspected the base was involved in nuclear testing; it was in fact simply observing cosmic rays interacting with the upper atmosphere (Colavito). Forty years later, the U.S. military would build its own Arctic atmospheric research station—the High Frequency Active Auroral Research Program, or HAARP, in Alaska—which invited no end of conspiracy theories involving weather control, mind control, and space warfare.

I began research for this article in July 2019. I am finishing writing it in April 2020, in a world that seems as transformed by coronavirus as Simmons's Arctic by the death of the Tuunbaq. Conspiracy theories abound, thriving in a cultural ecosystem that HAARP helped to create in the 1990s. The president describes the pandemic as an invasion from Asia, much like that of the Inutos. People await the coming of summer, believing that, like Ithaqua, the virus thrives only in the cold. The isolation of social distancing drives people as mad as the mountains did to Danforth, and have more than once caused me to think on the final lonely days of Crozier and Andrée. But by far the most shocking realization that the stars are right and the Lovecraftian Arctic has a resounding influence was the news at the start of this month that the captain of the USS *Theodore Roosevelt* was relieved of command for warning that coronavirus was spreading across his crew.

The name of this officer whose warnings of a sickening crew were unheeded until it was too late?

Captain Crozier.

Thanks to Henrik Olav Mathiesen and Michael F. Robinson for replying to queries during the writing of this paper.

Works Cited

Bloom, Lisa. *Gender on Ice: American Ideologies of Polar Explorations*. Minneapolis: University of Minnesota Press, 1993.

Capelotti, P. J. *By Airship to the North Pole: An Archaeology of Human Exploration*. New Brunswick, NJ: Rutgers University Press, 1999.

———. *The Greatest Show in the Arctic: The American Exploration of Franz Josef Land, 1898–1905*. Norman: University of Oklahoma Press, 2016.

Cavell, Janice. "The Sea of Ice and the Icy Sea: The Arctic Frame of *Frankenstein*." *Arctic* 70 (2017): 295–307.

Colavito, Jason. "Ancient Astronauts, Soviet Geopolitics, and the Spitsbergen UFO Hoax." *JasonColavito.com*, 10 June 2012. http://www.jasoncolavito.com/blog/ancient-astronauts-soviet-geopolitics-and-the-spitsbergen-ufo-hoax

Crichton, Michael. *Eaters of the Dead*. 1976. New York: Ballantine, 1988.

Derleth, August. "Beyond the Threshold." 1941. In Robert M. Price, ed. *The Ithaqua Cycle*. Hayward, CA: Chaosium, 2006. 80–101.

———. "The Snow-Thing." 1941. In Robert M. Price, ed. *The Ithaqua Cycle*. Hayward, CA: Chaosium, 2006. 69–79.

———. "The Thing That Walked on the Wind." 1933. In Robert M. Price, ed. *The Ithaqua Cycle*. Hayward, CA: Chaosium, 2006. 58–67.

———. *The Trail of Cthulhu*. 1962. New York: Beagle, 1971.

Eren, Metin I.; Boulanger, Matthew T.; and O'Brien, Michael J. "The *Cinmar* Discovery and the Proposed Pre-Late Glacial Maximum Occupation of North America." *Journal of Archaeological Science: Reports* 2 (2015): 708–13.

Fagan, Brian M. *The Great Journey: The Peopling of Ancient America*. London: Thames & Hudson, 1987.

Faig, Kenneth W., Jr. *Lovecraftian Voyages*. New York: Hippocampus Press, 2017.

———. *The Unknown Lovecraft*. New York: Hippocampus Press, 2009.

Falnes, Oscar J. "New England Interest in Scandinavian Culture and the Norsemen." *New England Quarterly* 10 (1937): 211–42.

Goudsward, David. *Ancient Stone Sites of New England and Debate over Early European Exploration*. Jefferson, NC: McFarland, 2006.

Guimont, Edward. "H. P. Lovecraft and Block Island." *Block Island Times* 49, No. 9 (2 March 2 2019): 13.

Indick, Ben P. "A Note on Nicholas Roerich." *Crypt of Cthulhu* No. 37 (Candlemas 1986): 46–48, 59.

Ingstad, Helge. *Land under the Pole Star: A Voyage to the Norse Settlements of Greenland and the Saga of the People That Vanished*. New York: St. Martin's Press, 1966.

Joshi, S. T. *An Index to the Selected Letters of H. P. Lovecraft*. West Warwick, RI: Necronomicon Press, 1990.

———. "On 'Polaris.'" *Crypt of Cthulhu* No. 15 (Lammas 1983): 22–25.

Kolodny, Annette. *In Search of First Contact: The Vikings of Vinland, the Peoples of the Dawnland, and the Anglo-American Anxiety of Discovery*. Durham, NC: Duke University Press, 2012.

Lake, Simon. "The Development of the Under Ice Submarine." In Hubert Wilkins, ed. *Under the North Pole: The Wilkins-Ellsworth Submarine Expedition*. New York: Brewer, Warren & Putnam, 1931. 203–32.

LaValle, Victor. *The Ballad of Black Tom*. New York: Tor, 2016.

Lovecraft, H. P. *Letters to Elizabeth Toldridge and Anne Tillery Renshaw*. Ed. David E. Schultz and S. T. Joshi. New York: Hippocampus Press, 2014.

———. *Letters to James F. Morton*. Ed. David E. Schultz and S. T. Joshi. New York: Hippocampus Press, 2011.

———, and August Derleth. *Essential Solitude: The Letters of H. P. Lovecraft and August Derleth*. Ed. David E. Schultz and S. T. Joshi. New York: Hippocampus Press, 2009.

———, and Clark Ashton Smith. *Dawnward Spire, Lonely Hill: The Letters of H. P. Lovecraft and Clark Ashton Smith*. Ed. David E. Schultz and S. T. Joshi. New York: Hippocampus Press, 2017.

Lumley, Brian. *Spawn of the Winds*. New York: Jove, 1978.

Mathiesen, Henrik Olav. "Norwegians in America and Perceptions of Belonging, c. 1840–1870." M.A. thesis: University of Oslo, 2015.

McGovern, Thomas H. "The Demise of Norse Greenland." In William W. Fitzhugh and Elisabeth I. Ward, ed. *Vikings: The North Atlantic Saga*. Washington, DC: Smithsonian Institution Press, 2000. 327–39.

McLaren, Alfred S. "Under the Ice in Submarines." *Proceedings of the United States Naval Institute* 107 (1981): 105–9.

Merritt, A. "The People of the Pit." 1918. In Ann and Jeff VanderMeer, ed. *The Weird: A Compendium of Strange and Dark Stories*. New York: Tor, 2012. 101–9.

Navroth, John M. "Lovecraft and the Polar Myth." In *Lovecraft Annual* No. 3 (2009): 190–98.

Palmer, Henry Robinson. *Stonington by the Sea*. Stonington, CT: Palmer Press, 1957.

Poe, Edgar Allan. *The Narrative of Arthur Gordon Pym of Nantucket.* 1838. New York: Penguin, 1999.

Price, Robert M. "About "Beyond the Threshold"." In Robert M. Price, ed. *The Ithaqua Cycle.* Hayward, CA: Chaosium, 2006. 80.

Putnam, George Palmer. *Andrée: The Record of a Tragic Adventure.* New York: Brewer & Warren, 1930.

Robinson, Michael F. *The Coldest Crucible: Arctic Exploration and American Culture.* Chicago: University of Chicago Press, 2006.

———. *The Lost White Tribe: Explorers, Scientists, and the Theory That Changed a Continent.* Oxford: Oxford University Press, 2016.

Schell, Jennifer. "Ecogothic Extinction Fiction: The Extermination of the Alaskan Mammoth." In Dawn Keetley and Matthew Wynn Sivils, ed. *Ecogothic in Nineteenth-Century American Literature.* New York: Routledge, 2018. 175–90.

Simmons, Dan. *The Terror.* New York: Little, Brown, 2007.

Sollinger, Günther. *S. A. Andrée: The Beginning of Polar Aviation 1895–1897.* Moscow: Russian Academy of Sciences, 2005.

Stefánsson, Vilhjálmur. "The History of the Idea." In Hubert Wilkins, ed. *Under the North Pole: The Wilkins-Ellsworth Submarine Expedition.* New York: Brewer, Warren & Putnam, 1931. 3–51.

———. *My Life with the Eskimo.* 1913. New York: Collier, 1962.

The Terror. Season 1. Created by David Kajganich. AMC, 2018.

Tierney, Richard L. "Cthulhu in Southeast Alaska." 1976. *Crypt of Cthulhu* No. 9 (Hallowmas 1982): 18–19.

Vaughan, Ralph E. "The Horror of 'Polaris.'" *Crypt of Cthulhu* No. 15 (Lammas 1983): 26–27.

Wilkins, George H. *Flying the Arctic.* New York: G. P. Putnam's Sons, 1928.

Wilkinson, Alec. *The Ice Balloon: S. A. Andrée and the Heroic Age of Arctic Exploration.* New York: Alfred A. Knopf, 2011.

Winchell, Alexander. *Walks and Talks in the Geological Field.* New York: Phillips & Hunt, 1886.

Textual Sources and *Corrigenda Minora* to "A Living Heritage: Roman Architecture in Today's America"

César Guarde-Paz

"Take away the past, & the best art of the present & future vanishes as well!"
—Lovecraft to Robert E. Moe, 18 May 1935 (*MWM* 411)

It is well known that the so-called Arkham House Transcripts (AHT), a vast set of excerpts from the letters of H. P. Lovecraft prepared by Donald Wandrei and August Derleth soon after his death, and said to amount to forty-one volumes averaging 100 pages each, contain an important number of lacunae and typographical errors, most of which found their way into the ill-famed *Selected Letters* (1965–76). Numerous misreadings therein have now been corrected through careful collation with original sources and, when missing or not preserved, amended with acute philological suggestions, leading to the extensive publication of revised editions of Lovecraft's correspondence (Joshi and Schultz 147).

Essays only preserved through AHT, however, have received comparatively little attention in regard to the abundant typographical errors and lacunae haunting some of them. These include three early scientific texts—"The Moon" (26 November 1903; revised on 24 July 1906), "Third Annual Report of the Prov. Meteorological Station" (16 January 1907), and "Celestial Objects for All" (28 July 1907), collected in *CE 3*—and, more importantly, three late philosophical essays: "A Layman Looks at the Government" (22 November 1933), "The *Journal* and the New Deal" (13 April 1934), and "A Living Heritage: Roman

166

Architecture in Today's America" (11 December 1934), all collected in *CE* 5.

This brief research note seeks to provide corrections for some of the textual problems encountered in the second, unpublished section of "A Living Heritage," by far still the most defective of these texts despite recent corrections in *CE* 5 (119–40). Inasmuch as neither transcripts nor original manuscript copies of this essay are readily available, my first object of consideration should be given to the genesis of the text, with a brief detour into the documentary sources upon which Lovecraft built his discourse. This, I believe, may also provide support for future researchers and editors as they confront the lacunae and mistranscriptions within this essay. Next, attention will be drawn to defining the precise nature of these typographical errors and the process whereby they originated. Based on this analysis, and through comparison with instances of identical or similar words in Lovecraft's own handwriting, I shall provide a tentative list of minor corrections.

Genesis and Sources of "A Living Heritage"

Whereas the first introductory section of "A Living Heritage" (originally published in the *Californian* [Summer 1935] as "Heritage or Modernism: Common Sense in Art Forms") comprises a riotous denunciation of radical Modernist aesthetics and an equally fervent advocacy of antiquarianism and traditionalism in Western art, its second part is a more relaxed textbook illustration of the evolution of Roman architecture and its influence upon Western civilization. As it has been noted before (*IAP* 893), "A Living Heritage" was written in response to Maurice W. Moe's request to generate some writing for his students' magazine, but its publication never took place. Moe's invitation is mentioned in Lovecraft's response on Thanksgiving Day, 29 November 1934, where he laments his paucity of leisure time:

> Regarding literary contributions to the various magazines of your infant charges—bless me, but I don't know whether I'll have time to write anything fresh! I am having to curtail on extras, for the number of obligations surrounding me wou'd oth-

erwise become all-ingulphing. Would *old* material do? [. . .] The one bit of *new* writing which tempts me is that which I'd produce in response to the request for something on *Roman architecture*. There's a theme I'm really keen about, tho' I've never written on it. But I doubt whether I'll have much time before mid-December. (MWM 365)

Moe seems to have given him "a vague hint of the desirability" shortly after the aforequoted letter arrived (MWM 411), for Lovecraft soberly expressed similar thoughts about his aversion to Modernist aesthetics and mechanization in a letter he wrote to R. H. Barlow two days later, on 1 December: "I have very little enthusiasm for things based on mechanical or technological 'progress'" (*O Fortunate Floridian* 192). Interestingly enough, Lovecraft also mentions here the "Roman scenes" from a film he recently enjoyed, Cecil B. DeMille's *Cleopatra* (1934), which he considered to be "certainly [. . .] damn good." I would like to venture the possibility, however slight, that Lovecraft's suggestion to Moe may have been influenced by the powerful Roman imagery portrayed in this film.

In any case, the whole essay was finished by 10 or 11 December, as both the AHT and a letter to Robert E. Moe confirm (MWM 403). Since Lovecraft had been rather busy at the time—for instance, he had been struggling with the slow-pacedness of "The Shadow out of Time" (HPL to E. Hoffmann Price, 18 November 1934; SL 5.71), which almost occupied him the whole winter[1]—this means that he may not have had enough time at his disposal to document himself on this topic, even if he was not wholly unfamiliar with it, and may have relied on a rather comprehensive source to *copy down* the most detailed aspects of his account of Roman architecture. I shall return to this point shortly.

---

1. Cf. as well his letter to Price on the same issue, 30 December 1934: "Pressure of other duties has for the moment made any original writing impossible." See also HPL to Wilfred B. Talman, 10 November [1936] (*Letters to Wilfred B. Talman* 276): "like the season of 1934–35, when I wrote half a dozen things and destroyed all save 'The Shadow Out of Time.'" Also an unpublished letter to Hyman Bradofsky (15 November 1934; A.Ms., JHL): "by next spring I hope to have several new ones [stories] finished."

The fate of the text can be reconstructed from pieces scattered through Lovecraft's correspondence. The essay is referred to again in a letter to Moe dated 15 February 1935 (as it seems, this important reference went unnoticed before), where Lovecraft acknowledges the reception of Moe's typed text of his introductory "sloppy architectural screed" and complains about the "careless way it was really composed . . . . . the loose diction, unrhythmical paragraphs, unverified statements, general lack of planning, and what-all!" (MWM 372). Lovecraft goes on to suggest a series of seven corrections, all but one identical to our received text—"insert *ancestors*' before *tenacious*," he says, but our current text has "persistent" instead of the latter (CE 5.121)— and already incorporated into the carbon copy preserved in JHL. Although the fate of this essay in the students' magazine remains a mystery, Moe considered the text worth publishing in a serious journal and urged Lovecraft to submit it or allow him to do so on his behalf. Lovecraft, however, politely declined to do so, on the grounds of its multiple imperfections and lack of originality (MWM 373). The next mention appears in a letter to Moe's eldest son, Robert Ellis Moe (1912–1992),[2] dated 12 March 1935, with whom Lovecraft had started to correspond on 13 February of that year:

> Glad my harangues & article on antiquity proved of some interest. I'll have to ask the return of that hectographed copy some time—but no hurry. I'll let you see the rest (the greater part) of the text when your respected pater gets it duplicated & sends me a copy. No—your generous sire did *not* hold out on you— since this random & really impromptu essay was written on the 10th of last December. (MWM 403)

Lovecraft probably lent the original, uncorrected copy to Moe's son in person—who was not in Milwaukee with his father, but working in Bridgeport, Connecticut—together with some books, when he paid him a visit in Providence on March 2–3 (MWM

---

2. Dates for Robert Ellis Moe and Hyman Jacob Bradofsky, below, come from their WWII Draft Registration Card, available at www.ancestry.com, the obituary in *Tampa Bay Times* (16 September 1992): 131, and the National Archives (www.archives.gov), respectively.

376, 400, and 408).[3] At this point we are brought to an interesting conundrum, for Lovecraft attached another typed copy of the same introductory essay he had already given to Robert in a second letter sent to him on 18 May (the typed copy is stored, together with the letter, in JHL). This time, once more, he stated that this was his only copy and asked for its return at Robert's leisure:

> In this connection I can't resist enclosing the introductory section of my recent rambling observations on Roman architecture & its echoes in the present—an introduction in which I endeavor to present the case for traditionalism in aesthetics. As you will probably recognize, the hectographing & typing are of Mocratic source. I wrote the thing in my usual scrawl—in response to a vague hint of the desirability of some such article for one of your father's pupil's MS. magazines—but he thought it worth preserving in duplicated form .... hence the present text. He is doing the copying & duplicating in sections–this being the only copy I have. Since it is an only copy, I'll ask you to return it at your leisure—not the slightest hurry, though. (MWM 411)

This problem is easily solved if we consider that Lovecraft should have submitted a copy for its publication in the summer issue of the *Californian,* an amateur journal edited by his correspondent Hyman Jacob Bradofsky (1906–2002). Early in November Bradofsky had requested a 7500-word story for the summer issue of his journal, and Lovecraft suggested to him the possibility of including an article on an unspecified topic instead (HPL to Bradofsky, 15 November 1934; A.Ms., JHL). Time passed by, and barely one month after Robert's visit, Lovecraft decided to have "A Living Heritage" submitted to the *Californian* under the title "Heritage or Modernism":

> Enclosed, therefore, is some material for the summer *Californian.*
>   I couldn't get around to that spell of fiction-writing—& anyhow, the amateur public probably couldn't care for the sort of weird stuff I turn out. Therefore I am sending an *article* instead of a *story.* This thing—"Heritage or Modernism"—represents

---

3. Although these volumes could be the ones mentioned in an epistolary fragment dated 20 March 1935 (MWM 405).

my reaction to the "modernistic" junk which threatens to become so typical a nuisance in this generation. Hope you'll find it reasonably acceptable & appropriate. It was conceived as an introduction for a longer article dealing with Roman architecture & its influence in the present, but is complete in itself. The other article, not yet typed, is in the present custody of our fellow-amateur Moe. Later on I may let you see whether you'd care to print it. (HPL to Bradofsky, 5 April 1935; A.L.S., JHL)

And later on 16 April, he wrote back to Bradofsky:

Glad to hear that my article proved suitable for use in *The Californian*. As for its sequel—the rough draught is in Moe's hands, & as soon as he gets it typed & mimeographed I'll demand a copy to send to you. I might explain that the whole thing was prepared to assist in one of Moe's school projects. The subject being especially congenial to me, I developed it further than was expected; so that Moe decided to get the text mimeographed for limited distribution & possible professional submission. I told him, however, that such a thing would scarcely have a chance professionally. (HPL to Bradofsky, 16 April 1935; A.L.S., JHL)

This certainly was not the first time Lovecraft submitted a previously unpublished piece to Bradofsky, as it was the case with "Some Notes on Interplanetary Fiction" (composed in July 1934), which was originally written for one of William L. Crawford's magazines but appeared instead in the Winter 1935 issue of the *Californian* (IAP 892). Since the first copy—perhaps the one lent to Robert in early March—was uncorrected, Lovecraft's submission to Bradofsky's journal should have been the new duplicate typed by Maurice afterwards, a second copy of which would have been forwarded to Robert on 18 May. Lovecraft requested again a typed copy of the second part on January 1936, to be sent to Bradofsky for the next summer issue of the *Californian*. However, Maurice seems to have misplaced Lovecraft's text and, unable to dig it up in time, the publication never occurred (*MWM* 391). The current AHT text probably found its way to Derleth's quarters soon after Lovecraft's death, when he and Donald Wandrei visited Moe to acquire "the almost invaluable trove of Lovecraft material he had collected in the 25 years of correspondence with HPL" (*MWM* 22).

This being said, I would like to focus briefly on the sources of the second part of "A Living Heritage." If we consider the relative steadfastness with which an otherwise occupied Lovecraft managed to write down both parts of the text, it seems very likely that he didn't dedicate a great deal of time and resources to locating the rich information that constitutes this second part. Indeed, a quick look at the few books on Roman and English antiquities and architecture owned by Lovecraft shows that he didn't bother with any of them. Denton J. Snider's *Architecture as a Branch of Aesthetic, Psychologically Treated* (1905; *LL* 826), despite its promising title, has no connection with Lovecraft's essay, whereas W. H. Goodyear's *Roman and Medieval Art* (1897; *LL* 369) could have contributed to the general structure of the second part of the essay, but it was not a source for its contents. An attentive collation of the different passages and themes in "A Living Heritage" shows that Lovecraft derived almost all the information directly from two entries in his edition of the *Encyclopaedia Britannica* (= *EB*, 9th ed. 1896) and its companion *American Revisions and Additions to EB* (= *ARA*; *LL* 299): "Robert Adam" and, most importantly, "Architecture," the latter written by Thomas Hayter Lewis (1818–1898), then Professor of Architecture at King's College (London), and George Edmund Street (1824–1881), President of the Royal Institute of British Architecture. These were polished with minor notes extracted from other related entries in the same encyclopedia and, at least in one instance, with Harold Donaldson Eberlein's *The Architecture of Colonial America* (1921; *LL* 290). Related entries can also be found listed in another volume Lovecraft had in his library, James Baldwin's *A Guide to Systematic Readings in the Encyclopaedia Britannica* (1895; *LL* 62), where a complete list of entries related to architecture in *EB* matching Lovecraft's main points is provided.

Although the contents were indeed rewritten and assimilated into Lovecraft's main threat—the living presence of Roman architecture and aesthetics in modern, pre-functionalist English culture—the substance of the text remains the same, and the narrative follows the events, names and description in *EB*: pre-

Roman architecture (*CE* 5.127–30, from *EB* 2.414ff.); Filippo Brunelleschi, the five orders, Vitruvius, and the Renaissance (*CE* 5.133–34, from *EB* 2.436–38); Andrea Palladio and the European styles (*CE* 5.134, from *EB* 2.441); the Italo-Vitruvian architecture, examples from Spain, Germany, or Denmark, and Inigo Jones (*CE* 5.135, from *EB* 2.442–43); Charles II and Christopher Wren (*CE* 5.135–36, from *EB* 2.444 and *EB* 24.689–90); Pompeii and Herculaneum (*CE* 5.136, from *EB* 2.445); and Robert Adam (*CE* 5.136–37, from *EB* 1.139–40). For instance, compare Lovecraft's discussion on Christopher Wren's activities after the great fire of London of 1666—

> Having already been approached on architectural matters by the King, he was placed in charge of the rebuilding of St. Paul's Cathedral, as well as of fifty city churches and numerous secular edifices. Gradually devising a set of plans in accordance with his notions of Roman design as applied to English needs, he built the great domed cathedral between 1675 and 1710, and created such lesser masterpieces as the churches of St. Bride's; St. Michaels, Cornhill; St. Stephen's, Walbrook; and St. Mary le Bow, in whose steeples ring the famous and now newly reconditioned Bow Bells. (*CE* 5.135)

—with its eponymous entry in the *Britannica*:

> Just before the fire Wren was asked by Charles II to prepare a scheme for the restoration of old St Paul's. [. . .] The first stone of St Paul's was laid on June 21, 1675, the choir was opened for use December 2, 1697, and the last stone of the cathedral was set in 1710. [. . .] After the destruction of the city of London Wren was employed to make designs for rebuilding its fifty burnt churches, and he also prepared a scheme for lying out the whole city on a new plan, with some wide streets radiating from a central space. [. . .] Among Wren's city churches the most noteworthy are St Michel's, Cornhill, St Bride's and St Mary le Bow, Fleet Street, the latter remarkable for its graceful spire, and St Stephen's, Walbrook, with a plain exterior, but very elaborate and graceful interior. (*EB* 24.689)

The remaining pages, mainly discussing the classic revival in America (*CE* 5.137–39), seem to have been taken from Chapter

X of Eberlein's *Architecture* and the supplemental *ARA*, and include brief mentions to the Richardsonian Romanesque, the Columbian Exposition of 1893, or modern American architecture in general.

Corrigenda Minora

Although noted deficiencies marring the AHT as a whole were entirely the responsibility of the editors—incoherence, abridgements, etc.—typographical errors were not necessarily due to their negligence: these were, instead, the unintended consequence of Alice Conger's self-recognized unfamiliarity with "Lovecraft's miles of spider web script" and rich yet notoriously archaic vocabulary (Litersky 133; cf. Joshi, "Barbarism" 51). It was Alice J. Conger (1908–1983),[4] research assistant and typist for Arkham House since 1936/37, who prepared the transcripts of Lovecraft's excerpted letters and selected tales from materials chosen by the editors (Derleth 2), "armed with reference books, dictionaries, and magnifying glass" as well as a tremendous well of patience (Litersky 133). This means that the transcriber behind the AHT did respect the original text to the best of her ability, and that errors in these texts represent the nearest educated guess to the otherwise unknown or strange vocabulary Lovecraft may have used. For instance, a well-known mistake in "The *Journal* and the New Deal" is the word "irrate" in the line "The preceding administration of irrate Hamiltons in Jefferson's clothing grudged even the dole," which could be tentatively corrected to "innate" based on the similarity of the letters "r" and "n" in Lovecraft's handwriting. Taking this into consideration, and with the sources at our disposal, I provide below a short list of important corrections without which the text, paraphrasing Lovecraft, "would convey ideas which I do not mean to convey" (*MWM* 373).

caleriole: The text should read "cabriole" (a type of curved leg in furniture resembling an animal's pawn), with the letter "b" being mistaken for "le" due to its similarity, as it can be seen in

---

4. See her obituary in the *Madison Wisconsin State Journal* (8 November 1983): 23.

Lovecraft's own handwriting of similar words: "Inside the houses there will be paneling with pilasters, and mock-pediments and arched concave niches, and much of the furniture will be of graceful cabriole outlines" (CE 5.125).

low-cast: It should be corrected to "law-court": "The capacious basilica, or law-court with nave and pillared aisles, dates from the second century B.C." (CE 5.128). Compare with the following text in the *Britannica*, from where the sentence above may have been rewritten (the nave and the isles appear also mentioned in the next lines):

> BASILICA, a term denoting (1) in civil architecture, a court of law [. . .]. From this circumstance the term appears to have gained currency as the designation of a law-court, in which sense was adopted by the Romans. The introduction of the *basilicae* into Rome was not very early. [. . .] The earliest named is that erected by M. Porcius Cato, the censor, 183 B.C. (*EB* 3.412)

washing: Already doubted by S. T. Joshi. Context seems to suggest a word related to "moulding" (cf. *EB* 2.415), for which I suggest "working," based on the similarity between the letters "-ash-" and "-ork-" in Lovecraft's handwriting: "These last-named tendencies, found most often in late or provincial edifices, violate the austere theory of 'functionalism' more than any other forms in classical architecture—being in effect a working of Roman arch construction by an appearance of Grecian column-and-architrave construction" (CE 5.130).

Brunelleschi: A lacuna in the following text can be tentatively supplied by comparison with the *Britannica*:

> No sounder theory could possibly have been conceived, and upon this the famous Brunelleschi proceeded to act . . . a generation before the birth of Columbus. (CE 5.133)

> The first step taken towards the revolution of architecture was by Filippo Brunelleschi, a Florentine architect, who was employed to finish the cathedral of his native city early in the 15th century; a work which had been commenced more than a cen-

tury before on the designs of Arnolfo. (*EB* 2.436)

Brunelleschi started working of the Cathedral of Florence approximately "a generation before the birth of Columbus," and the lacuna probably mentioned the famous building.

Lenore: What seems to be an obscure reference to Gottfried August Bürger's poem (or perhaps Edgar Allan Poe's) should in fact be corrected to "Louvre": "The old Louvre being demolished in 1527, its classical successor was under way within a decade" (*CE* 5.134). Cf. the *Britannica:* "Between 1527 and 1540 Francis I demolished the old Louvre, and in 1541 Pierre Lescot began a new palace four times as large, which was not finished till the reign of Louis XIV" (*EB* 18.290).

Halo-Vitruvian: Appearing in four occasions (*CE* 5.134, 135, and 136), this common typographical error should be corrected to "Italo-Vitruvian," given the similarity of "It" with an "H" in Lovecraft's handwriting. For instance:

> In the eighteenth century a severer Roman taste produced the Pantheon, and since then there has been ceaseless conflict between the archaeological and the localised "Italo-Vitruvian" spirit. [. .] Spain adopted and abused the revival; one of its typical early products being the gloomy Escurial, whilst later developments touched the nadir of extravagance. (*CE* 5.134)

> Spain received but soon modified the Italo-Vitruvian architecture, and has never recovered from the architectural excesses into which her architects plunged when the wealth of their countrymen in the 16th and 17th centuries enabled them to accomplish such enormous works. [. .] the Escorial, a vast palace built upon the ingeniously rural plan of a gridiron. It is a vast but bare, cold, and repulsive building. (*EB* 2.442)

Likewise, **Halian** should be corrected to Italian, as in the following passage: "Wren, a thorough student of Roman, Italian, and French forms, was virtually the first architect to react sharply from the solecisms and extravagances of the Italo-Vitruvians" (*CE* 5.135).

authenia: The correct term here is "anthemia," plural form of "anthemion," a decorative motif also known as palmette in the shape of the petals of a flower or palm-tree leaves:

> Adam-period architecture, with its delicate straight lines, classically exact mouldings, and tasteful ornaments in low relief—urns, ovals, spandrel fans, anthemia, and pendent husks—forms the high-water mark of domestic design, and employs the decorative principles of the Romans with maximum effectiveness. [. . .] Samuel McIntire of Salem and Charles Bulfinch of Boston are its best-known practitioners on this side of the water, though John Holden Greene of Providence ought not to be overlooked. (CE 5.137)

Compare with Eberlein's The Architecture of Colonial America:

> In New England, under the influence of such men as Charles Bulfinch and Samuel McIntire, the delicate proportions and fascinatingly refined details brought into English architecture by the Brothers Adam remained in favour until well into the nineteenth century and exercised a beneficial effect that has not yet lost its force. With excellent taste both Bulfinch and McIntire employed the Adam heritage of urns, pendent husks, anthemia, ovals, spandril fans and all the rest of the Pompeian refinements, and McIntire unhesitatingly lengthened out the proportions of pillars and pilasters until he had removed all suggestion of grossness from his design and imparted a slender grace to all his work. (112)

Pernerian: Appearing in a list of art styles, I believe this term should be read, in fact, as "Peruvian": "All known styles from Egyptian to Romanesque, Persian to Renaissance, Grecian to Gothic, Peruvian to Algerian, were exaggerated, parodied, and mixed in one and the same building" (CE 5.138). Peruvian architecture is mentioned near the end of the Britannica's article on "Architecture" (EB 2.451), although this seems to be Lovecraft's own attempt of criticism of the American Gothic revival and its distancing from the comfort of familiar traditions. Peruvian art is also mentioned within this context in Lovecraft correspondence:

> That is why I believe a Georgian doorway has more real signifi-

178   César Guarde-Paz

cance for an ordinary American than an Inca masque or Italian primitive has. In order to make the Inca or Renaissance object of equal significance—of equal relationship, that is, to the actual experience & tradition stream of the beholder—one would have to take exhaustive & specialised courses in Peruvian anthropology & cinquecento art & life. (HPL to Frank Belknap Long, 27 February 1931; *SL* 3.325)

Works Cited

Baldwin, James. *A Guide to Systematic Readings in the Encyclopaedia Britannica.* Chicago: Werner Co., 1895.

Derleth, August. *Thirty Years of Arkham House, 1939–1969: A History and Bibliography.* Sauk City, WI: Arkham House, 1970.

Eberlein, Harold Donaldson. *The Architecture of Colonial America.* Boston: Little, Brown, 1921.

The Encyclopaedia Britannica: A Dictionary of the Arts, Sciences, and General Literature. With additions by W. H. De Puy. 9th ed. Chicago: Werner Co., 1896.

Litersky, Dorothy M. Grobe. *Derleth: Hawk . . . and Dove.* Aurora, CO: National Writers Press, 1997.

Joshi, S. T. "Barbarism vs. Civilization: Robert E. Howard and H. P. Lovecraft in Their Correspondence." In Darrell Schweitzer, ed. *The Robert E. Howard Reader.* San Bernardino, CA: Borgo Press, 2010. 51–81.

———, and David E. Schultz. *An H. P. Lovecraft Encyclopedia.* Westport, CT: Greenwood Press, 2001.

Lovecraft, H. P. *O Fortunate Floridian. H. P. Lovecraft's Letters to R. H. Barlow.* Ed. S. T. Joshi and David E. Schultz. Tampa, FL: University of Tampa Press, 2007.

———. *Letters to Maurice W. Moe and Others.* Ed. David E. Schultz and S. T. Joshi. New York: Hippocampus Press, 2018. [Abbreviated in the text as *MWM.*]

———. *Letters to Wilfred B. Talman and Helen V. and Genevieve Sully.* Ed. David E. Schultz and S. T. Joshi. New York: Hippocampus Press, 2019.

On Hawthorne's Unwitting "Children": The Strange Case of H. P. Lovecraft

Simone Turco

If one were to search among H. P. Lovecraft's works for direct references to or even mild hints at authors who had a significant impact on his narrative, Hawthorne's name would hardly be found. Although Lovecraft analyzes Hawthorne extensively in "Supernatural Horror in Literature," he does so in what seems an ultra-objective, almost detached way.

The Providence author openly credits European Gothic writers such as Arthur Machen and Lord Dunsany (who were his contemporaries) as a source of inspiration. Apart from his critical works, he often mentions such authors in fiction. Among the Americans, Poe is the one who stands out most notably. In fact, Poe's style and stylemes echo in the pages of Lovecraft's best-known Gothic-structured tales. On the other hand, Hawthorne seems to play the part of the great absentee. Nonetheless, a certain affinity can be recognized. Peter Cannon famously noted that "while outside the genre he may be a pygmy beside such classical giants as Poe, Hawthorne, and Melville, Lovecraft in the darkness of his vision can be compared as their spiritual heir" (125). Throughout his treatise, Cannon actually does much to redeem Lovecraft from his reputation as a "pygmy" and a "pulp fiction" author, in comparison with his great predecessors. In particular, however, the comparative study of Lovecraft and Hawthorne, the latter being a notable component of the nineteenth-century American triad, has not been carried out to a satisfactory degree. It is our hope that this brief paper may move specialists to initiate a more comprehensive and specific study of those interrelations. We shall start by first referring to Poe, who played a major role in the development of Lovecraft's aesthetics.

In Lovecraft's works, Gothicism entwines with exquisitely New World themes, the most prominent one being America's Puritan record. In Poe, East Coast culture is often hinted at but largely remains in the background, providing the basis for the development of plots that tend to the grotesque and, ultimately, the fantastic. Indeed, Poe revolutionizes the tenets of Romantic realism, but most of his productions feature fantastic elements that, in the end, are recognizable precisely as fantastic, that is, as no longer realistic. Despite his tendency to reproduce Poe's style, Lovecraft follows the pattern set by his contemporary Machen in making it his goal to present the reader with a completely factual narration of events, characters, and motifs recounted and developed in purely realistic terms. In so doing, he is able to trespass the divide between fancy and reality without implicitly furthering the idea that what is being recounted is a piece of fantastic narrative.

A foremost example of Poe's tendency to mingle reality and unreality can be seen in "The Devil in the Belfry" (1839), where the estranging atmosphere causes the reader immediately to situate the story in a fantastic, unreal—and unrealistic—setting. In this respect, Poe and Hawthorne are at the antipodes in the narrative tradition of the American Renaissance. Poe is a writer of weird fantasy; Hawthorne is a writer of fantastic or magical realism, in that he sees in reality the possibility of expressing a magical or psychological side of the real that would be neglected by using the techniques of narrative realism in the strict sense.

Magical realism springs from the need to show a side of the real that pragmatic tenets, such as those that contributed to positivism, tended to deny as a Romantic and unverifiable surplus. Hawthorne strives to reject a systematization of reality as uniquely depending on physiological phenomena. He belongs, as Lovecraft put it, to "the tradition of moral values, gentle restraint, and mild, leisurely phantasy tinged more or less with the whimsical," where "we have none of the violence, the daring, the high colouring, the intense dramatic sense, the cosmic malignity, and the undivided and impersonal artistry of Poe" (CE 2.104). Central to his thinking is, of course, the reflection on the notion of evil, which later matured in younger authors such as Melville, whose work in any case Hawthorne did not fully appreciate. But Hawthorne's approach to evil is different from Poe's and his immediate "disciples": "Evil, a very real force to Hawthorne, appears on every hand as a lurking and conquering adversary; and the visible world becomes in his fancy a theatre of infinite tragedy and woe . . . but he was not disinterested enough to value impressions, sensations, and beauties of narration for their own sake" (CE 2.104). Lovecraft acutely concludes: "Supernatural horror . . . is never a primary object with Hawthorne; though its impulses were so deeply woven into his personality that he cannot help suggesting it with the force of genius when he calls upon the unreal world to illustrate the pensive sermon he wishes to preach" (CE 2.105).

Hawthorne's lesson in "narrative plenty" was, at times, unwittingly received and interiorized by the next generation of writers; even Henry James, whose style and language are so innovative as to draw the reader's attention away from the plots of his narratives, owes much to him in terms of *Lust zu fabulieren* (the "pleasure of narrating" for narration's sake). Nevertheless, after Hawthorne's death, his settings and stylemes fell into a kind of oblivion, as if all that was to be said concerning such themes as evil, redemption, retribution, and sin had been fully explored in his works. Becoming a classic, his work also became somewhat crystallized, to the point of being criticized for the prevalence of descriptions and personal, narratorial observations over an extensive construction of character psychology (which, instead, is evident in James).

Formally, the only connection between Lovecraft and Hawthorne is their Puritan background. Though defining himself an atheist, Lovecraft seems actually to profess a form of "hard" agnosticism. Hawthorne's rapport with religion is still unclear, although he is certainly not an atheist. And yet, from a comparative point of view, the way Lovecraft devised his literary endeavor follows the pattern of Hawthorne's experience with his forefathers' religious faith, at the base of which stood the concept of evil as a pervasive and relentless, obscure will that transcended any positive effort to constrain it within the realm of materiality.

The reason why Puritanism so haunted Hawthorne's mind is known through his often-mentioned biography. The responsibility of one of his ancestors in the Salem events left such a deep impression on his imagination that to him those events were like the true originating factor of New England's history, the exposure of its true set of values and the dangers of following it. Hence, the issue of witchcraft and the legacy of witch-hunts by the Puritans surely played a prominent role in the evolution of his themes. Though suspending his judgment on the truthfulness of witch-related occurrences, Hawthorne's reflection is based upon the assumption that the stricter the rule, the lesser will be the ability of reason to avert totalitarian impulses, such as the violent turn taken by the Salem community in 1692.[1]

The sin the Fathers so strongly wished to uproot and atone for had manifested itself in the cure they employed to get rid of sin itself; it became a major sin that in turn would haunt the descendants of those overly zealous Puritans for many generations to come. Lovecraft, on his part, was born in a city that had been shielded from the application of rigid Puritan rules and even became a haven for anti-Puritan intellectual revolters (see Lovecraft, *Against Religion* 142). As he himself recognized, as a youth Lovecraft benefited from this atmosphere. The environment of the household in which he grew up was equally free. He availed himself of the great quantity of books present, forming a taste both for more recent or even current thinking and literature and for older, more "mysterious" collections he found in the attic. Eventually his readings, coupled with a nearly morbid isolation experienced during his teenage years, contributed to his developing a frame of mind and a view of reality that we may call "anti-materialistic." He lived as if plunged into a world of pagan deities, of fauns and dryads, to the point of developing a kind of rational paganism that dominated his life and works. It is possible to argue that such a pagan influence, along with the great freedom enjoyed in terms of cultural and intellectual stimuli, caused him to become oblivious to the very notion of sin, which

---

1. At the same, time, Hawthorne conceived of sin as an element "not in the least subject to human volition . . . thus stressing its purely accidental nature" (Hansen 34). Therefore, his view of sin is to a large extent fatalistic.

is one of Hawthorne's main preoccupations and an exquisitely Jewish and Christian idea.

Donald R. Burleson, one of the few critics concerned with initiating a comparative analysis of the authors, observes: "Hawthorne's recurrent notion of 'unpardonable sin' . . . must have been virtually meaningless to Lovecraft" (36), who does not have a good relationship with Christianity. His experience with religion draws a parable totally contrary to Hawthorne's, who in the end seems to reconcile with a Protestant (though still very "customized") idea of God. As Burleson points out: "Lovecraft digested Hawthorne's corpus of works" and "described him in terms of genius, though harboring a marked distaste for Hawthorne's allegorical didacticism and moralizing" (36). This is a substantial aspect. Hawthorne uses New England as an allegory of intimate and familiar life disturbed by the dark shadow of sin crouching at the door. Basically, his outlook on East Coast culture is positive, though marred by the "necessity" of sin and corruption, which he attempts to rationalize in symbolic terms and thereby make an example of. His style bends to such a goal; extensive descriptions and narratorial insertions, which also correspond to a certain Romantic sensibility, aim at reconstructing reality as a complex allegorical system. Therefore, his style comes to be affected by the main tenets upon which the work is built.

An instance of Hawthorne's allegoric leanings can be seen in *The Marble Faun* (1860), which, though set in Rome, has many Puritan and New England-related themes and elements. Such a "narratorial abundance" divests the narrative of its realistic value and turns it, in many ways, into a psychological drama, where reality and fantasy merge and appear to the reader as an elaboration of the narrator's or the characters' thoughts and sentiments. Why would Lovecraft have disdained such an allegorical approach? For the sake of realism. Though founding his work primarily on New England's traditions, Lovecraft devises a material world that is far more obscure than written and official history would pinpoint.

New England (which Lovecraft loved very much) becomes the repository, the focal point of an alternative history of mankind, steeped in witchcraft and evil practices, of which the Puritans would be a mere historical manifestation. His narrators often remark that along with their Protestant faith, the *Mayflower* pilgrims also carried over from Europe terrible traditions that the isolation of the New World would have caused to develop into new and twisted forms. His New England, therefore, is not "intimistic" or psychology-oriented. Rather, it is open to extrovert interpretations of Puritan history and of current reality in neo-mythological terms, which elicit the feeling that what the reader is experiencing is true, factual, and verifiable. It cannot be confused with a psychological drama or a dreamy experience, as sometimes happens in Hawthorne, who lingers on individual and narratorial sensations in order to produce his allegory of things.

To Lovecraft, things are *as* and *what* they are; they do not refer to something else, or, better, their figural power is objective and real, not translated, transposed, or exemplary. Overall, however, both authors are comparable as to the notion of history's obscurity or incomprehensibility. The characters of their respective works seem to fluctuate in a cosmos where individual choices are determined by powers not entirely understandable by purely human means. Whether it be the force of Fate, as in Hawthorne, or the legacy of a mythical and fear-inspiring past, as in Lovecraft, the end result is the same: the inability to peer into the past to understand one's individual and collective present and its rationale. An instance of these differences and convergences can be detected by briefly comparing aspects of *The House of the Seven Gables* (1851) and "The Shadow over Innsmouth" (1931).

In *The House of the Seven Gables*, the seven-gabled dwelling represents those elements of the past that withstand the operation of time. It is the repository of a family tradition, a monument to the family's unique past. It is time-eaten but still standing; its inhabitants live under a curse dictated by the unjust action of their common ancestor, who seized the house from a man who was accused of being a sorcerer and was executed. The protagonists' actions are almost totally determined or affected by that single past act, and although they still attempt to use their own free will, they are always constrained by a superior force. The ancestral house becomes the focus of their actions and wishes, of their common destiny and existential demise.

In "The Shadow over Innsmouth," Lovecraft masterfully develops the theme of mankind's mythical and fearful past. The narrator-protagonist wanders about in the waste town of Innsmouth, where half the population is the result of interbreeding with an ancient race of non-human submarine and eternal beings. The houses where such 'children of the gods' live are shut, bleak, and rotten. Even the houses of the rich upper-class members of society undergo the same process; they are the objective correlative representing the consuming of what is exterior to pursue a higher, though terrible, goal.[2] Those who inhabit them, in fact, are transforming into sea creatures that will soon join their ancestors in the deep. By observing such a decay, the unaware protagonist reflects on the effect of time and decadence on human affairs, but he also finds out that he himself is partly a product of that interbreeding and is turning into a creature of the abyss.

The two works differ notably from a stylistic point of view. The *tropos* of the house is developed to some extent by Poe in "The Fall of the House of Usher" (1839), where the building is closely identified with the family and with Usher himself. However, in "The Shadow over Innsmouth" we find the theme of blood-related, "genetic" decadence and of the crooked ancestral influence, which Hawthorne is the only one to develop so incisively in an American context prior to Lovecraft. While Lovecraft derived from Poe the taste for grotesque, gloomy, and even horror-arousing settings and stylemes, it is undeniable that he absorbed Hawthorne's tendency to elaborate largely on the topic of family decay and degradation.

The house, which is often a New England dwelling, or the house-theme occurs many times in both authors, both in negative and in positive acceptations. Hawthorne was fascinated by New England manses and homes overgrown with ivy and mosses, around which many of his characters' lives revolve. In Lovecraft, the house is often a terrible place where horrible things

---

2. As S. T. Joshi observes, "Lovecraft never achieved a greater atmosphere of insidious decay than in 'The Shadow over Innsmouth,'" where "the cosmic and the local, the past and the present, the internal and the external, and self and the other are all fused into an inextricable unity" (167).

happen (as in "The Shunned House"), since they represent the space of intimacy that is often full of fearful aspects to be hidden from the public eye.

For both Hawthorne and Lovecraft, the house is a virtual mystery, having a symbolic significance difficult to interpret and referring to a set of symbols that we may comprise in the so-called collective unconscious. At the same time, our authors display a remarkable ambivalence. Lovecraft writes about New England as the center of untold horrors, and yet he is fascinated by and attracted to it. Here, aesthetic attraction wins over repulsion. Hawthorne, for his part, feels distraught at New England's dull and totalitarian past. And yet, especially in his *French and Italian Note-Books*, he incessantly criticizes European life and customs while extolling and yearning for East Coast homes, woodland, and habits. This attraction-repulsion interplay is, in our view, at the core of both authors' approach to existence and, consequently, a major factor in the development of their work; a work where Gothicism mingles at various degrees with realism.

Stylistically speaking, as mentioned, Lovecraft is a pure realist. This approach to the fantastic enables his work to be perceived as truthful despite its rationally implausible features. In this respect, he is an absolute innovator. Hawthorne, as Lovecraft himself noted, is more "suggestive" and less direct. When he speaks of demons, witches, and the supernatural, he is more than cautious and, at times, even suspicious or ironical. As an heir of the Transcendentalist tradition, which he absorbed to some extent, he does not let supernatural inputs trespass the realm of the imagination and take a full hold of the senses. Simply put, he remains anchored to a rational ground into which he grafts the individual psychologies of his characters. In this way, the divide between dream and reality, plausibility and impossibility, becomes blurred, and factual truth does not stand out. Lovecraft, instead, implicitly declares all the recounted "matter" as truthful, even when it is presented to the reader by psychologically disturbed characters. The sense of horror and doubt is thus accrued, as are the realistic aspect and the sense of estrangement.

Aside from direct influences of one author on the other, it

will not be amiss briefly to examine the possible, common *inter-médiaires* between the two. It appears that both Hawthorne and Lovecraft drew on similar types of readings. In Hawthorne's case, it was a normal custom of his time to be educated at reading seventeenth and eighteenth-century English renditions of classical and ecclesiastical Latin and Greek works, which he also utilized to produce his versions of Greek myths. He was also acquainted with English classics and, of course, with English and American Protestant authors, such as Bunyan and the Mathers.

Curiously, though living at a much later time, young Lovecraft became an avid reader of seventeenth and eighteenth-century literature, which had a lasting impression on the way he conceived of language, style, and expression. In his early teens, he was even able to write and speak English in an eighteenth-century fashion, which he favored over modern usage. Clearly, he was an exception in his time. It does not come as a surprise that his style and themes are so distant from then-current literature and so much closer to Brockden Brown's, Poe's, and, of course, Hawthorne's writing styles.

It would be an interesting undertaking to analyze and compare the contents of Lovecraft's and Hawthorne's respective libraries to seek in-depth a consonance in terms of motifs, plots, and themes. Above all, what Hawthorne and Lovecraft hold in common is the "prejudice" against the progression of history, which, in their view, amounted to no progress at all. Their common, general view could be thus summarized: despite the danger and darkness presented by the past, the future has much worse things in store. Hawthorne sometimes resorts to the notion of Golden Age to express the desire to go back to a time when things were fixed and immutable. In reality, though, as in *The Marble Faun,* he recognizes that no such era ever existed, and that the only possible Golden Age is the space and time of the present, where familiar ways and custom give sense to individual existence and steadfastly root man in the ever-changing scenery of history. Lovecraft, who narrates of abysmal past in dreadful terms, nonetheless yearns to return to the era of the Fathers, to a century where modern thinking and values (which he views as disvalues) were nonexistent and did not present a risk for tradition. This one is, in fact, the sole force that enables man to withstand the swirling stream of time.

In conclusion, it is beneficial again to refer to Burleson's analysis: "Lovecraft, despite all the influences that helped shape him, was a highly individual writer who transcended those influences to weave his own dark tales in his own distinctive manner." And he adds: "The cosmicism of Lovecraft's fiction is unlike anything that preceded him" (43). Yet, as the critic also recognizes, if Hawthorne were to read Lovecraft he would find themes, stylemes, places, and a sense of existence very familiar to him. Hawthorne and Lovecraft are therefore comparable due to their picturing man as alone on the brink of time and space and as capable of fighting off solitude by a melancholic retraction into historical tradition and domestic myth. Such an approach also enables them to analyze modernity and criticize it from a unique perspective.

As brought out at the outset, it is our wish that the study of Hawthorne's and Lovecraft's approach to history, myth, and the past become again a topic for further study and research, in relation both to their common sources and to the perils and risks they saw in the progression and triumph of Time.

Works Cited

Burleson, Donald R. "Hawthorne's Influence on Lovecraft." In Robert H. Waugh, ed. *Lovecraft and Influence: His Predecessors and Successors*. Lanham, MD: Scarecrow Press, 2013. 35–44.

Cannon, Peter. *H. P. Lovecraft*. Boston: Twayne, 1989.

Hansen, Klaus P. *Sin and Sympathy: Nathaniel Hawthorne's Sentimental Religion*. Bern: Peter Lang, 1991.

Joshi, S. T. *A Subtler Magick: The Writings and Philosophy of H. P. Lovecraft*. San Bernardino, CA: Borgo Press, 1996.

Lovecraft, H. P. *Against Religion: The Atheist Writings of H. P. Lovecraft*. Ed. S. T. Joshi. New York: Sporting Gentlemen, 2010.

Zeitgeist and *Untoten:*
Lovecraft and the Walking Dead

Duncan Norris

The animate human dead are one of the commonest, perhaps even original, tropes of both horror literature and the folktales, myth, and legendry that preceded it. Certain schools of anthropological thought have even theorized that funerary rituals developed as much out of apotropaic measures against the fear of the returning dead as for the obvious needs in tangible expressions of mourning, although likely all these factors play indivisible parts. H. P. Lovecraft was no exception to this usage of the undead in horror fiction, although it is not generally considered one of his more important or common leitmotifs, and pales against the Cyclopean edifice that continues in the ever-expanding Cthulhu Mythos. Yet the animate dead make a surprisingly large appearance in his work when considered as a whole and, paradoxically for a writer noted for his outré cosmological perspective, Lovecraft did in his very first paid prose writing commission create a perfect template for the specific trope of the cannibalistic human corpse returned from the grave that has become instantly recognizable to the modern Western audience as a zombie.

This is not to suggest that Lovecraft invented the cannibalistic undead out of whole cloth, or was the first to use this particular manifestation: monsters that eat humans are perhaps an even hoarier trope than the undead, and their commingling is inevitable. The Mesopotamian Epic of Gilgamesh, one of earliest extant pieces of human literature, includes the very particular and specific threat issued by the goddess Ishtar that she "will bring up the dead to eat the living" (Tablet VII). The cannibal corpse or spirit is found throughout the ages in myth and legend across the world. The very Father of History, Herodotus, gives us the word anthropophagi ("man-eaters") from the alleged tribe of monstrous cannibals near Scythia (*Histories* 4.106.1), albeit shorn of the overtly supernatural aspects. Yet Lovecraft, in a work commonly seen as semi-parodic and deliberately comical in the iridium blackest of senses, created an undead prototype that has continued to resonate, as it has been enlarged upon and endlessly disseminated into the popular culture down to the present day. Thus this monograph shall examine jointly both the broad usage of the corporeal undead in Lovecraft's fiction and demonstrate how, in a most curious set of circumstances, he presciently created the modern Western conception of the zombie.

Before commencing this broad survey of the undead in Lovecraft's fiction it is important to show the differential in the understanding of terminology between that utilized in his day and the evolution of understanding of those words in contemporary society. The very word undead is a relatively modern coinage and, as a random yet illustrative sampling, editions of *Webster's Dictionary* (1959), *The Concise Oxford Dictionary* (1971), and *The American Heritage Dictionary* (1992) do not have an entry for it. Nor did Lovecraft himself use the word even once in his overview of genre fiction in "Supernatural Horror in Literature." While the usage of undead as a descriptor is traceable to an origin in about the fifteenth century, the definition there was of something "neither dead nor alive" (*Online Etymology Dictionary*), a slight yet important differentiation.

The word in the sense of dead creature still having some of the functions of a living being can be traced directly to Bram Stoker's *Dracula* (1897). Indeed, a title originally mooted by Stoker for his novel was *The Dead Un-Dead,* and until shortly before publication *The Un-Dead* was the title the manuscript bore (Stoker 184n3). The popularity of this novel is directly responsible for, among many other things, the distribution of the word as descriptor and metonym for a vampire, and over time its attendant meaning has broadened to encompass all manner of creatures seen to be conceptually related, such as zombies or ghosts. Thus in the twenty-first century the undead, in large part due to modern popular cultural adaptation, have evolved to become a very specific type of monster, with solidly established traits. This has been especially prevalent due to the enormous rise in popularity of fantasy, science fiction, and horror role-playing and video games, which necessitate codification of otherwise intangible ideas as a requirement of game mechanics. While variation is extremely common, many follow the concepts promulgated by the seminal role-playing game Dungeons & Dragons model, with the undead as a precise classification of monster, being in some way the returned spirit or body of a dead creature retaining some aspect of the living, such a motion, speech, intelligence, hunger, etc. Such classifications of the undead thus tend to have certain specific commonalities, such as immunity to poisons and natural events, a general vulnerability to sunlight, ability to be repelled by holy symbols, and a host of other collective traits.

However, this ideation was not anywhere near as distinct or legalistic in folklore. For example, the traditional Balkan term *vrykolakas* has been used to describe both vampires and werewolves (Summers 20–21), while the *dhampir* is the child of a vampire whose reproductive status is generally considered moot in many modern interpretations (Guiley 101–2). Or rather it was, until the sexually generative vampire revival in the paranormal romance genre of literature of which the *Twilight* saga is either the acme or the nadir, depending on one's preferences. Thus, in the original and continuing development of literary and cultural ideas and depictions of the undead, the boundaries between what is a living monster or an undead creature was once far more fluid as the various terms and genres developed, diverged, evolved, accreted, and eventually calcified. The following triumvirate of examples concerning the seemingly familiar zombie, vampire, and ghoul will demonstrate the inherent difficulties in classifications of fundamentally mythological terms and ideas that evolve over time, and particularly in trying to comprehend them in any given prior era in the light of modern understandings.

The zombie, with variant spellings, was of course a term known during Lovecraft's lifetime, albeit with some dissimilarities in meaning. After the success of *The Magic Island* by W. B. Seabrook in 1929, filled with lurid sensations about Haiti, the word zombie began most frequently to refer to the reanimated slaves of Haitian Voodoo origin. Curiously, there is a specific if tangential Lovecraft/Seabrook connection, as the Old Gent actually had a story, "The Music of Erich Zann," published in Dashiell Hammett's anthology *Creeps by Night: Chills and Thrills* (1931), which also contained Seabrook's story "The Witch's Vengeance." (Technically one might say Lovecraft was published with Seabrook twice, as the abridged edition of the book, titled *Modern Tales of Horror* [1932], also contained both their stories.)

This codification of the idea of a zombie was typified and substantially helped by the 1932 motion picture *White Zombie*, which also borrowed a significant amount conceptually from Seabrook's travelogue. This often overlooked movie stars no less a horror luminary than the seminal 1931 Count Dracula himself, Bela Lugosi, and is widely considered the first zombie film.[1] Sadly, *White Zombie* is underappreciated for good reason: while atmospheric, it is not a stellar exemplar of the art of filmmaking. The thematic underpinnings of the film are likewise odious enough that *White Zombie* has the added dubious distinction of being one of the limited number of American horror movies approved for German audiences by the Nazis (Rhodes 233). In the film Lugosi plays the evil Murder Legendre, a voodoo priest running his sugar cane mill on the cheap using traditionally controlled zombies, and having in addition various wicked designs on the film's heroine.

Lovecraft's friend and contemporary *Weird Tales* author Robert E. Howard wrote a short story in 1934 entitled "Pigeons from Hell" in which a zombie variant, the female zuvembie, appears; but in common with the thinking of the time, this creation too is tied to ideas of voodoo and with only a certain repetitive intelligence. This also intersects with the definition given by linguistic scholar Maximilian Schele de Vere in his 1872 book *Americanisms: The English of the New World*, in which he states that a *Zombi* is "a phantom or a ghost, not unfrequently heard in the Southern States in nurseries and among the servants" (138). Schele de Vere, curiously, gives it an etymological root in the Spanish term *sombra* ("shadow" or "shade"),

---

1. Arguments could be made for other films deserving of this title, such as French director Abel Gance's *J'accuse* (1919), with its massed battle-dead returning to their home, but such is not the point of the current work.

"which at times has the same meaning," presumably in a more metaphorical sense such as the translation might be used in English, i.e., shade as a synonym for ghost or spirit. Howard, it should be remembered, was a native Texan with deep Southern roots and an abiding interest in all aspects the folklore of his region. He also owned all five of Seabrook's published works by the time of his own death in 1936 (Burke) and actively recommended them to Lovecraft in a letter earlier the same year, albeit for understanding the politics of French colonial policy (*A Means to Freedom* 940).

Lovecraft himself mentions Seabrook by name twice in 1933 letters to R. H. Barlow—"a friend of yours, like William B. Seabrook, has come into first-hand contact with the horrors of Damballa & his serpents"; "Thanks tremendously for the voodoo report, which I've read with extreme interest. Your friend seems to have been quite an amateur Wm. B. Seabrook"[2] (*O Fortunate Floridian* 83, 85)—in contexts that indicate he was at least familiar with the concepts contained in *The Magic Island* and may even have read this highly popular work. Yet our modern idea of the zombie as an undead reanimated cannibal was in fact a Lovecraft creation both predating and eventually eclipsing Seabrook, although the word was retroactively rather than contemporaneously applied, as shall be demonstrated below.

The literary and popular vampire archetype, extant under various names and attributes for millennia, rapidly became cemented into a distinct codification in the popular mindset following *Dracula*'s enormous success. In fact, the alleged rules for vampires were established so swiftly that a reader wrote to *Weird Tales* to complain about Robert E. Howard's "four flagrant breaches" of this apparent canon in his 1932 tale "The Horror from the Mound" (Howard, *Horror Stories* xxii). Such pedantry often ends up in a tangle of clashing understandings and contradictions. For example, it is a common popular view—heavily promulgated by films beginning with the seminal (and unauthorized) *Dracula* adaptation *Nosferatu* (1922), in which the titular

---

2. Amusingly, very few persons today attach the label professional to Seabrook's activities and writings. Even in 1932 *Time* referred to them as "romantic fibs."

vampire is disintegrated by the rising sun—that vampires cannot go out by day, and that they are even destroyed by sunlight. This runs directly counter to both some traditional folklore (Summers 205) and the actions of the modern progenitor of the vampire archetype Dracula, who in his eponymous novel is clearly described going abroad during the day. Likewise, modern films frequently use ultraviolet light as a weapon against vampires, the thinking being that as a major component of sunlight this can be artificially created, ignoring the original mystical elements specifically associated with the sun that (supposedly) makes the light efficacious as a weapon against the walking dead. After a certain point applying logic to the supernatural becomes inherently illogical.

To use a more specific set of real-world examples, modern scholarship has interpreted the ancient Greeks conceptualizations of ghosts as falling into four main categories: *Aôroi, Bi(ai)othanatoi, Agamoi,* and *Ataphoi.* Respectively these are "those dead before their time" (commonly perceived as that of as infants and children), "those dead by violence," "those dead before marriage" (an exceptionally bitter loss for women, as marital motherhood was one of their few rights in classical times), and "those deprived of burial" (Ogden 146). Yet even these high specialized conceptions by their very nature are somewhat arbitrary, highly culturally based, and somewhat fluid in application, crossing over frequently one into another. Thus, with that exemplar as caveat, for the purposes of our analysis, we shall examine the undead in Lovecraft's literary corpus as being classifiable into two main types. Allowing that premise, without appearing unnecessarily authoritative or pedantic, these categories can be distilled into the revenant and the resurrected. This dualistic approach will at least offer a guide and framework upon which to hang the broader undead picture for the purposes of this examination. Yet, citing the model above, a word of explanation must be made concerning the nature of the ghoul, a modern archetypical undead creature.

Ghouls are of course immediately familiar to readers of Lovecraft, as they make several distinct appearances in both "Pickman's Model" and *The Dream-Quest of Unknown Kadath,* having a particular prolonged presence in the latter work. Yet it is quite clear that in Lovecraft's writings these creatures, while forming a distinct racial group, are not necessarily undead in the generally accepted term of a reanimated human body, but perhaps form a separate variety of monstrous classification. The artist Pickman's degeneration into one (implied to be due to biological heritage from a tainted changeling in his family line), and the mention of ghoul communities, seem to confirm this hypothesis, but the exact nature of ghouls is never made explicit. Lovecraft also uses the term "ghoul" as a more poetical descriptor in connection with grave-robbery in "The Hound," with the narrator defensively stating of their actions that "we were no vulgar ghouls" (CF 1.341) and describing the occupant of the grave the protagonists seek to despoil as someone "who had himself been a ghoul in his time and had stolen a potent thing from a mighty sepulchre" (CF 1.342). Yet it is clear in both tangible and metaphoric description that concerning ghouls Lovecraft, who read the *Arabian Nights*[3] as a child, is drawing here on the Arabic tradition of the *ghūl* whence both the English word and concept evolved.

There is also likely a significant influence of William Beckford's orientalist *Vathek*, which Lovecraft read in 1921, although he does write of having "read of ghouls" in a 1919 letter that predates his acquiring of a copy of *Vathek* (SL 1.97). Lovecraft singles out *Vathek* for praise in both letters and in "Supernatural Horror in Literature," and more significantly its immediate influence can be clearly demonstrated in the line from "Herbert West—Reanimator" (1921–22) about the origin of the typhoid epidemic coming "like a noxious afrite from the halls of Eblis" (CF 1.297), terms and connotations directly culled from Beckford's novel. The term ghoul actually appears in for the first time in English in the translation of *Vathek* from the French, but the *Arabian Nights* brought the term into European literature via the French translation that influenced Beckford. The ghouls of *Vathek* are thus heavily influenced by those in the *Arabian Nights*, and Lovecraft himself admits modeling his structure for *The Dream-Quest of Unknown Kadath* upon *Vathek* (SL 2.94)

---

3. Although commonly referred to today as *One Thousand and One Nights*, I have taken the liberty of utilizing the title HPL himself knew and called the work at that time.

and cribbed other information from it, such as the Arabic name from the *Necronomicon* from the notes on the text by Samuel Henley (*JVS* 319).

While there is a scholarly argument that much of the Western conception of ghouls comes from errors, artistic licence, and elaborations in translations from the Arabic, the effect the ideas had moving forward remains the same. To quote from the aforementioned *Arabian Nights*, using two different translations to convey the differences and similarities:

> a ghoul—one of those demons which, as your Highness is aware, wander about the country making their lairs in deserted buildings and springing out upon unwary travellers whose flesh they eat. If no live being goes their way, they then betake themselves to the cemeteries, and feed upon the dead bodies. (Andrew Lang)

> Thy Highness wotteth well that Ghuls be of the race of devils; to wit, they are unclean spirits which inhabit ruins and which terrify solitary wayfarers and at times seizing them feed upon their flesh; and if by day they find not any traveller to eat they go by night to the graveyards and dig out and devour dead bodies. (Richard Burton)

In their original milieu both female and male terms for the creatures exist, and very human familial concepts such as husband and wife are associated with them. Despite being correlated with one of the archetypical lairs of the undead, the cemetery, it is for reason of provender rather than an intrinsic connection with graves per se. Such a creature as the hybrid folkloric/literary ghoul thus presented in English is distinctly more monstrous or demonic than undead, and its defining character is, above all, the eating of human flesh. The infamous Comics Code of 1954, a censorious list of prohibitions and requirements for comic books induced by a moral panic, includes that no depictions be made of the "walking dead, torture, vampires and vampirism, ghouls, cannibalism, and werewolfism" (Part B, Section 5), in which the juxtaposition of the ghoul to the undead and cannibalism could not be clearer.

Thus while a ghoul could be, and frequently is, construed as undead, it is not intrinsically throughout this whole period, and indeed in part thanks to Lovecraft, not absolutely so today. For our analysis, while a ghoul is thus certainly a monstrous yet humanoid creature that needs or desires to feed upon the physical bodies of human beings, it is not portrayed in Lovecraft as a specifically dead creature doing do. In fact, to the contrary, in "The Outsider" the most common interpretation is that the narrator is an undead creature returned from a familial crypt to its old living habitation in the classical revenant model, yet the story specifically mentions ghouls, ambiguously as poetical terminology or perhaps literally given the context, as if they were a different type of being at the end of the tale. Interestingly, and although not directly germane to the point but certainly illustrating the inherent ambiguity in the terms, in the movie generally held responsible for popularizing many of the ideas of the modern zombie, *Night of the Living Dead* (1968), the word zombie is never uttered, but rather the term ghoul is used to indicate the ravenous undead.

Returning to our chosen dyadic undead categorization, revenants are the classic Western undead model, although they are also frequently, almost ubiquitously, encountered across all human cultures, and as noted previously can be traced back to the earliest extant Sumerian writings. Fundamentally, a revenant is an animate corpse come back to plague the living: the very name revenant, which begins to appear in literature in the Middle Ages, comes from the old French for "returning" (*Online Etymology Dictionary*). The term retains enough connection to the original concept that the 2015 film in which famed actor Leonardo DiCaprio won his first Academy Award, portraying the eponymous character coming back from the grave (into which it should be mentioned he was prematurely interred) for revenge, was called *The Revenant*. Accounts of this type of undead are particularly widespread throughout myth, legend, folklore, and even in historical accounts from otherwise reliable authorities such as the twelfth-century English chroniclers Walter Map and William of Newbury.

The incorporeal version of this manifestation is the classical humanoid ghost, and these tend to be more specific and limited as to their haunts, such as the archetypical haunted house of Athenodorus Cananite described in Pliny (*Letters* 7.27). These creatures' motivations and appearances vary, but are often self-willed, generally to a specific purpose, or acted upon by perceived cosmic supernatural forces or laws. As such they frequently have specific weaknesses to defeat them. Common reasons for return include evil in life, suicide, a lack of proper funerary rites, curses, and to avenge a great wrong upon them. Also included in this broad heading for our purposes are those undead that have eternal unliving immortality, such as the deathless lich-sorcerer sustained by dark magic or creature who preys upon the living for sustenance. Examples of more classifiable entities include the aforementioned traditional folkloric vampire (before its rebirth in literary guise under Bram Stoker, which places it more straddling this definition and that of the resurrected cited below), the *preta* ('hungry ghosts', 餓鬼 in Chinese) of Buddhism and across various other traditional Asian religions, and the *draugr,* a dead Norse warrior who generally protects the treasure of his burial mound; but variations on these archetypes are encountered across the breath of European and indeed world mythologies. This idea of the revenant is the undead most frequent encountered in Lovecraft's writings.

The second broad type of undead in our classification is the resurrected, which as the name implies is a corpse resurrected directly at the will of another being. This is a classic trope connected with the sorcerer or witch, the punishment of the gods, literary ideas of vampires raising minion vampires under their control, and includes the traditional Haitian zombie of myth and religion. Mary Shelley's seminal *Frankenstein* added the scientific resurrection of the formerly dead to the undead canon, a classification related to but wholly distinct from the created living being such as the homunculus or life-endowed inorganic matter such as the Golem. The Frankenstein idea famously captured the public imagination and has been pursued in scientific, folkloric, and literary aspects in an ever-expanding circle since Shelley's novel was first published in 1818. Again, this is a particular type that will recur in Lovecraft's writings and is central to the largest impact Lovecraft's undead have had in popular culture since his own time.

It is important to note that Lovecraft, despite using this concept of the corporal undead frequently in whatever guise chosen, never resorts to the traditional non-corporeal human ghost, although the swapping of personalities (or souls, if one chooses to interpret such from a religious perspective) does recur as a trope. It is hard to imagine that as a purely material atheist he felt that any terror or other feeling could be evoked by such an anthropocentric artefact as a disembodied returning soul, and the few tales in which (ahem) shades of this trope appears are often considered among his weaker efforts. For a like reason we shall largely exclude Lovecraft's revision works, which often have more conventional undead themes forced upon him by the necessities of being a ghostwriter.

In a chronological appraisal of Lovecraft's fictional canon it is difficult, yet given the frequently insubstantial and enshrouded nature of the topic somewhat apt, to characterize the first appearance of the undead with unquestionable exactitude. The immortal sorcerer trope is certainly present in his terrible Gothic juvenilia of "The Alchemist" (1908). This story, which is charitably described as a poor and slavish imitation of the traditional Gothic form, concerns within its meager plot the pedestrianly named Charles le Sorcerer, who invents immortality only to waste his time waiting to kill the descendants of those who wronged him every twenty-nine years. Yet perhaps such lack of innovation in a notoriously sheltered and immature eighteen-year-old author can reasonably be excused, and in a broad general reading of the tale it seems more correct to state that Charles simply never died, rather than having passed into death and returned. Contrary to "The Alchemist" in the best Gothic and classic-form ghost tales, there is often a distinct hint, or occasionally abundance, of ambiguity concerning supernatural aspects and a lack of directness to add to the mystery of the tale. Speaking directly to this point decades later in "Supernatural Horror in Literature," Lovecraft openly and extravagantly praises the work of Ann Radcliffe yet importantly notes she "set new and higher standards in the domain of macabre and fear-inspiring atmosphere despite a provoking custom of destroying her own phantoms at the last through laboured mechanical explanations" (CE

2.89). Avoiding this is a lesson Lovecraft most certainly took to heart in the years since writing "The Alchemist," and this deliberateness of hinting and vagary as a storytelling device across the entire corpus of his fictional writings can be easily seen when contrasted with his distinctively direct and unambiguous writings in letters and other miscellaneous nonfiction.

"The Tomb" (1917), the next extant story since "The Alchemist," at first glance seems to invoke the undead directly. After all, the narrator speaks openly of "nocturnal meetings with the dead" (CF 1.50–51) and spends his time visiting with them in their abode in the eponymous tomb. Yet the story is deliberately vague as to the details and mechanism of what is actually occurring. It seems rather that the narrator is through some violation of natural law transported, either mentally, as a duplicate or otherwise, to those entombed ancestral dead while they were still living rather than their being with him while dead in his present reality. Indeed, the paradox between what the narrator experiences and the reports of those who have watched his actions distinctly adds to the overall weirdness of the tale.

Yet as ever with Lovecraft there are hidden depths, in this case buried in the classical allusions with which the tale, and many others, are replete and which are unearthed in detail in Robinson Peter Krämer's "Classical Antiquity and the Timeless Horrors of H. P. Lovecraft." The epigraph for the tale, "Sedibus ut saltem placidis in morte quiescam," speaks directly to the plot of the story, reading in various translations "That at least in death I may find a quiet resting-place" or "Until (least gift!) death bring me peace and calm" (Virgil, *Aeneid* 6.337). Yet there is greater meaning again to this phrase when it is placed back in its original context in the *Aeneid*. The line is spoken in the Underworld to Aeneas by Palinurus, his martyred helmsman who was lost at sea as an offering to the gods to ensure the Trojans safe passage to Italy. This is the embodiment of the Roman ideal of the individual sacrificing for the greater good, literally stated in the text as "one life in lieu of many" (5.814–15). Yet Aeneas, not understanding the role of the gods in the death of Palinurus, thinks him negligent in his duties. Palinurus is now in the characteristic liminal zone of the disembodied revenant, dead yet unable to cross into the Underworld proper because his body remains unburied near Velia in Italy where he was cast ashore and subsequently murdered.

It is noteworthy that Lovecraft, who in general exalted the more original Greeks over the often pastiching Romans in matters of artistic endeavor (SL 3.283, 5.351), chose Palinurus over his equivalent in the *Odyssey*. In that work it is the young sailor Elpenor who is the first shade to greet Ulysses on the latter's trip into the Underworld, and who similarly asks for burial rites that he may be at peace. It may be that the Latin rather than Greek epigram was more suited to the Gothic tradition of which "The Tomb" is clearly a part, yet this seems unlikely to be the sole reason. Elpenor died wastefully of an accident arising from drink, unlike the more heroically motivated death of Palinurus. This idea of the misunderstood martyr intersecting with the unquiet dead ties directly into the fate of Jervas Dudley, who compares himself by name to Palinurus in final paragraphs of the story, hoping not to share his fate and arranging to be laid properly to rest with a certain hope of a final peace. This further parallels the post-mortem fate of Palinurus, who, as predicted by the Cumaean Sybil, will eventually be given a proper burial and have the land about named after him,[4] an event determined but yet to come in the *Aeneid*, rather than the cremation of Elpenor that Odysseus actually performs inside the events of *The Odyssey*.

The luminous entity that possesses Joe Slater (or Slaader) in "Beyond the Wall of Sleep" (1919) is certainly more of an alien, inhuman creature rather than anything resembling the traditional and religious notions of the disembodied human soul or ghost. In fact, Lovecraft is likely making a satirical dig at customary conceptions of heaven as the afterlife repository of souls: the entity and narrator communicate "soul to soul" in an "elysian realm" (CF 1.81), the term being a common synonym for heaven and originating in the blessed place for heroes in the afterlife in Greek mythology; yet this elysian realm is described as "the stupendous spectacle of ultimate beauty. Walls, columns, and architraves of living fire blazed effulgently around the spot

---

4. Which incidentally it remains so named to this day.

where I seemed to float in air; extending upward to an infinitely high vaulted dome of indescribable splendour" (CF 1.80–81), with fire of course being the standard bale, punishment, and primary aspect of hell. The entity does declare that "the cosmic and planet souls rightly should never meet" (CF 1.83), and this perhaps conveys shades of mystical ideas of projection of the astral form which were undergoing a revival in belief in the early twentieth century, but again this is far from the conventional ideas of the more orthodox specter.

It is clear that the time spent in an earthly vessel is a negative experience for the cosmic entity, "a degrading periodic bondage" (CF 1.81), and that it is not its natural or preferred state. This being does temporarily use Slater's dead body in a classically possessive manner as a means to communicate briefly with the narrator, and this makes it undead, from a certain point of view. Yet this is somewhat akin to filtering a signal through an imperfect radio receiver, parallel to the telepathy device the narrator utilizes in the tale, or a (slightly) more benign alien version of a controlling demonic infestation, rather than truly infusing Slater with undead animation in the more conventionally understood sense. The possessive entity definitively declares Slater dead, but Slater himself is certainly not present, and his body's unnatural vitality fits uneasily into simple categorization. Even in this early tale the false trichotomy of trying to classify Lovecraft as solely a writer of science fiction, fantasy, or horror is patently laid bare.

"The White Ship" (1919), and in an almost identical context the later *The Dream-Quest of Unknown Kadath*, make mention of the eidolon Lathi as the ruler of Thalarion. Again this may refer to an undead creature, as eidolon in English means specter or phantom, but without further indicators in a noted "daemon-city" (CF 1.81) such characterization is far from a certainty. The term eidolon is often used in ancient Greek literature as a spirit-image of both a living or dead person, or a spirit likeness of the human shape, and in modern usage can also be the personification of an idea or an ideal: indeed, the word is part of the root of the modern English "idol."

It may be the massacred beings of Ib that return for vengeance in "The Doom That Came to Sarnath" (1919) are undead, yet again clearly they are not the human dead. One possible, even likely explanation is that is bodies of the slain, which were pushed "into the lake with long spears" (CF 1.124) and had their idols cast in after them, were animated to unnatural vigor once more to be agents of the DOOM. It is certain that fell forces were at work in the lake itself, for "the shadows that descended from the gibbous moon into the lake, and the damnable green mists that arose from the lake to meet the moon" (CF 1.129). But even this idea of undead beings of Ib is certainly open to other interpretation, such as them being bought back to actual life for a night by the powers of Bokrug, the murdered beings displaced to come forward from their time living through some strange alchemy of the dreamlands, being vengeful members of the same race enlisted for the grisly work of that night of horror, or some admixture of some or any of these possibilities.

While the nature of the being who speaks to the eponymous character at the end of "The Statement of Randolph Carter" (1919) is technically unknown, its being some form of undead being seems possible or, even to the most skeptical listener, the likeliest explanation. This certainly connects with the mention of the purpose of Harley Warren and the titular author in investigating the cemetery in the story, being "*why certain corpses never decay, but rest firm and fat in their tombs for a thousand years*" (CF 1.133–34). This corresponds with information later cited from the *Necronomicon* that "it is of old rumour that the soul of the devil-bought hastes not from his charnel clay, but fats and instructs *the very worm that gnaws*" (CF 1.417). Allowing this to be true, the unknown speaker from inside the sepulcher is quite possibly some sort of undead sorcerous revenant. This idea is reinforced by Warren's admission from inside the sepulcher to Carter that "no man could know it and live" (CF 1.137), which leads the reader to infer either an undead being or a decidedly nonhuman one. This ambiguity is backed up by Warren's last statement "*Curse these hellish things—legions*" (CF 1.138), as the two main inhabitants of hell are the malign dead and demons. Legions likewise are often associated with demons in medieval demonology generally, where the number of lesser minions each demonic master controls are given in such enumeration and terminology, and "Legion" is famously the name given by the demonic entities subsequently cast out by Jesus as related in the Gospels, specifically Mark 5:9 and Luke 8:30. The particular term legions in this chthonic context will appear again in Lovecraft's work.

Adding to this opacity of meaning, the dream transcription in an 11 December 1919 letter, which is effectively an in-person first draft of "The Statement of Randolph Carter," mentions the term "ghouls—mould shades" in connection with "the hideous voice at the last," and Lovecraft himself confesses, "I don't know yet what it was all about" (SL 1.97). Note the judicious and tantalizing usage of the word "yet." While the (admittedly only potential) undead may not be fully presented, as is so often with Lovecraft's fiction, with many of his creations precise definitions are by design elusive, yet their presence is distinctly felt in the meticulously crafted negative space that remains unoccupied by fuller explanation. As a final comment it is worth observing that the suggested alternative figure to accompany the delver in the dream in the dream transcription, cut from the published version, is given as one "Dr. Burke" (SL 1.96). While highly speculative, Burke is one-half of the infamous duo of nineteenth-century resurrectionists (grave-robbers who sold corpses to medical teaching facilities) turned murderers Burke and Hare, who sold their victims to Dr. Knox, and it is tempting to see a subconscious conflation of the names and titles in the swirl of dream imagery of such a nature.

The misfortunate thieves who come to such a brutal end in "The Terrible Old Man" (1920) seem likely to have encountered the dead bought back corporally; but again, as with the near contemporaneously written "The Statement of Randolph Carter," this possibility is intentionally kept unseen for storytelling dramatics. More interesting is the manner of occult converse the eponymous ship captain has with what seem to have been former crewman or companions. There is a long tradition of both captured human spirits and less knowable entities being held in bottles. The classic archetype is the genie from the *Arabian Nights* mentioned earlier. But Lovecraft was probably also conversant with the "witch bottle" of New England folklore, recorded at least as far back as Increase and Cotton Mather, whose works he accessed as a child through familial copies. The pendulum has been used in divinatory practices since classical times.

However, all such aspects of contacting the perceived otherworld beyond saw an increase in both use and the public consciousness with the unprecedented deaths of so many by violence in the First World War following on from the revived interest in spiritualism which has been present in the late Victorian and Edwardian eras. Likewise, necromancy, perhaps most commonly associated with the conjured undead in modern popular culture, has a long history with divination, including for the location of lost treasures. (To quote the article on magic from the 9th edition of the *Encyclopaedia Britannica,* which we know Lovecraft read as he drew from it liberally in "The Horror at Red Hook": "Thus the ghosts of the dead are called up by the necromancer to give oracles or discover hidden treasures.") Those who traffic in such magics often have unnaturally prolonged lives as well. A conflation of all these ideas seems to be at work in "The Terrible Old Man," and its brushings against the ideas of undeath add a far deeper power than its scant 1142 words might otherwise be reasonably expected to convey.

"The Tree" (1920) has revenge from the grave as its central motif but is conceptually far more akin to an admixture of the mythic or legendary fireside tale with that of the Gothic tale "dressed in Greek toga" (Norris 17). Yet it might be cogently argued that no truly human corpse is the direct agent of this vengeance. Rather it is the eponymous tree growing from twigs placed in the grave at the head of a murder victim by his treacherous friend and killer, although the "singularly prodigious" scion of the olive groves is noted as having an aspect "so weirdly human" (CF 1.150). This tree is clearly the author of the final destruction of the perfidious Musides, presumably being either figuratively, by a supernatural proxy, or most likely literally animated by Kalos' desire for retribution.

The tropes of both the Gothic and classic ghost story are present in abundance: Musides' singular stance of being simultaneously "fascinated and repelled" (CF 1.148) by the tree he is clearly unwilling to harm or leave; his dread of being alone; the tree "sending out a singularly heavy branch above the apartment in which Musides laboured" (CF 1.149) as a spy and portent of doom, while the aural component of "the bleak mountain wind, sighing through the olive grove and the tomb-tree, had an uncanny way of forming vaguely articulate sounds" (CF 1.149) holds the paradoxical imagery being both distinct and original while simultaneously a heavy cliché.

"The Tree" also has the typical layers of deeper darkness in the final analysis that is something of a feature of a Lovecraftian tale. Allowing that the tree is in fact animated by Kalos' spirit, the final lines about the branches whispering "to one another in the night wind" (CF 1.150) would imply that his revenge has come at the cost of his own transition into the afterlife, and thus his own murder exacts a doubly high price. Yet, as would be characteristic of Lovecraft and continually refined in his later works, the exact details are left tantalizingly vague. The reader's imagination filling in the narrative gaps so pointedly left after strong direction down a predetermined path is a far more effective tool than mere description. Lovecraft here demonstrates he has learnt the lesson of the flaws of compete explanation, about which he lamented in Section III of "Supernatural Horror in Literature," so common to the Gothic novel whose form is somewhat imitated in the tale.

"The Temple" (1920) may have a more traditional undead figure in the form of the unknown "young, rather dark, and very handsome" (CF 1.157) seamen clinging dead to U-29's railing after the latter's sinking of the *Victory*. In a classic Gothic manner his dead eyes "gazed steadily and mockingly at Schmidt and Zimmer" (CF 1.157) as his body was prepared to be thrown into the ocean and the boatswain Müller swore that the corpse swam away; but implications of other divine or diabolic preternatural attributes to him cannot be discounted.

Consider the further visions of Müller, who "babbled of some illusion of dead bodies drifting past the undersea portholes; bodies which looked at him intensely, and which he recognised in spite of bloating as having seen dying during some of our victorious German exploits. And he said that the young man we had found and tossed overboard was their leader" (CF 1.158). This points as much to hallucination as reality, and it is worth pedantically noting as a factual point that a bloated body would probably have risen to the surface rather than drifting past the portholes. This "dead dark youth" who looks at the remaining ordinary sailors and drives them to madness before swimming away harks back equally to the classic retributive agency of the Gothic revenant and to the mythic divine transgressor. Yet his visage may simply be the luckless agency through which the embodiment of the curse of the ivory carving is enacted, he may be lineally connected to the god depicted, or both, or something else entirely. In fact, given that the conclusion of the story has the Lieutenant-Commander going bodily into an undersea fane that is implied to be the source of their predicament, a divine attribution as cause seems perhaps the most likely explanation for the youth's apparent survival beyond the limits of mortality and human endurance.

"The Nameless City" (1921) is another of Lovecraft's tales filled with ideas of the undead which defy easy categorization. The ideas of such things lurking in the ruins are cleverly foreshadowed by the city's appearance "protruding uncannily above the sands as parts of a corpse may protrude from an ill-made grave" (CF 1.231) and the earliest appearance of the famous couplet, later confirmed to be from the *Necronomicon*, "'That is not dead which can eternal lie, And with strange aeons even death may die'" (CF 1.232). The reptilians who raised their city in ancient times had "no pictures to represent deaths or funeral customs, save such as were related to wars, violence, and plagues," being, at base, "death-hating" (CF 1.241, 244). The ideas encapsulated in the couplet clearly hints at the undead, the potentially transient nature of death itself, and ideas beyond the regimented human understanding of the universe in which death is by definition a permanent state. The very abstruseness of the quotation gives it power, yet that same abstruseness in the denouement of the tale leaves it rather muddled, the extremely fine balance betwixt keeping the mystery and explaining the events cogently slightly askew.

It is clear that a manifestation of the now-vanished reptilian race of the nameless city is returning to literally haunt its former

demesne, filled with a fury all the more terrifying for being unable to act as corporeal beings, attempting to drag the interposing
narrator into their abyssal home. The moaning mentioned in the
fourth paragraph is recontextualized as unambiguously quite literal, eventually becoming language even if the speech itself is
still unintelligible to the narrator, and the wind is shown by the
"luminous aether of the abyss" (CF 1.247) to be the spectral
forms of the departed inhabitants of the city. This is perhaps the
closest Lovecraft ever comes to the stereotypical ghost in one of
his original tales: he even has the narrator characterize them as
"wind-wraiths" (CF 1.246). Yet these wind-wraiths are far removed from the sheeted phantom of common lore. They are the
collective incarnation of a perished race who were malefic in life,
horrific in form, and clearly still filled with malignant intent, but
hampered by the impotence of their incorporeal form. This may
even be the natural final fate of their species as it went into extinction, for the story specifically notes that "the forms of the people—
always represented by the sacred reptiles—appeared to be gradually wasting away, though their spirit as shewn hovering about the
ruins by moonlight gained in proportion" (CF 1.242). Thus, while
their exact nature is elusive, they clearly fit the mold of the revenant, returning in lessened form by night to the site of their fallen
glory to the detriment of any who encounter them.

Allowing the preceding analyses to be sound, "The Outsider"
(1921) thus counts as the first definitive and unambiguous actual appearance of the human undead in Lovecraft's adult fiction,
a being once a corpse and now given life anew for reasons and
by powers unknown. Keats's poem used in the epigraph, *The Eve
of St. Agnes,* concerning lovers illicitly escaping from a castle
filled with revellers, is a curious choice. It is possible to interpret
the Outsider as the returning of that poem's Porphyro or one of
his scions as punishment, or less literally as someone from a like
situation, or as the idea of the punishment for such transgressive
behavior. St. Agnes Eve is a date on which dreams of the future
are common, and it could be that is what is meant by the use of
the epigraphic segment linking past and present, although such
prophetic dreams in this context are traditionally of the marriage prospects of young virgins, and the linkages suggested

above are highly tenuous. It is more likely that Lovecraft, who rated Keats a master poet of the highest order (*SL* 2.314), simply used the darkest lines from an otherwise erotically charged poem to create a suitable dark, Gothic, and (paradoxically) Poe-like atmosphere.

What is certain is that the titular Outsider is fundamentally the classic revenant, the returned who was once dead and carries with it the decay and detestation of the grave as it returns to a place no longer its own. Nor is this a random occurrence or location. The Outsider is patently a relation or likely ancestor of those inhabiting the castle, which he remembers from a more barbarous time when a moat and defensive towers were necessities. He is truly a medieval revenant, although his cause or reason for his returning is distinctly unclear, at least to the reader. The Outsider speaks of his understanding of what has occurred, even as he follows that swiftly with a releasing forgetfulness, and subsequently of his own detestation and escape to other lands and riding with "the mocking and friendly ghouls" (*CF* 1.272). What the Outsider is, besides a returned dead man, is not made clear, but by that implication he is not one of the ghouls' intrinsically necrophagous ilk, although it is also implied he may partake of their provender in "the unnamed feasts of Nitokris" (*CF* 1.272).

Interestingly, the Outsider's preceding habitat as understood in the origin of his own narrative is not that of simply awakening in a coffin or mausoleum as might be expected. Somewhat surreally, these environs and their description are structured to the extent that the entire first half of the tale might upon an initial reading be (mis)interpreted as a solely mental dying/afterlife/revival narrative. It also echoes classical Greek journeys connected to the underworld, the difficult ascent from chthonic depths in the form of an inverted *katabasis*,[5] a dead person leaving rather than a living person descending for (hopefully) a round trip. Significantly, this underworld landscape, mental or actual, is not one to which the Outsider can return after emerging again into the mundane world. Such returns from the underworld rarely work out well, as in the infamous case of Orpheus, a figure tangentially

---

5. Technically this could be perhaps be termed an *anabasis*, but the word holds different connotations in Greek history.

connected to the "The Tree" written the year before and with whom Lovecraft was obviously familiar.

As ever in Lovecraft, judicious parceling out of information adds to wider ambiguity and creates a stronger story thereby. How the journey is achieved is far less important to Lovecraft than the feelings it evokes. A final fact of note is that the viewpoint of the story is exclusively from the outlook of the Outsider. It is solely from the monster's own point of view that we get the tale told, and thus there are gaps in our understanding both due to the narrator's limited knowledge in some aspects and by what he chooses to withhold from the reader. All this adds a curious perspective to the story that the author himself considered one of its best aspects (*SL* 3.379). In fact, Lovecraft would recrudesce many of the base elements of "The Outsider"—the perspective being of the monster not revealed to either reader or narrator until the end of the tale, the return to a familial place having unknown consequences, the acceptance of one's dark fate, the fleeing to a place of safety with one's ilk—in the classic "The Shadow over Innsmouth."

It is possible to read "The Picture in the House" (1920) as having in the old man of ill-kempt aspect an undead cannibal, but a closer reading of the text merely suggests that he has unnaturally prolonged his life with "more the same" (*CF* 1.217) in his diet rather than having come back from the dead to prey upon the living. "The Music of Erich Zann" (1921) again has the undead in a minor but crucial role, with the viol player continuing on with his performance to drown out the other sounds past the point of mortality. The moment of realization of this fact alone is a semi-climactic event in the tale. This emphasizes the limits and flaws of the dualistic undead model introduced earlier, but for the sake of simplicity let us consider it as case of the revenant, continuing to act with purpose superseding the limits of natural life. Yet again, in his deft manner Lovecraft suggests that the true horror is not the cold corpse playing frantically in a darkened room, assuredly a nightmarish circumstance in itself, but the hideous things *outside* that are the reason that it is driven beyond death to play.

Chronologically "Herbert West—Reanimator" (1921–22)

would be next, but given its importance to the general concept of the undead in popular culture and the necessity of the fullest explanation it will be reserved until after the totality of Lovecraft's work can be surveyed.

"The Hound" (1922) seems at its essence the classic Gothic tale of the revenant, the evil sorcerer who rises from his grave to retrieve a vital possession lifted from him by the two protagonists. Interestingly, while the Hound is motivated by vengeance and a distinct malevolence, its key purpose seems to be recovering the stolen amulet. This "oddly conventionalised figure of a crouching winged hound, or sphinx with a semi-canine face" (CF 1.343) is clearly is an artefact of some power. The body of the inhabitant of the grave is intact ("much—amazingly much—was left of the object despite the lapse of five hundred years" [CF 1.342]), which is often considered a supernatural sign in various traditions, possibly indicative of saintliness in Catholic belief or of the balefulness of the excommunicate in Orthodox credence, for example. Likewise, the skeleton bears the marks of its violent death at the jaws of a beast, and it may be that the vengeful figure who rises from the grave is as much a victim of the amulet as anyone else in the tale. While brutally killing both St. John (who, given his superior position in his relationship with the narrator, almost certainly took the amulet of the deceased himself) and the family of thieves who actually possessed it when the revenant came a-calling, the Hound then retreats to his grave. It does not attack the narrator even when he re-disturbs its rest, and although it is implied at the end that it is now coming for him, this may be a result of the second desecration rather than any other motivation, although a vicious sadism in the manner of the conte cruel may equally be at work here.

There is also an isolated reference, from the *Necronomicon*, to the shape of the stolen amulet as "the ghastly soul-symbol of the corpse-eating cult of inaccessible Leng . . . drawn from some obscure supernatural manifestation of the souls of those who vexed and gnawed at the dead" (CF 1.343). This has a curious intersection with the traditional Jikiniki ("human-eating ghosts," 食人鬼 in Japanese) of Japan. Such a being notably appears in Lafcadio Hearn's *Kwaidan: Stories and Studies of Strange Things*

(1904) in the eponymous story found therein and does indeed eat a corpse laid out for it as provender. Lovecraft lavishes praise on Hearn in letters and in "Supernatural Horror in Literature," and owned a copy of the aforementioned *Kwaidan,* albeit one published in 1930. Such talk of soul-symbols and corpse-eating cults is all highly atmospheric and intoxicatingly esoteric in the manner of such lore, both deliberately fictional and otherwise. It simultaneously implies a large theological underpinning yet one that is inaccessible in the absence of other information, and as such is powerful as an artistic conjuration in the context of a supernatural tale. It certainly brushes up against ideas of survival beyond death, and the line in the final paragraph—"claws and teeth sharpened on centuries of corpses" (CF 1.348)—seems to harken back to these ideas. However, it doesn't seem to point to any definitive occurrence, other than perhaps to effect the reanimation of the inhabitant of the grave himself as already discussed.

Interestingly, the next three tales both direct address the nature of the ghost tale, albeit in different ways. "The Lurking Fear" (1922) has the narrator conclude after his first few experiences that "I now believed that the lurking fear was no material thing, but a wolf-fanged ghost that rode the midnight lightning. And I believed, because of the masses of local tradition I had unearthed in my search with Arthur Munroe, that the ghost was that of Jan Martense, who died in 1762" (CF 1.362). This is later shown to be a fallacy, and Lovecraft both as author and narrator makes a comment on this by describing his actions on the re-exhumation of the grave as "digging idiotically" (CF 1.362). Further to the same point in his next tale, "The Rats in the Walls" (1923), Lovecraft makes what may be a dry critique or perhaps a call back to the classic ghost tale with a suggestive line juxtaposition ("part of the old Gothic structure. I realise how trite this sounds—like the inevitable dog in the ghost story, which always growls before his master sees the sheeted figure" [CF 1.382]), but rather deftly subverts expectations with the true horrors unveiled at the conclusion. Notably, dogs as heroic detectors of, and defenders from, the unnatural is a recurrent theme in Lovecraft's writings, such as their howling at Curwen's use of magic in *The Case of Charles Dexter Ward,* hatred toward and eventual killing of Wilbur Whateley in "The Dunwich Horror," their battles with the Mi-Go in "The Whisperer in Darkness," and forewarning antipathy to the Elder Things in *At the Mountains of Madness*. This is all the more significant given Lovecraft's famed ailurophilia, and likely is a distant echo of this ghost story trope.

"The Unnamable" (1923) is perhaps Lovecraft's attempt at a deconstructionist ghost tale, and from the opening paragraph he actually discusses the nature of the fictional supernatural story in some detail. In it he advocates a series of straw man arguments in the mouth of one of the protagonists for conventional supernatural manifestations and uses it to highlight the nonsensical nature of such supernatural categorizing before recrudescing the facts and pouring them forth as the titular unnamable. What it really is can be debated. The creature is mentioned as having died and "with the years the legends take on a spectral character" (CF 1.402). The folkloric remedy of burying the bones to dispel the lingering haunt is notable here only for its decided ineffectualness. Overall the story certainly brushes up against the concepts of the undead as physical manifestation "moulded by the dead brain of a hybrid nightmare" (CF 1.403), and the narrator relates that in the "noxious rush of noisome frigid air" outward from the creature's tomb "my fancy peopled the rayless gloom with Miltonic legions of the misshapen damned" (CF 1.404). The mechanics of the attacking creature seem to indicate some sort of semi-orthodox revenant based upon the physical form of the now dead being, with the skull of the being indicating "it had four-inch horns" and their injuries leading doctors to describe them as "the victims of a vicious bull" (CF 1.403, 405). But the true horror of "The Unnamable" is far more cosmic in its outlook in that certain things, "religious intuitions" (CF 1.397) notwithstanding, are in truth beyond description.

The undead literally teem underneath the sands of Egypt in "Under the Pyramids" (1924), but their exact nature is, as ever, suitably mysterious. Khephren and Nitokris appear to be archetypal revenants, undead immortals presumably sustained by the "inner mysteries and antique powers" (CF 1.432) boasted of by the former after the binding of Houdini. They certainly lead the composite mummies of the netherworld, although how much those creatures are animated by the spells and preparations of the mortuary priests, the will of Khephren "intoning endless formulae with the hollow voice of the dead" (CF 1.448), the Unknown God of the Dead or their own returning *ka* unnaturally blended with animal bodies is tantalizingly unclear. These composite mummies are a particularly innovative element and seem to be drawn from a combination of the therianthropic depictions of the gods in Egyptian art (commonly misunderstood as literal by modern observers) and the unnatural blendings of human "parts joined to organic matter other than human" (CF 1.320) as practiced by Herbert West.

Significantly, but typical of Lovecraft, he avoids and subverts the common tropes of the mummy at his time. There is no mention of classic revenant intervention because of treasures plundered or to be protected, while the romantic notions of the mummy connected with separated lovers, which were once the most common trope of the genre and would for example play a central role in the 1932 film *The Mummy*, are thoroughly mocked by the nightmarish visage of Nitokris as Khephren's bride. Intriguingly, Lovecraft's conceit of the immortal or resurrected Khephren masquerading as the guide Abdul Reis el Drogman is almost directly duplicated by Boris Karloff's revived mummy Imhotep posing as the local archaeological guide Ardeth Bay in the aforementioned Universal Studios film. This may be purely coincidental, as the trope of the returned villain in a new guise is once again hoary with age. Yet the screenwriter of *The Mummy*, John L. Balderston, was one much prone to adaptation of others works, including a 1927 play of *Dracula* that was the basis of the 1931 film which he also wrote, along with scripts for *Frankenstein* and *Bride of Frankenstein*. *The Mummy* itself was adapted from a smaller treatment, although little of that work survives into the film.

This adaptation of horror novels into movies wasn't accidental. Using a literary source gave the horror film a greater veneer of respectability, much as Victorian painters of nudes drew on Greek mythical sources to allow such depictions without censure. By the time of *The Mummy's Ghost* (1944) the Egyptian priests involved

now hail from Arkam [*sic*], a change from the real Egyptian Kar-
nack necessitated by wartime political concerns (Worland 55),
although the screenplay was not connected with Balderston.
Even more peculiarly in the unpredictable and unfathomable in-
tersections of art, Balderston's *Berkeley Square,* of which he wrote
both the original play and film adaptation, is credited by S. T.
Joshi as an influence on "The Shadow out of Time" (*IAP* 898).

"The Shunned House" (1924) is Lovecraft's riff on the legend of the vampire, and in a typical fashion he excludes most of
the traditional tropes and explanations. Here he is blending
folkloric horror and science, reimagining ancient superstitions in
the light of the modern scientific method and understanding,
but the mix is not as fully or smoothly amalgamated as in later
stories. There is no explicitly unambiguous supernatural aspect
presented by the protagonist, with his pseudo-scientific explanations taking their place, and it is modern science and chemistry
rather than faith that create a positive resolution. Yet the re-
working still rests on the foundations of the older lore even
while Lovecraft recrudesces it: the vampiric monster only affects
those living in the house directly upon his grave, and he comes
out in the form of a noxious destructive vapor; both actions are
directly stated by the servant Ann White, who "alleg[es] that
there must lie buried beneath the house one of those vampires—the dead who retain their bodily form and live on the
blood or breath of the living—whose hideous legions send their
preying shapes or spirits abroad by night" (*CF* 1.462), and in the
lore concerning "some vampirish vapour such as Exeter rustics
tell of as lurking over certain churchyards" (*CF* 1.477). Disap-
pointingly, the servant White is completely correct in her as-
sumptions.

Connecting directly with these comments, Lovecraft actually
cites New England's most infamous vampire case, that of Mercy
Brown. Although not named in the text, her exhumation and
the burning of her heart in Exeter in 1892 are undoubtedly the
events referenced in almost exactly those words by the narrator.
Yet it is also important to remember that the term vampire was
not actually used by the rustics in the Mercy Brown incident: it
was the similarity of the practices with Eastern European tradi-

tional lore that led outsiders to make the connection (Bell). "The Shunned House" is on some levels a precursor to the antiquarian horrors lying in the lost graves of the Providence past that will figure so centrally in *The Case of Charles Dexter Ward*. While purely speculative, the choice of the re-use of the name Tillinghast, first seen in the demented Crawford Tillinghast in "From Beyond," in the later novel for the maternal ancestor of Charles Ward may hold a double resonance aside from its renown and fecundity in colonial times and beyond: the Tillinghast family of Exeter suffered another suspected vampire exhumation some 100 years before Mercy Brown ("Vampire Case").

"The Horror at Red Hook" (1925) is a somewhat dubious mishmash of assorted mythological and anthropological ideas squeezed through the oculus of a patent racism, and Lovecraft's normally deft story painting with glimpses of larger horrors and hintings of a greater whole is instead simply muddled and unclear. Insinuations of undeath are implied by the repeated lines in the incantation concerning the being "who wanderest in the midst of shades amongst the tombs" (CF 1.492–93), an evocative quotation Lovecraft took directly from the 9th edition of the *Encyclopaedia Britannica*.[6] Curious borrowings from ancient sources in modern texts for greater verisimilitude aside, the undead make a definitive if brief manifestation in the tale. The final act of Robert Suydam is when his corpse, now revealed to be gangrenous (presumably through decomposition over time) and having again his earlier corpulent and white-haired appearance, is briefly animated again with his own will and acts to destroy the ritual to which it is clearly no longer a willing participant. He appears to fulfill the standard position of the resurrected, and in the classic trope of the ensorceled who overthrows his

---

6. As an aside—and probably unknown to HPL, as the citation in the text says it is only "preserved by an early Christian writer"—the invocation originates in Hippolytus' *Refutation of All Heresies*, a Christian polemic of the early third century. An alternative translation of the same line "wading 'mid corpses through tombs of lifeless dust" is less evocative of the undead, but no less darkly compelling. However, when the lines are placed back in the original text, with its aim of exposing the "knavery of the magician" and their various tricks to fool the gullible, it naturally has a somewhat less ominous resonance.

master or uses their power against them.

"He" (1925) is another of Lovecraft's hateful philippics against the New York he detested, and is not generally held in any particular esteem. The tale feels distinctly autobiographical, with blatant lines such as "My coming to New York had been a mistake . . . I had found instead only a sense of horror and oppression which threatened to master, paralyse, and annihilate me," "The disillusion had been gradual," and "But success and happiness were not to be" (CF 1.506, 507); and this feeling is not lessened by the knowledge that Lovecraft was in fact wont to wander the city in the wee hours hunting hidden architectural antiquities as the narrator does. The story itself deals with a pedestrian trope and involves a sorcerer who invites the narrator back to his manse but is felled by a ghastly incarnation of those Native Americans the time-warped mage murdered long ago for their magic. "He" is perhaps the closest Lovecraft comes to a genuine human ghost in his original stories.

Yet as with the reptilian wind-wraiths of "The Nameless City," there is no typical white-sheeted figure, but rather a collective multitude. The sounds on the stairs "as with the ascent of a barefoot or skin-shod horde" (CF 1.515) and the appearance of a tomahawk cleaving through the door clearly tell the reader the nature of the ingressing supernal agency, yet when it appears it is not the human ghosts of murdered natives bearing weapons but "a colossal, shapeless influx of inky substance starred with shining, malevolent eyes" (CF 1.516) that carries the malefactor away to a nameless doom, leaving the narrator shaken but unharmed. This description holds certain similarities with the eponymous being of "The Unnamable" seen by Joel Manton as "a gelatin—a slime—yet it had shapes, a thousand shapes of horror beyond all memory. There were eyes—and a blemish" (CF 1.405). This existence of the identifying nature of the blemish and tomahawk seems to indicate that these horrors from beyond the grave carry only traces of their previous selves with them. That the wizard himself was some kind of dead man sustained by a similar magic seems likely given his dissolution: "the black thing facing me had become only a head with eyes, impotently trying to wriggle across the sinking floor in my direction, and occasionally emitting feeble little spits of immortal malice" (*CF* 1.516).

"He" also contains the classic ghost story trope of the house seemingly of a different age that decays along with the owner and cannot be located later, although it should be noted that the protagonist has no wish to find it. This idea of sudden unnatural decay was seen in his immediately preceding story with the corpse of Robert Suydam (although other interpretations may be interpolated here with equal validity) and will be present again far less ambiguously at the second dissolution of Dr. Muñoz in "Cool Air." As often the case with Lovecraft, this haunted house motif is recycled from a recent story of his own, the aforementioned "The Shunned House." It is a rare instance of the later story being a lesser work arising from a similar idea, although he will fully redeem the concept with the Federal Hill church in "The Haunter of the Dark."

More important to the current theme is Lovecraft's undeniable usage of the revenant archetype of vengeful Native American spirits on the usurping Europeans, a narrative of the locale-specific lingering curse inherited by descendants of the settlers of those who displaced the aboriginal inhabitants which first begins to find expression in nineteenth-century American folktales and literature. Given the recurrent attempts by certain critics to falsely distill Lovecraft into a caricature of racism, it is worth observing in passing that the unarguable thrust of the story is of the evil invading white warlock suffering a morally justified retribution at the hands of the wronged Native Americans, who significantly do not harm the blameless narrator who chances to be there. Darryl V. Caterine posits in "Heirs through Fear" that "Lovecraft thus reinterpreted Puritan demonology for the twentieth century, transforming bedevilled Christian sites into paranormal terrains stalked by monsters" (45), and draws a tantalizing series of links betwixt Lovecraft's work and the writing of *The Amityville Horror*. This infamous paranormal work is a fictionalized version of an allegedly true account of a haunted house in New York that has spawned a supernatural demi-genre still going strong today, and has at its root a highly dubious connection to alleged Native American practices on the site. In addition to more than twenty film versions of the ghostly goings on connected with Amityville and countless supernatural investigation documentaries, the popular *Conjuring Universe* film series also purports to draw upon the case files of the initial investigators of the Amityville haunting, and the idea of the haunted "Indian Burial Ground" is a now well-established horror trope, to the point of cliché. Lovecraft's influence is often found in the most curious quarters.

"In the Vault" (1925) is perhaps Lovecraft's most blatantly prosaic and clichéd horror premise. Another classic incarnation of the revenant, it deals with a dishonest undertaker getting his just desserts literally at the hands of dead person whose body he has dishonored after becoming trapped in the burial vault with it. There is nothing original in the storyline and by its nature little possible in the execution, and the tale is only somewhat redeemed by a certainly quality to the writing, especially in the opening paragraph, which elevates what is other a distinctly pedestrian tale. Considering these facts, it is interesting to note that the story idea was not one of Lovecraft's own. Rather it was suggested to him by a colleague in the amateur press, Charles W. Smith, who first published it and to whom it is dedicated for the suggestion.

"Cool Air" (1926) is the last of the New York polemics, and is a curious admixture of Edgar Allan Poe's "The Facts in the Case of M. Valdemar" and, by Lovecraft's own admission (Joshi and Schultz 47), Arthur Machen's "Novel of the White Powder" from *The Three Impostors; or, The Transmutations*. Both the aforementioned tales have in their climax the dissolution of a human being into a corrupt putrescence, and the influence of both authors on Lovecraft is too well known to require further exposition here. It is interesting to note, given Lovecraft's generally more cosmic, outré, and weird focus, that in addition to the obvious fact that these are all lesser stories by an unhappy man, there is a distinct uniformity of the human undead clustering in these New York tales. Dr. Muñoz is clearly a literary offspring of the immortal lich sorcerer, using a blend (dare one say Frankenstein-ing?) of the scientific and occult to effect his unnatural longevity.

Unlike the purely material actions of the scientific Herbert West, whom Lovecraft had created four years earlier and will be discussed below, Dr. Muñoz seems to be blending the occult with more traditionally scientific practices. Ideas he posits include "that will and consciousness are stronger than organic life itself, so that if a bodily frame be but originally healthy and carefully preserved, it may through a scientific enhancement of these qualities retain a kind of nervous animation despite the most serious impairments, defects, or even absences in the battery of specific organs" (CF 2.15), but he has on his bookshelves volumes containing "the incantations of the mediaevalists, since he believed these cryptic formulae to contain rare psychological stimuli which might conceivably have singular effects on the substance of a nervous system from which organic pulsations had fled" (CF 2.16).

Likewise, the sudden catastrophic decay of Dr. Muñoz after the failure of his attempts to remain cool evokes ideas of falsely denied natural forces suddenly and vehemently reasserting themselves over unnatural tampering. (An obliquely related fate also occurs to the main character in "The Quest of Iranon" [1921] when he ages instantly upon discovery of the truth of his quest.) This mixture of formulae and scientific method in "Cool Air" in regard to the preternatural extension of life and resurrection of the dead will ultimately find a final expression in the hideous works of Joseph Curwen and his companions in *The Case of Charles Dexter Ward*. It is interesting to note that "Cool Air," along with "In the Vault," "The Shunned House," and "The Terrible Old Man," were the only completed non-revision horror tales excised from the three-volume release of all Lovecraft's work in the Grafton/Harper Collins paperbacks in international markets in 1985–94. With the (possible) exception of "The Shunned House" these are generally considered decidedly lesser stories, and it may be that their largely more conventional undead horror aspects may have been a factor (conscious or otherwise) in the decision to exclude them.

It would be somewhat heretical to many purists to consider dread Cthulhu in "The Call of Cthulhu" (1926) as an undead being, and given its alien nature this conception does seem a rather poor characterization. Cthulhu certainly is physically destroyed by the charge of the *Alert* and thus theoretically "dead" as humans in a similar situation might be so categorized, before "nebulously recombining" (CF 2.54) into its original shape. Yet of course Cthulhu was already dead in its tomb when it rose up and attacked the crew of the *Alert* in the first instance, so as ever applying logic to the weird beyond certain limits becomes both illogical and analytically unhelpful. More germane to the argument is the famous couplet of the mad Arab Alhazred, "That is not dead which can eternal lie, / And with strange aeons even death may die" (CF 2.40). This first appears in the "The Nameless City" as noted above but is later applied to Cthulhu in its titular story. It is the mutable ambiguity of the phrase that allows the easy yet naturalistic and unforced repurposing of the quotation and its underlying ideas, and lays plain Lovecraft's mastery of the paradoxically definitive and equally inexplicable in a manner that promotes wonder and deeper mystery rather than annoyance. Yet the clearly ultramundane being of Cthulhu is not in the spirit of the ideas of the undead as commonly understood, and will thus be left with only a mention as an experiment, partially in legalism and largely as an alternative thought and a way to reconsider the parameters of genre, as Lovecraft was ever wont to do.

"Pickman's Model" (1926) deals with ghouls, but as noted earlier these are not presented as undead creatures and thus for all their import fall outside the scope of this monograph, as does their reappearance in *The Dream-Quest of Unknown Kadath* (1926–27). Such cannot be said of the *The Case of Charles Dexter Ward* (1927), in which the trope of the resurrected sorcerer and his likewise restored minions are given predominant position in the novella. As an aside it is worth noting the defense of the practice of having and utilizing the "essential Saltes of humane Dust" to "call up the Shape of any dead Ancestour" given by Borellus is that it may be done "without any criminal Necromancy" (CF 2.214). This perfectly illustrates the confusion inherent in supernaturally based ideas both intrinsically and as understandings change over time as discussed in the introduction. To a modern perception, raising the dead is Necromancy

101. When Borellus was writing, necromancy was seen as a far more innately connected with demonology and demonolatry, and the method he describes, not utilizing these types of intermediary agents, thus would be considered a more "natural" magic or even as science, and hence not proscribed in the same fashion.

While the dead brought back bodily is the central conceit of the story, their nature is decidedly under-explained. This literary technique is of course a deliberate commonplace, some might even say a defining aspect of Lovecraft's writing. Yet in *The Case of Charles Dexter Ward* this may be partially a result of an unfleshed-out final conception never undergoing a true final revision for publication (*SL* 4.152–53) as much as Lovecraft's deliberate obfuscation to allow building in shadows and for the reader's always more potent imagination, for the mechanics of the resurrected are often unmistakably contradictory, as will be demonstrated below. In the initial paragraphs the resurrected Curwen posing as Ward is described physiologically:

> his organic processes shewed a certain queerness of proportion which nothing in medical experience can parallel. Respiration and heart action had a baffling lack of symmetry . . . digestion was incredibly prolonged and minimised, and neural reactions to standard stimuli bore no relation at all to anything heretofore recorded, either normal or pathological. The skin had a morbid chill and dryness, and the cellular structure of the tissue seemed exaggeratedly coarse and loosely knit. (*CF* 2.215)

This is Lovecraft all but telling us that the being described is not a true living man, but in such a way that it is impossible to miss on a second reading yet bafflingly obtuse upon the first.

Those called back from their essential Saltes, it appears, no longer need sustenance in the manner of living creatures and, in a darkly comedic moment (at least from the teller's perspective), Curwen declaims as much with his statement "Damn 'em, they *do* eat, but they *don't need to!*" (*CF* 2.352). This assertion is also supported by Dr. Bowen's autopsy of the resurrected Daniel Green: "the digestive tracts of the huge man seemed never to have been in use" (*CF* 2.251). (As common sense tells us that he was hardly in a position to have eaten often in his post-resurrection circumstances, this is hardly the first thought of a reader when other connections are clearly being proffered.)

This lack of the vital needs of the living in the resurrected also accounts for the undying existence of those beings made of imperfect Saltes ("Noth'g butt ye liveliest Awfulness" [CF 2.251]), such as the creature in the oubliette glimpsed by Willett or that seen in the Pawtuxet river by the fishermen of Curwen's day, which "half cried out although its condition had greatly departed from that of objects which normally cry out" (CF 2.247). Yet patently these resurrected were capable of expiring anew: the body of Green being found dead on the ice flows in the river, the oubliette creature perhaps as a result of eating the torch Willett dropped and, by admittedly pure supposition, the absence of further mention of those things swept down the Pawtuxet river. More disturbingly, they were clearly capable of experiencing emotion, judging from the "horror-bulging eyes" (CF 2.250) of the unfortunate blacksmith Green and the "alternately raging and sullen" (CF 2.244) individual questioned about the Limoges Massacre, and physical pain, given the endless moaning of the creatures in the catacombs, the cries and groans heard above ground from the same locale and the presence of instruments of torture therein.

All this established information brings up a question as to the nature of the Guards Curwen utilized. It is certain from the pre-raid consumption of animals at Curwen's farm that many of those kine were going to feed them, as Hutchinson's letter implies their ravenous nature in that they were "eat'g off their Heads" (CF 2.342) to the extent it was burdensome. Yet given that the resurrected need not eat, there is an implication that such guards were likely pacified and controlled by the feeding of their hungers, which can be inferred as a side-effect of the resurrection process. Curwen's need that he "must have it red for three months" (CF 2.327) and the vampirism he clearly perpetrated to this effect certainly support these ideas. This apparent necessity (if true; Curwen is hardly a reliable source of unbiased information) holds grim inferences for the more benign being who saves Dr. Willett and attends to the deaths of Hutchinson and Orne, and might be a factor in why such resurrection cannot ultimately be anything other than an evil undertaking.

As a linguistic aside, Lovecraft specifically links Curwen to these attacks by using the word ravenous, which only appears twice in the entire tale, first to describe Ward's apparent sudden upswing in appetite as he is feeding Curwen in secret and then to describe in the vampiric attacks with (naturally enough to Lovecraft) the adverbial version of the same word. However, it is possible that the guards are in fact not resurrected humans, but something more sinister still. The ambiguity in Hutchinson's letter about the nature of what was called up from the Sarcophagus of the Five Sphinxes is telling. Hutchinson clearly writes that he was told of the location of said sarcophagus by "He whome I call'd up," but that he spoke thrice "with *What was therein inhum'd*" (CF 2.323). The implication that not all the resurrected are human is another disturbing layer to the tale, yet even this may not be the source of the Guards. Depending on one's reading of the same Hutchinson letter, it could be understood that the author's pleasure that Curwen no longer traffics as much "with *Those Outside*" (CF 2.323) is referring directly to the abandoning of keeping of the "Guards in Shape" (CF 2.323).

In a final look at this wonderfully fruitful letter the unexplained phrase "Legions from Underneath" (CF 2.324) comes shortly after the mention of Memphis and harks back textually to two distinct mentions of the undead legions beneath the sands of Egypt in "Under the Pyramids," one of which is an objective reality as seen by the narrator Houdini. Yet this could just as easily be interpreted as a recrudescence of the former inhabitants of the Nameless City or another order of beings entirely; and, as noted earlier, Harley Warren also uses the term legions to describe the beings he encounters under the cemetery in "The Statement of Randolph Carter." While *The Case of Charles Dexter Ward* masterfully uses the undead as a key plot constituent, their presence seamlessly enmeshed as the more explicable element in a larger, more outré and alien universe of implied, half-seen, and potential horrors gives strength to both and elevates the story far more than either would alone.

As a side note, there is a distinct subversion of the tradition of cremating a body to rid it of supernatural agency. Charles's last frantic letter specifically instructs Dr. Willet to shoot Curwen (disguised as Dr. Allen) and afterward to "*dissolve his body in acid*. Don't burn it" (CF 2.306). This echoes the even darker and dreadfully matter-of-fact advice of Edward Hutchinson to do the same to Charles if he grows too squeamish. Presumably this is to prevent the creation of ashes as a nucleus for later resurrection, and if so it may be a subtle knock at the theology of the Catholic Church at the time, which considered cremation to be anathema and a denial of the divine resurrection promised in their doctrine.

The undead make only one incontestable appearance in Lovecraft's original fiction after *The Case of Charles Dexter Ward*, and it is a notable trend of his work that his own ideas and creations tend to become more and more dominant as time progressed. Yet a small detour to the ghostwritten piece "The Mound" (1929) is highly suggestive of the author's thoughts upon the conventional ghost story. As is well known, "The Mound" is technically written on behalf of Zealia Bishop, but her actual input was limited to the plot-germ "There is an Indian mound near here, which is haunted by a headless ghost. Sometimes it is a woman" (Joshi 192). In a piece of wry meta-commentary on either the synopsis, the conventional ghost story, or both, Lovecraft actually notes in the story, after a series of tantalizing and decidedly outré events, that "so short is human memory—the mound was almost a joke; and the tame story of the murdered squaw began to displace darker whispers" (CF 4.167–68).

At the Mountains of Madness (1931) is, at a superficial glance, an unlikely story to include in a listing of the undead in Lovecraft's work. After all, the antagonists of the tale, if one can use the term in this context, are decidedly alien in nature and, while certainly unnatural in that sense, are equally decidedly living creatures. Even if one chooses to see the shoggoths through the lens of science fiction terminology, they are emphatically biological constructs and not the reanimated dead. Yet the underlying tropes of the undead are deftly remolded into a new purpose in this tale in such a manner as almost completely to obscure their origins. The Elder Things are creatures disturbed as a result of the Lake sub-expedition's delving in their unhallowed graves; and they awaken from a state initially indistinguishable from death to inflict a terrifying retribution on their disturbers. They actively draw sustenance from eating human flesh, are seemly immune to the conditions that would slay ordinary life, and are filled with unknowable purpose. Replace the term "Elder Things" with any variety of other terms such as vampire, mummy, or zombie, and the nucleus of an endless number of stories dealing with the undead is revealed. Lovecraft's transcendence of genre and convention again highlights his brilliance and mastery in the creation of original ideas and concepts out of the ashes of clichés and tropes.

"The Thing on the Doorstep" (1933) is the last of Lovecraft's stories truly to utilize the animate dead. It is also, in the words of preeminent Lovecraft scholar S. T. Joshi, "one of his poorest later efforts" (IAP 861). The trite cliché of the explicit mechanism of transference of souls is the key plot element, and it has such commonplaces in supernatural stories as the necessity of the body being cremated to destroy the lingering evil associated with it. This sits rather oddly and in a decidedly traditional and humancentric position amidst the uncaring and inexplicable horrors of the malignly indifferent cosmos that underpins much of Lovecraft's other writing. Indeed, Lovecraft himself would create a far more original and atheistic idea of mental transference of personalities in "The Shadow out of Time" (1934–35). Yet for all its flaws "The Thing on the Doorstep" invokes and distills many of the key tropes that shallowly stereotype Lovecraft's works in the broadest sense, almost a Lovecraftian pastiche as actually written by Lovecraft: the tale starting with the climax half-revealed, a narrated story from the secondary participant after the event, characters slowly descending into madness, hidden cults in the New England woods, ominous final notes, and smugly ineffectual lawmen.

Echoes of previous stories fill the writing: the opening paragraph narrated from the admitted patient in an insane asylum is reminiscent of "The Tomb," while the end is an even darker echo of the inmate finale of "The Rats in the Walls"; the idea of the hardcore skeptic turned believer is analogous to Francis

Wayland Thurston from "The Call of Cthulhu"; the identification of the decomposed body via dental records is taken from "The Horror at Red Hook." Yet the undead horror connected with the twin climaxes of the tale is rather effective. The awfulness of poor Derby's soul pushed out of his living body into the corpse of the wife he had murdered in order to be free of the predations of the evil sorcerer who in turn inhabited her is one that grows the more it is dwelt upon. This in turn feeds the true horrific and undetermined outcome of that murder and repossession, that Daniel Upton is now actively fighting against the same fate, even as the story finishes and thus draws a dark veil over whatever conclusion this will have. For a clichéd premise Lovecraft breathes life anew into tired ideas.

The final and most significant tale of the undead is the aforementioned "Herbert West—Reanimator." For numerous reasons it is an unlikely choice for such a momentous role as the progenitor and archetype of the pop cultural cannibalistic zombie. In both creation and style it is a marked departure from the rest of Lovecraft's oeuvre, and is regarded by many as among the author's poorest work; Lovecraft himself literally described it so in a 1922 letter to Clark Ashton Smith (*SL* 1.201). Indeed, it is filled with a dark humor that leads many to think of the work as a parody, particularly of *Frankenstein*, rather than a straight horror tale. The casual and blunt racism of the story in places likewise doesn't endear it to the twenty-first-century audience, although this too perhaps should be viewed as a deliberate aspect of the consciously overblown and parodic characteristics of the tale. Yet for all these openly admitted flaws the tale has a vitality and momentum that gives it a distinct appeal, and it holds numerous instances of either immediate or lingering horror.

Written to order as a serial run in the vulgar[7] magazine *Home Brew*, "Herbert West—Reanimator" is most unusually broken into six distinct chapters, each with a distinct climax, and each new chapter begins with a summary of the events of the preceding sections. Yet it is not the narrative flow that is the main concern to the topic under discussion, although it will prove rel-

---

7. HPL's own words (*SL* 1.201).

evant, but rather the ideas the story contains. One of the key elements is that the resurrection of the dead is achieved without any of the occult trappings or supernatural elements commonly ascribed to such events in the preceding fictions of other (and indeed many later) authors. This harkening back to *Frankenstein* is both deliberate and demonstrable, albeit in a rather arcane way. Lovecraft relates a dream in a 1920 letter that clearly influenced the creation of "Herbert West—Reanimator." In it Lovecraft is not himself but rather an American Civil War army surgeon named Dr. Eben Spencer, best friend of another surgeon who was performing nameless medical experiments on human remains to the end of achieving some sort of reanimation (*SL* 1.100–102). The dream was clearly a vivid and powerful one, as Lovecraft notes many intricate details in relating it and, in addition to being the clear model from which "Herbert West—Reanimator" had its genesis, shades of it can be found in other stories.

The description of the changes in the character of Crawford Tillinghast in "From Beyond" are likely an echo of the changes of the dream character of Dr. Chester, while aspects of events and characters in *The Case of Charles Dexter Ward*—the obsessive studying behind locked doors, hints of great revelations to be made, displacement in time, and emphasis on odor—show that the residue of the dream had not left Lovecraft unmarked many years later. Yet by Lovecraft's own admission in the same letter, this dream was inspired by an impending (or perhaps commenced; the language is slightly ambiguous) re-reading of *Frankenstein*. This simplistic yet probably not inaccurate self-psychoanalysis as to the broad origin of specific dreams that were foundational to later stories appears over and again in Lovecraft's letters. For example, he credits the inspiration for the dream transcription that would eventually be published after his death as "The Very Old Folk" as coming from re-reading the *Aeneid* and the surrounding Halloween season festivities (*SL* 2.189). Yet even a cursory knowledge of those two sources will reveal there is still an enormous amount of purely Lovecraftian invention and creativity in the resultant writing. For such an imaginative person, Lovecraft was occasionally surprisingly straightforward and prosaic in his self-reflection, and as ever habitually modest about his achievements.

At this point it is worth noting two interesting, and somewhat conflicting, academic theories concerning the primary inspiration for "Herbert West—Reanimator." Elizabeth Outka in *Viral Modernism: The Influenza Pandemic and Interwar Literature* posits that Lovecraft was heavily influenced by the 1918 influenza pandemic in his writing of this tale in particular, while in *Wasteland: The Great War and the Origins of Modern Horror* W. Scott Poole states that the First World War was the underlying genesis. Of course, an epidemic and the war assuredly make appearances in the story, and both authors make cogent circumstantial arguments as to their reasoning. Yet lacking for either is any direct evidence of influence as cited by Lovecraft himself, not unsurprisingly as the topics of the Great War and following pandemic make little impression in his extant letters of the period. Absent a more tangible connection, it is as likely that Lovecraft simply used these aspects for atmosphere and the air of verisimilitude he habitually added to his tales. Outka and Poole each also cite "Nyarlathotep" as originating from their proffered perspective with equal logical validity, and more curiously both authors associate Lovecraft and *The Waste Land* by T. S. Eliot. This was a work and writer Lovecraft was not favorably disposed to (*SL* 2.96). He went as far as to call *The Waste Land* "grotesque chaos" (*SL* 2.251), Eliot's writings generally as a "pathetic farce" (*SL* 2.231), and took note of the author's appearance upon attending a reading ("He is now 45, and looks every inch of it......... unlike the pictures commonly in circulation" [*JVS* 126]): in all some harsh criticism from the generally politely disposed Old Gent of Providence. In any event, *The Waste Land* was first published (*Criterion*, October 1922) months after Lovecraft finished writing his serial tale.

Returning to the dream inspiration initiated by Lovecraft's unconscious meditations on *Frankenstein*, the novel's scientific approach to reanimation is echoed in West's creation of the reagent being posited in such a manner that the reader is invited to believe such a thing is indeed possible. Indeed, given the subsequent creation of techniques such as Cardiopulmonary Resuscitation (CPR) and anti-opiate injections of Naloxone to revive those who have fatally overdosed, such an idea falls with the realms of the plausible, at least within a fictional context. After West, in his fiction Lovecraft will inevitably mix in a certain occult, ultramundane aspect to any resurrection, and this seems to be a deliberate decision. After all, if one can scientifically make a solution to revive the dead perfectly it will swiftly cease to be a horror tale.

Yet fortunately, for the sake of the horror reader at least, the results in "Herbert West—Reanimator" are monsters of various kinds, most often maniacally violent. As West perfects his solution, infamously at the price of murder, this does not remove or mitigate the violent tendencies of those resurrected, but merely allows them greater control. Given the importance of the template Lovecraft creates for the modern zombie, it is worth looking at the broadest traits they possess, as seen by the reanimated person whose actions we learn the most about, the ill-fated dean of Miskatonic University, Allan Halsey. The immediate aftermath of his resurrection is violence, although curiously not fatal to our protagonists. In common with the unnamed drowned farmhand, Halsey first returned to the scene of his burial, with an almost instinctual deliberateness, and this desire may have saved our protagonists, though this is probably more a narrative necessity than indicative of any deeper meaning. Yet the idea of the undead connected with their grave is of course long established in folklore, and while seemingly having no logical connective tissue here Lovecraft almost unconsciously draws upon this folkloric well to carry forth the idea of the unnatural and new associations for the dead reborn.

Halsey's cunning and violence are both on display over the following days and nights, for he is capable of hiding well enough to escape pursuit but cannot help coming in to slaughter and more importantly to rend with cannibal intent. And its voiceless savagery to itself in its cell for sixteen years speaks of an arrested, unchanging, and unchangeable element caused by its unnatural vitality. Halsey is the very model of the modern zombie seen across all spectrums of contemporary media.

Most of the other creatures in this tale are variants on this basic theme of a linked body whose individual parts retain independent yet interconnected vitality and limited feral intelligence:

the cannibal boxer who comes to West as the place where his body last lay as the others come to their properly anointed final resting places, largely savage but able to attempt at least to open the door, a hideous parody of a dog returning a tossed stick with the dead child's hand in its mouth; the final memory of the murdered traveling salesman articulated; the body of Sir Eric Moreland Clapham-Lee, D.S.O., with his parts still controlled centrally despite decapitation; the unknown giant functional despite the partially eaten face. Even the idea of the zombie as contagion is present, albeit in a curious form, for Clapham-Lee was versed in West's own lore and the latter "used to make shuddering conjectures about the possible actions of a headless physician with the power of reanimating the dead" (CF 1.321), which Clapham-Lee indeed appears to have done. A modern reader unfamiliar with the composition date of "Herbert West—Reanimator" would easily be forgiven for assuming it a contemporary work merely utilizing the most common tropes of today to create an unoriginal period story, rather than being the seminal work that created, codified, or helped cement those tropes.

Lovecraft's technical standing as the font of the creation of the modern zombie is unchallengeable, but the directness and extent of the influence going forward is a tantalizing question. Spanish author Enrique Gaspar y Rimbau's 1887 work El Anacronópete (roughly meaning "flies backward through time" or "he who flies against time"; the word itself is Rimbau's neologism) is a serious candidate for being the first novel involving a time travel machine. El Anacronópete predates by a year the publication of H. G. Wells's first time travel machine story "The Chronic Argonauts," which itself would be the prototype and predecessor of his own seminal and enormously influential The Time Machine (1895). Yet Rimbau's unquestionable precedence notwithstanding, his actual wider legacy has been severely limited. The novel was not even translated into English (as The Time Ship: A Chrononautical Journey) until the twenty-first century, and Paul J. Nahin's authoritative Time Machines: Time Travel in Physics, Metaphysics and Science Fiction, as but one ex-

ample of many, fails even to mention the work.[8] The most
common image of Frankenstein's monster derives not from Shelley's original hideous yet articulate and intelligent creation but
from the lumbering portrayal by Boris Karloff in the film *Frankenstein* (1931) in Jack Pierce's iconic makeup. Likewise to the
same point, and largely for the same reason, few picture Count
Dracula with the hairy palms and unibrow that he is clearly described having in the original Stoker novel. In dealing with generative inspiration additional to merely lineal precedence such
often highly esoteric considerations must be included.

While Lovecraft's enormous effect on both contemporary
and future generations of writers and other creative artists is too
well known to need elucidation here and could be seen in and of
itself as sufficient confirmation of the natural absorption and influence of "Herbert West—Reanimator," it is impossible to ascertain with any true degree of accuracy the impact this tale
specifically had in the slumbering collective consciousness of
those in creative fields or the wider public. For example, how
can the effect the (rather truncated and unfaithful) comic book
rendition of the tale as "Experiment . . . in Death" in the May–
June 1950 edition of *Weird Science* may have had be quantifiably
determined? George A. Romero, whose *Night of the Living Dead*
(1968) is widely regarded as seminal in creating the modern zombie archetype, openly admitted his love of and influence from the
horror comics of the 1950s, as did script co-writer John Russo
(Kane 111, 138). These comics regularly directly adapted Lovecraft and are filled with "Herbert West—Reanimator"
knockoffs, clones, and facsimiles.

Romero's love of the E.C. Comics was no passing childhood
fancy. He would eventually create a horror comedy anthology film
in homage, *Creepshow* (1982). This featured a segment, "The
Lonesome Death of Jordy Verrill," starring horror author and
Creepshow screenplay writer Stephen King,[9] based on one of his
own own short stories, "Weeds," a tale that was itself clearly a riff

---

8. In Nahin's defense it must be noted that his book is deliberately focused on
literature in English, but again it is the lack of distribution of *El Anacronópete*
that is rather the point being made.

9. As an actor King is an excellent writer.

on the "The Colour out of Space." Yet Romero openly stated that his biggest inspiration was the seminal 1954 vampire novel *I Am Legend* by Richard Matheson and its 1964 film adaptation *The Last Man on Earth* (Kane 22,65). Given that Lovecraft's friend and protégé Robert Bloch thought enough of Matheson to have written the introduction to the latter's first short story collection *Born of Man and Woman* (1954), it is almost certain that Bloch would have brought Lovecraft's work to Matheson's attention even if his own interests or having his work appearing in *Weird Tales* had not already done so. Yet while it is interesting to speculate endlessly upon possible influence, this digression is far from the primary topic at hand, and in truth there is little in Matheson's work reminiscent of Lovecraft (Joshi 267).

Addressing more demonstrable connections, the late Stuart Gordon, who was to direct the film adaptation of the Herbert West story that became a cult classic as *Re-Animator,* states that prior to the genesis of the film he was unfamiliar with the tale despite being well versed in Lovecraft and had great difficulty in obtaining a copy in 1983, eventually having to go to the Special Collections division of the Chicago Public Library. Yet he had heard of the tale in the first place from an unnamed woman who drew his attention to it when Gordon complained at a party about a lack of good Frankenstein movies (Gordon).

The interplay and interaction of artistic inspiration and creation are almost infinitely multifarious, with many of the strands making any specific piece of complex art opaque, unconscious, or invisible. Consider *Alien* (1979), a justly famed original science fiction horror film widely considered to be one of the best Lovecraftian forays into the realm of movies. Yet it draws very clearly upon such of its filmic predecessors as *It! The Terror from Beyond Space* (1958) and *Planet of the Vampires* (1968) among numerous others (McIntee 19), and was similar enough in part to A. E. van Vogt's short story "Black Destroyer" (*Astounding Science-Fiction,* July 1939) that 20th Century Fox had to reach an out-of-court settlement with the author (Van Vogt). Famously, the design of the eponymous alien itself was a creation of Swiss artist H. R. Giger, after the director saw some of Giger's artworks for his *Necronomicon* exhibition, whose inspiration in Lovecraft is patent.

Less patent but equally connected at a remove from Lovecraft is the inspiration cited by the *Alien* screenwriter from *The
Thing from Another World* (1951) (McIntee 19). The film is
based on the John W. Campbell novella "Who Goes There?,"
which appeared in *Astounding Science-Fiction* (August 1938) and
which clearly owes a great deal to Lovecraft's *At the Mountains
of Madness*, published in the same magazine in 1936. Not coin-
cidentally, *The Thing from Another World* is the film Romero
credited with starting his attraction to horror (Kane 24). All this
is not to cast shade at all and sundry involved in the still less
than exhaustive examination of sources and inspirations as
demi-plagiarists: Lovecraft himself was one to openly homage
and drew liberally from writers and writings which inspired him.
It is just to demonstrate the convolutions involved in how something comes into being and how it will resonate in the culture.

Alien, however, has little obviously in common thematically
with the zombie film. There is a tangential reference in that one
character mocks another over her fear of the dead "facehugger"
alien by pointing out this isn't a zombie, although the import of
this small aside will be made clear presently. To return to our
primary topic and put this into an even tighter perspective,
modern Western folklore strongly associates zombies specifically
with the eating of brains rather than with a more indiscreet
cannibalism, to the point where variations on a joke about being
safe in a zombie uprising because a particular person has no
brains is very much a tired cliché. Yet this diet of *cerveau humain*
is a belief that can be traced to a specific source, the 1985 film
Return of the Living Dead. The film's plot is rather simple. The
dead are reanimated by chemical means and hunt the characters
of the film until the army, which created the chemical in the
first instance, eventually intervenes and issues a nuclear strike
on the location. It is in this film that the dead specifically make
the first strident calling for "Brains!" The tarman zombie explicitly hunts the heroine with this chant, among numerous other
zombies doing the same, while later a captive zombie explains
that they eat brains to alleviate the pain of being dead. *Return of
the Living Dead* certainly enjoyed an immediately evident success, making a respectable $14 million in ticket sales, yet it was

only the 64th ranked film at the North American domestic box office of its year (*Domestic Box Office for 1985*) so the spread of the belief in brain-eating zombies of necessity must have been disseminated more by people who had not seen the film than those who had. The film eventually spawned four sequels, is commonly regarded today as a cult classic, and certainly has more cultural cachet than other of its contemporaries such as the now largely culturally forgotten *Murphy's Romance*, a film from the same year with more than double the box office of *Return of the Living Dead* and which was nominated for two Academy Awards (IMDb).

As two pieces of anecdotal evidence of *Return of the Living Dead*'s influence and penetration, I had a neighbor for whom *Return of the Living Dead* was his favorite film, yet this neighbor was a child in the Soviet Union at the time of the movie's release and obviously not in a position to access the film easily, while I myself distinctly remember seeing the cover of the film in video stores ubiquitously throughout the second half of the 1980s and beyond. To attempt to codify this idea of fundamentally intangible cultural resonance as a number, *Murphy's Romance* and *Return of the Living Dead* both have similar score audience scores on review aggregator site Rotten Tomatoes, but with roughly 6,500 audience ratings for the former and more than 55,000 for the latter.

Yet this exemplar is not picked wholly from thin air. The film was one of two separate sequel branches emanating from the above-mentioned seminal *Night of the Living Dead*, a curious situation arising from legal complications in connection with the rights of the first film. The writer and director of *Return of the Living Dead*, Dan O'Bannon, was probably most famous as the co-creator of the story and screenplay writer of the aforementioned *Alien*, a film with deep Lovecraftian tendrils. But this is not a case of a one-off or tangential connection. O'Bannon was a man with an enormous Lovecraft pedigree, often in convoluted and esoteric ways. He worked with John Carpenter, perhaps cinema's most Lovecraftian director, in numerous roles (including co-writing and acting) for Carpenter's early hit *Dark Star* (1974), co-scripted *Lifeforce* (1985) and the much-delayed production of *Bleeders* (1997; a.k.a. *Hemoglobin*), adaptations of the

Colin Wilson's highly Lovecraftian *The Space Vampires* and
Lovecraft's own "The Lurking Fear" respectively. O'Bannon
himself eventually followed up *Return of the Living Dead* as a di-
rector with a 1991 adaptation of *The Case of Charles Dexter
Ward* as *The Resurrected*. Directly germane to the impact of
Lovecraft in the creation of the modern zombie conception,
O'Bannon is credited as the co-writer for the script for *Dead and
Buried* (1981), in which the local coroner murders and then res-
urrects the local townsfolk under his control. Or, as Christian
Sellers and Gary Smart succinctly said of O'Bannon, "Dan was a
total Lovecraft freak" (186).

The zombies in *Return of the Living Dead* are clearly modeled
on those poor misfortunes bought back to this mortal coil by
Herbert West. They are reanimated without resorting to the supernatural by a chemical concoction, 2-4-5 Trioxin, are violent
and cannibalistic, can be returned to a partial state of dissolution, dissection, or decay, have varying states of intelligence but
are able to communicate verbally at need, and are capable of a
full range of motion including running. This is all very distinct
from the Romero zombies, with their characteristic slow, jerky
movements, almost nonexistent intelligence (especially in their
first two incarnations) and unknown origin.[10] Significantly, as a
storytelling device O'Bannon has a character in *Return of the Living Dead* relate the events of *Night of the Living Dead* as a true story to set the stage for the events to unfold, following the usage of
the expositional preface as a literary device in each installment of
"Herbert West—Reanimator." Equally as important is the mix of
black humor and extreme horror that pervades the film, echoing
that in Lovecraft's original tale, down to the nihilistic endings
with the monsters undefeated both film and story possess.

Of course, this seeping into the public consciousness of
Lovecraft's seminal undead creation did not occur in a vacuum.
Romero's third zombie film in his *The Dead* series, *Day of the
Dead*, was released in July of the same year, a month and half
before *Return of the Living Dead*, and featured a scientist experi-
menting on the zombies in an attempt to make them controlla-

---

10. There is a nod to Matheson's *I Am Legend* virus-caused vampires in a reporter's comments in *Night of the Living Dead*, but a cause is never stated explicitly.

ble, and the dead are now shown to have glimmerings of human intelligence remaining. Just over two months after the release of *Return of the Living Dead* came another work based upon the same fundamental Lovecraftian source, this time openly acknowledging its fountainhead. Originally released as *Re-Animator* with H. P. Lovecraft's name prominently on the movie poster, the connection is emphasized to such an extent that it is also commonly known and marketed as *H. P. Lovecraft's Re-Animator*. More faithful to the spirit of the story than literal, the film nonetheless really captured the black humor and extreme gore present in the original, as well as the less than happy ending. More importantly, it carried over the idea of the swift, anthropophagous, frenziedly violent, and sometimes more intelligent zombie resurrected by science, which was to become a standard trope in the genre moving forward. *Re-Animator* is itself almost a cottage industry, with two sequels, an Italian remake, a stage musical, at least fifty-seven comic books featuring various incarnations of Herbert West stemming from the movie version of the character, multiple action figure lines, and penetration into the wider culture to the point where it was referenced by characters in the Academy Award–winning *American Beauty* (1999).

Two of these films above unarguably have their genesis firmly in the reanimation reagent in the hands of Dr. Herbert West, and the modern zombie owes a distinct lineage to their presentation of the walking dead, even as traces of Lovecraft can be noted in Romero's work. There is no doubt of the influence of these films on the modern conception of the zombie, and it is common to see the ideas mixed with staggering Romero-style zombies lurching and stating "Brains!," such as in the classic episode of *The Simpsons*, "Treehouse of Horror Episode III" (1992). Likewise, the Italian film *Zombi 2* (1979), an unauthorized sequel to Romero's own *Night of the Living Dead* sequel *Dawn of the Dead* (1978), has voodoo as the cause of the undead, but in following trends the in-name-only further sequel *Zombi 3* (1988) uses a serum to reanimate the dead and even steals the idea of the smoke from cremated remains as an infectious agent from the end of *Return of the Living Dead*.

Overall, as is often the case with Lovecraft, there is a hidden depth to certain aspects of his work that has a tendency to get over-looked due to the vibrancy and resonance of his most famous creations, and his usage of the undead is certainly among that number. As ever, he added to the conventions, subverted them or made their usage in such a way as to infuse a life of his own into their fallen forms, and his influence echoes ever more loudly to generations who have never knowingly read a word of his work. "Herbert West—Reanimator" clearly first unleashed the vengeful ravening corpse bent on cannibalism back from the dead through twisted science in literary form, and his progeny ever continue to flourish.

Works Cited

The American Heritage Dictionary of the English Language. 3rd ed. Boston: Houghton Mifflin, 1992.

Beckford, William. *Vathek: An Arabian Tale.* 1786. London: Lawrence & Bullen, 1893.

Bell, Michael B. "Real Vampires in New England?" In *Seacoast New Hampshire,* www.seacoastnh.com/Places-%26-Events/The-Grave-Site/Real-Vampires-in-New-England?/

Burke, Rusty. *The Robert E. Howard Bookshelf.* howardhistory.com/the-robert-e-howard-bookshelf/

Caterine, Darryl V. "Heirs through Fear: Indian Curses, Accused Indian Lands, and White Christian Sovereignty in America." *Nova Religio: The Journal of Alternative and Emergent Religions* 18, No. 1 (August 2014): 37–57.

The Comics Code of 1954, cbldf.org/the-comics-code-of-1954/

The Concise Oxford Dictionary of Current English. 5th ed. Oxford: Oxford University Press, 1964.

Domestic Box Office for 1985. Box Office Mojo, www.boxofficemojo.com/year/1985/

Encyclopaedia Britannica. 9th ed. Volume 15. Edinburgh: Adam & Charles Black, 1883.

"Experiment . . . in Death." *Weird Science* No. 12 (May–June 1950).

Gaspar, Enrique. *The Time Ship: A Chrononautical Journey.* Tr. Andrea Bell and Yolanda Molina-Gavilán, Yolanda. Middletown, CT: Wesleyan University Press, 2012.

Gordon, Stuart. "Episode 24: Herbert West: Reanimator, Part 1." *The H. P. Lovecraft Literary Podcast, Hosts Chad Fifer and*

Chris Lackey, hppodcraft.com/2009/12/17/episode-24-herbert-west-reanimator-part-1/

Guiley, Rosemary Ellen. *The Encyclopedia of Vampires, Werewolves, and Other Monsters.* New York: Facts on File, 2005.

Heard, Lafcadio. *Kwaidan: Stories and Studies of Strange Things.* Boston: Houghton Mifflin, 1904.

Herodotus. *The Histories.* Tr. A. D. Godley. Cambridge, MA: Harvard University Press, 1920.

Hippolytus. *Philosophumena; or, The Refutation of All Heresies.* Tr. F. Legge. New York: Macmillan, 1921.

Howard, Robert E. *The Horror Stories of Robert E. Howard.* New York, Ballantine, 2008.

Homer. *The Odyssey.* Tr. A. T. Murray. Cambridge, MA: Harvard University Press, 1919.

Joshi, S. T. *A Subtler Magick: The Writings and Philosophy of H. P. Lovecraft.* San Bernardino, CA: Borgo Press, 1996.

———, and David E. Schultz. *An H. P. Lovecraft Encyclopedia.* Westport, CT: Greenwood Press, 2001.

Kane, Joe. *Night of the Living Dead: Behind the Scenes of the Most Terrifying Zombie Movie Ever.* New York: Citadel Press, 2010.

Kovacs, Maureen Gallery, tr. *The Epic of Gilgamesh.* Wolf Carnahan Electronic Edition, 1998 www.ancienttexts.org/library/mesopotamian/gilgamesh/

Krämer, Robinson Peter. "Classical Antiquity and the Timeless Horrors of H. P. Lovecraft." In Brett M. Rogers and Benjamin Eldon Stevens, ed. *Classic Traditions in Modern Fantasy.* London: Oxford University Press, 2017. 92–117.

Lovecraft, H. P. *O Fortunate Floridian: H. P. Lovecraft's Letters to R. H. Barlow.* Ed. S. T. Joshi and David E. Schultz. Tampa, FL: University of Tampa Press, 2007.

———, and Robert E. Howard. *A Means to Freedom: The Letters of H. P. Lovecraft and Robert E. Howard.* Ed. S. T. Joshi, David E. Schultz, and Rusty Burke. New York: Hippocampus Press, 2009.

McIntee, David. *Beautiful Monsters: The Unofficial and Unauthorized Guide to the Alien and Predator Films.* Tolworth, UK: Telos Publishing, 2005.

Murphy's Romance. IMDb, www.imdb.com/title/tt0089643/

Nahin, Paul J. *Time Machines: Time Travel in Physics, Metaphysics and Science Fiction.* 2nd ed. New York: Springer-Verlag, 1993.

Norris, Duncan. "Lovecraft's Greek Tragedy." *Lovecraft Annual* No. 11 (2017): 7–22.

Ogden, Daniel. *Magic, Witchcraft, and Ghosts in the Greek and Roman Worlds: A Sourcebook.* Oxford: Oxford University Press, 2002.

One Thousand and One Nights: The Complete Collection. Tr. Richard Francis Burton et al. n.p.: Delphi Classics, 2015.

Online Etymology Dictionary, www.etymonline.com

Outka, Elizabeth. *Viral Modernism: The Influenza Pandemic and Interwar Literature.* New York: Columbia University Press, 2020.

Poole, W. Scott. *Wasteland: The Great War and the Origins of Modern Horror.* Berkeley, CA: Counterpoint, 2018.

Rhodes, Gary D. *White Zombie: Anatomy of a Horror Film.* Jefferson, NC: McFarland, 2001.

Rotten Tomatoes, www.rottentomatoes.com/

Schele De Vere, Maximillian. *Americanisms: The English of the New World.* New York: Charles Scribner & Co., 1872.

Seabrook, W. B. *The Magic Island.* New York: Literary Guild of America, 1929.

Sellers, Christian, and Gary Smart. *The Complete History of The Return of the Living Dead.* London: Pleuxus Publishing, 2016.

Stoker, Bram. *Dracula.* Ed. Nina Auerbach and David J. Skal. New York: W. W. Norton, 1997.

Summers, Montague. *The Vampire: His Kith and Kin.* London: Kegal Paul, Trench & Trübner, 1928.

"Theatre: New Plays in Manhattan." *Time* (10 February 1932).

"The Vampire Case of Sarah Tillinghast," locationsoflore.com/2018/07/26/the-vampire-case-of-sarah-tillinghast/

Van Vogt, A. E. "1950: The Voyage of the Space Beagle." *My Science Fiction Life: The Story of Science Fiction in Britain,* www.bbc.co.uk/dna/mysciencefictionlife/A20258336

Virgil (P. Vergilius Maro). *Aeneid.* Tr. Theodore C. Williams. Boston: Houghton Mifflin, 1910.

Webster's New World Dictionary of the American Language, Encyclopedic Edition. Cleveland: World Publishing Co., 1951.

Worland, Rick. "OWI Meets the Monsters: Hollywood Horror Films and War Propaganda 1942–1945." *Cinema Journal* 37, No. 1 (Autumn, 1997): 47–65.

Reviews

H. P. LOVECRAFT. *Letters with Donald and Hoard Wandrei and to Emil Petaja.* Edited by S. T. Joshi and David E. Schultz. New York: Hippocampus Press, 2019. 553 pp. $30.00 tpb. Reviewed by D. H. Olson.

Some years ago Hippocampus Press embarked on what has become its most significant, and certainly most historically important, long term project: the collection and publication of H. P. Lovecraft's lifetime of correspondence, or at least of all that is known to have survived. The entire body of it, complete and unabridged. His letters, and those of his correspondents to the extent they were available. Compiled from various sources over decades, scrupulously transcribed from copies often illegible in cases where the originals had been subsequently lost or damaged. Collated, edited, copiously footnoted . . . A massive undertaking.

That first Hippocampus edition, *Essential Solitude,* was released in 2008, but its roots, and the basis of all subsequent and future volumes, go back decades before that. To the 1970s at least, when two young scholars, S. T. Joshi and David E. Schultz, began to assemble the archive that made it all possible. Beyond that even, way back to 1937, when Donald Wandrei and August Derleth first thought to collect Lovecraft's letters from correspondents, preserve and transcribe them for future use and possible publication.

Their view was limited, however, and less comprehensive. It resulted in the five-volume *Selected Letters,* which finally saw its way into print through Arkham House during the 1960s and '70s. Joshi and Schultz had a grander design but lacked the wherewithal to achieve it, at least until Hippocampus came along. Some of their earliest efforts, short but important, were published by Necronomicon Press during the 1980s and '90s. Two more fulsome efforts, more in line with their vision, were released by Night

Shade Books in 2002 and 2005. There the template was set. It is only now, however, thanks to Hippocampus, that the full scope of that goal is finally on its way to becoming reality.

Which brings us to the volume at hand. The Wandrei/Lovecraft correspondence is important on many levels. It is also one of the most comprehensive, for few letters are missing on either side. The editors considered them significant enough to make them the first volume of their initial Night Shade offering back in 2002, under the title *Mysteries of Time and Spirit*. The Hippocampus version is an improvement over that earlier effort only in the sense that it has been expanded to include other material, some related to Donald Wandrei and some not.

The primary text of this book is divided into three parts: the complete correspondence between HPL and Donald Wandrei; the surviving, extant correspondence between HPL and Donald's younger brother Howard; and the letters Lovecraft wrote to a young fan named Emil Petaja who would himself, eventually, become a writer of some note. To these are added several appendices of value. Though there are gaps and omissions, none are the fault of the editors, for they were limited by the vagaries of historic preservation. Thus, these are the most comprehensive collections of these three correspondence cycles one is ever likely to see.

The main selling point, of course, is the Donald Wandrei section, which takes up about two-thirds of the book. Those who have the Night Shade edition will find little new in this section. Though the introduction has been changed and the notes slightly updated, there are no new, previously unknown letters included. In spite of that, it's still worth a re-read, for the correspondence is intense and revealing. It is especially important in the light it sheds upon the development of Donald Wandrei as a writer and a poet. When it begins Wandrei is a mere nineteen years old, a fan but little more. By its end Wandrei is a well-established and successful pulp author. The Student, in some sense, had surpassed the Master. Little wonder, given the mentor relationship, that Wandrei would later play such a significant role in preserving and popularizing Lovecraft's own work.

Nor was the relationship entirely one-sided, for in these letters we see how Wandrei's sonnet cycles inspired Lovecraft's own *Fungi from Yuggoth*, and how the more commercially successful Wandrei conspired to help his former mentor make certain sales.

If there's a sadness to this section it's that the correspondence eventually trails off, becoming increasingly one-sided. Wandrei had matured and moved on. Though his connection to Lovecraft remained heartfelt, his life was too hectic and busy to allow for lengthy correspondence. Then, the most poignant cut of all: the letter that closes out this section was written, by Wandrei to Lovecraft, after a long hiatus, on March 17, 1937—two days after HPL had passed, but with Wandrei still unaware of the fact.

The Howard Wandrei section is spottier and less comprehensive. Part of this is because Howard corresponded with Lovecraft far less often than his brother and was less open and chatty when he did so. Ironic, in a way, for Howard Wandrei, like Howard Lovecraft, was fully capable of writing twenty-, thirty-, and even seventy-page letters on occasion. He just never availed himself of that in his correspondence with Lovecraft, most likely because he was too busy working to put food on the table. Lovecraft was similarly restrained. Worse, his letters to Howard were eventually sold off, piecemeal, a few years after Donald Wandrei's death. Presumably many are still extant, but their status remains uncertain. A list of known, missing letters is included in an Appendix in the latter part of the book. Though we can hope these will eventually resurface, they were clearly unavailable for inclusion in this book. A loss, but not a huge one, for Howard Wandrei was only a minor correspondent. His letters to August Derleth, still unpublished and uncollected, are of substantially more historical interest.

The third portion of this book collects Lovecraft's letters to Emil Petaja. Again the reader has to approach this section with a certain degree of disappointment. Petaja was but a teenage fan at this point. Lovecraft corresponded heavily with him during the last few years of his life but does not appear to have retained any of Petaja's letters to him. Thus, in this section, the reader experiences a distinctly one-sided conversation. Such is of interest, of course, to Lovecraft fans and scholars, but there are moments of frustration where Lovecraft's comments can't help but leave the reader cocking an eyebrow and wanting more. One such example is in a letter from October 1936 in which Lovecraft mentions, in passing, "Taves," "Woodard," and "Parrish." He's responding to something Petaja wrote a week or two before in which he'd described recent recent visitors to his hometown in Montana. It's an important moment, for that missing letter would have included details of Petaja's first meeting with Hannes Bok—then still going by his birth name of Wayne Woodard—on his way back to Seattle from New York, after a visit to Maxfield Parrish and several Big City editors. Though the moment is immortalized in Petaja's memoir of Bok (*And Flights of Angels,* 1968), it would have been nice to have a contemporaneous account. Not least as Petaja's later recollections are not to be entirely trusted. And also because Petaja's involvement with Bok's literary estate during the 1960s and '70s so closely paralleled what Wandrei and Derleth had done for Lovecraft decades before.

Beyond the listing of known but missing Lovecraft letters to Howard Wandrei, the appendices include an early interview with Donald Wandrei, a selection of poems and other writings by Emil Petaja, a "Glossary of Frequently Mentioned Names," an extensive bibliography, and a useful if not entirely comprehensive index.

As with all the other books in the series, it is a worthwhile addition to the library of any serious Lovecraft fan or scholar. As a fan of the Wandrei brothers in particular, I'm especially glad to see this material being made available in an affordable form.

OOBMAB. *The Flock of Ba-Hui and Other Stories.* Translated by Arthur Meursault and Akira. Manchester, UK: Camphor Press, 2020. xvii, 234 pp. $24.99 hc; $14.99 tpb. Reviewed by S. T. Joshi.

If anyone doubts the worldwide reach of H. P. Lovecraft's tales and conceptions, this volume would provide definitive refutation. What we have here are four stories—three of them of 50 or 60 pages, the other of about 25 pages—in which key Lovecraftian motifs and, at times, actual creations are utilized by a Chinese author who masks himself under the pseudonym "Oobmab" (read the name backwards to grasp its significance). These stories not only reveal a striking grasp of the essence of Lovecraftian cosmic horror, but are skillful narratives in their own right, carrying the reader along from beginning to end with an ever-increasing crescendo of terror.

Lovecraft's presence in China has long been suspected, but that largely closed society has made it difficult to ascertain with precision how and when his work has been disseminated there. John H. Stanley, the former curator of the H. P. Lovecraft Collection at the John Hay Library of Brown University, has discovered a volume of Lovecraft's stories translated into Chinese dating to 2005. Possibly there were earlier editions.

In two separate prefaces, the translators of this book provide hints about Lovecraft's popularity in China. We learn that the nation "has a healthy and burgeoning online-fiction scene," and one website, *The Ring of Wonder,* is specifically devoted to Lovecraft-inspired tales. This is where the stories of Oobmab appeared.

The four stories in the book are narrated in the first person by anonymous figures designed only as the Researcher, the Dreamer, the Historian, and the Anthropologist. The first story, "The Flock of Ba-Hui," tells the complex tale of Zhang Cunmeng, a postdoctoral researcher who has found evidence of a previously unknown prehistoric civilization in Sichuan province. He had met with Dr. David T. Whitener of the Cabot Museum in Boston (from Lovecraft's "Out of the Aeons"), who had in his possession a "leather scroll of unknown origin." This civilization worshipped the god Ba-Hui ("the Great Serpent"), which at a later point is explicitly identified with Yig and Kukulkan. The narrator—a friend of Zhang's who seeks to retrace the course of his research—later comes upon a cave with huge murals depicting the history of the unknown society (highly reminiscent of Dyer and Danforth's exploration of the city of the Old Ones in *At the Mountains of Madness*). The story continues to its powerful and grim conclusion, justifying the narrator's comment that he has found information that "could capsize history as we know it."

"Nadir" is set in Lovecraft's Dreamlands, where an artist named Nebuchadnezzar becomes interested in a tower north of the city where he is residing. (One suspects that a Western writer would not have used a character name so loaded with historical and religious associations, but it may simply have struck

Oobmab as a charming and evocative name.) He seeks to portray the vivid vistas of his hometown that have come to him in dreams, but feels that his paintings fail to capture the essence of his vision; he believes that by ascending the tower he may be able to see his visions again. But he sees something very different: "It was not the blue skies of his dream that appeared on the other side of the portal, but a frightening expanse of bright stars." How can we not think of "The Music of Erich Zann"? There are further visions denoting a cosmic cataclysm.

In "Black Taisui," police are puzzled to discover the decomposed body of Lao Mingchang, an elderly man from the city of Qingdao who had become interested in family history. His nineteenth-century ancestors appeared to have an uncanny knowledge of incidents in the remote past. The family in fact claims to have come upon the secret of immortality. Lao's great-grandfather, Lao Gelin, was both a businessman and a student of the occult (just like Joseph Curwen). But in 1909 twenty-eight members of the Lao family were found in a decomposed state; only one member, a five-year-old boy, had survived. Lao Mingchang locates the residence and starts living in it. He finds manuscripts describing conversations with ancestors who must have been long dead. One of these, Lao Fu, the progenitor of the family, tells of finding a strange substance called taisui and eating it. This substance, he is told, is "the ancestor of all life" on earth. It is unsurprising that later investigators find a shoggoth-like creature in the sewers near the Lao residence.

"The Ancient Tower" is set in Tibet, where an anthropologist comes upon a tower that the local residents believe is the home of "ghosts and evil spirits [who] were trapped within." When exploring the tower, the anthropologist has visions of all manner of strange entities within it, including the Great Race (cited by name) from "The Shadow out of Time." He sees a series of kaleidoscopic visions: "I saw ghostly jungles of innumerable weird plants flourishing under a sky of surging whitewater vapor that then withered and degenerated into a vast and sinister swamp."

It is evident that Oobmab has been significantly influenced by *At the Mountains of Madness*, "The Shadow out of Time," "The Haunter of the Dark," *The Case of Charles Dexter Ward*, and several other key stories; indeed, he exhibits a thorough familiarity with the entire corpus of Lovecraft's work. But these stories are hardly mechanical pastiches; they reveal a true grasp of Lovecraftian cosmicism and an enviable gift for conveying a sense of terror and dread. The lengthier stories develop a fine sense of cumulative horror, and their spectacular climaxes fully justify their length.

The translators have done an outstanding job in presenting these stories for an English-speaking audience. They provide helpful footnotes identifying the author's numerous references to Chinese history, mythology, and culture, and their translations, while occasionally faulty in points of grammar and style, are fluent and eminently readable. This volume is a revelation to students of H. P. Lovecraft—but more than that, it is a thoroughly enjoyable read.

H. P. LOVECRAFT. *Letters to Alfred Galpin and Others*. Edited by S. T. Joshi and David E. Schultz. New York: Hippocampus Press, 2020. 495 pp. $25 tpb. Reviewed by Martin Andersson.

Letters to Alfred Galpin was the first tentative volume from Hippocampus Press of Lovecraft's uncut letters, published in 2003, and it has now been expanded and upgraded to fit in properly with the rest of the series. The 200+ new pages include a few recently surfaced epistles to Galpin and an expanded appendix of secondary texts of interest, but most importantly, letters to (and in one case from) no fewer than *three* Lovecraft correspondents have been added; hence the *and Others* of the new title. The new additions are amateur journalist Edward H. Cole (who later had the sad distinction of being one of the few guests at Lovecraft's funeral), amateur journalist John T. Dunn (later a priest of the Roman Catholic Church), and revision client Adolphe de Castro (a prolific writer on a number of subjects, and a friend of Ambrose Bierce). The letters to Dunn were previously published in an issue of *Books at Brown* that is long out of print; the letters to de Castro were published in a 1987 issue of *Crypt of Cthulhu;* the letters to Cole appear here for the first time. Editors Joshi and Schultz provide their usual incisive and information-packed introduction and notes.

With three of the four correspondents connected to the amateur journalist movement, amateur matters necessarily loom large, but as always in his correspondence, Lovecraft's intellect ranges wide and far. Topics include the linguistic situation in Roman Britain, philosophy, cats, literature, Colonial architecture (of course!), and the historical existence or non-existence of Jesus Christ, and everything is delivered with the usual Lovecraftian stylistic flair and wit, sometimes even utilizing the archaick long s. The letters to Cole's infant son Sherman are an especial delight with their solemn humor, as when Lovecraft congratulates Sherman on his first tooth, writing: "You will need teeth very much if you are to become a literary critick; since the prefent ftate of literature calls for much gnafhing on ye part of thofe who furvey it." In the case of the de Castro correspondence, the reader also has the added luxury of seeing some of de Castro's side of the correspondence (de Castro could not hold a candle to Lovecraft as an epistolarian, but his letters are nevertheless of interest in that they shed light on their business relationship).

All four correspondents are interesting in their own right, and because they bring out different facets of Lovecraft's personality. This means that Lovecraft sometimes does not show himself from his best side, as when he is—somewhat heavy-handedly and insensitively—defending the English presence in Ireland to the Irishman Dunn; fortunately, Dunn seems to have been able to give as good as he got. Then again, he also shows a more human side, particularly in his old age, as when he poignantly discusses the melancholy duty of scattering the ashes of Mrs. Dowe, whose daughter, Lovecraft's friend Edith Miniter, herself had died and was thus unable to fulfill her mother's wishes. But the *pièce de résistance* of the book still remains the letters to Galpin. Alfred Galpin was the first of Lovecraft's many "grandsons," and Lovecraft's surviving letters to him (alas, Galpin himself destroyed many of the pre-1930 letters, "apparently ashamed of some of his youthful enthusiasms," according to the introduction) indicate that Lovecraft found him one of the most brilliant. Indeed, Galpin was a kindred spirit, as Lovecraft wrote to Rheinhart Kleiner: "Our minds are cast in precisely the same mould, save that his is finer." The fine sampling of Galpin's own writings in the appendix bears this out, even though no letters from Galpin to Lovecraft are extant. Lovecraft needed a correspondent of his own calibre to bring out the best in him, and Galpin certainly was one of those.

The appendix contains a number of texts—stories, articles, and poems—by and about the correspondents; this is one of the many strengths of the volume (and indeed of the Letters series as a whole), since the vast majority of these texts were published in amateur journals and are very difficult for most readers to find on their own. Only John T. Dunn is not represented, which is a pity; it would have been both fun and interesting to see what this early acquaintance, described by Lovecraft as being "among the cleverest of the United [Amateur Press Association]'s humorous writers," wrote.

Now the question is: Is it worth the price to get the upgrade to someone who already has the original *Letters to Alfred Galpin*? The answer is emphatically "yes," to the mind of this reviewer. Lovecraft was a complex character, emphasizing different sides of himself to various people, and only by absorbing as many of his correspondence cycles as possible is it possible to at least come close to grasping the multifaceted jewel that was Howard Phillips Lovecraft, gentleman, writer, and human being.

H. P. LOVECRAFT. *Letters to Wilfred B. Talman and Helen V. and Genevieve Sully*. Edited by David E. Schultz and S. T. Joshi. New York: Hippocampus Press, 2019. 576 pp. $25.00 tpb. Reviewed by Leigh Blackmore.

The publication of this volume of Lovecraft's correspondence sees a continuation of the project by the editors to see into print the entirety of Lovecraft's enormous correspondence, or such of it as survives. Here we have the letters to one of Lovecraft's male correspondents and literary collaborators (Talman), together with Lovecraft's missives to two women (Helen V. Sully and her mother, Genevieve), which add to the store of published letters to female acquaintances of Lovecraft already published by Hippocampus Press—those to Anne Tillery Renshaw and Elizabeth Toldridge, to C. L. Moore, and to Jonquil Leiber. It will be interesting to see if the future holds a volume or volumes of Lovecraft's correspondence with such other female figures (major and minor) as Ida C. Haughton, Anna Helen Crofts, Winifred Virginia Jackson, Edith Miniter, and Hazel Pratt Adams. We know that there is no prospect of Hazel Heald's letters from Lovecraft being published, for she did not keep them. However, I digress.

Wilfred Blanch Talman was a member of the Kalem Club, the literary group in which Lovecraft participated during his years of "New York exile" (1924–26). His brief but touching memoir *The Normal Lovecraft* (Gerry de la Ree, 1973) was a refreshing antidote to the then-prevalent view of HPL as a morbid eccentric, showing Lovecraft as a wittily engaging speaker and friendly "regular guy." Talman notably published four stories in *Weird Tales*. There are 107 letters here from Lovecraft to Talman, occupying very nearly half this generously sized volume. Thirty or more pages are occupied in the appendices by Talman's poetry, *Cloisonné and Other Verses* (reprinted from what may be the only surviving copy of the booklet) and some short fiction (with the exception of the tale Lovecraft revised for him, "Two Black Bottles," readily available elsewhere). Additionally, there are some interesting oddments: firstly, reproductions of three bookplate designs drawn by Talman—one for himself, one for HPL's correspondent James F. Morton, and the famous one for Lovecraft featuring the half-open colonial doorway, stair-rail, and fanlight window; secondly, a piece titled "Lovecraft Revisited"—not a memoir, but the record of a word association test participated in by Talman, Lovecraft, and F. B. Long (first published in a 1960 issue of *Fresco*); and lastly, three letters Talman published in *Weird Tales*.

Of Lovecraft's letters to Helen V. Sully, a friend of Clark Ashton Smith's who actually journeyed from California to Providence to see Lovecraft, there are but 25 letters, but most of them are lengthy and this correspondence occupies 175 pages of the volume. Helen, a music and drawing teacher, was one of the two daughters of Genevieve Sully, the other being Marion. The family all lived in Auburn, California. Lovecraft wrote but a few letters (four to be precise) to Genevieve Sully, from 1934 to 1937. The editors also supply reprints of two letters that Genevieve Sully published in *Weird Tales*.

To both Talman and Sully, Lovecraft wrote extensively of his antiquarian travels, which formed one of his chief passions. He waxes rhapsodic to Sully about various aspects of Quebec and Charleston in particular, giving her detailed information about sights she absolutely must not miss on her visits there.

But we also see in all these sets of letters the expansive wit and learning that made Lovecraft so charming a correspondent with all his close acquaintants. If the subject be the divisions of the moon and their relation to astrology, as it is in a couple of letters to Talman, then Lovecraft holds forth with all his erudition. If the subject be the dating systems of the Greeks and Egyptians, then HPL was up to the task of discussing them with Talman in detail. If the subject be Talman's resumption of musical endeavors, then Lovecraft would congratulate and encourage his friend despite his own relative inability in that sphere of the arts.

Likewise, with Helen Sully and her mother, Lovecraft was both informative and always capable of putting his correspondent at their ease. His knowledge of the history of foreign settlement in various parts of the US was extensive, and though he might at times express (to other correspondents than these) his grievances over the erosion of what he saw as New England values, he could write to Genevieve Sully of Russian and Spanish influences in American settlement, and without any undue modesty admit to minor areas of deficiency in his otherwise wide-ranging knowledge.

A letter [No. 47] of September 1930 to Talman contains several fascinating tidbits: "I have just inspected a full-grown embalmed *whale* exhibited in a great flat car in the freight yards behind the Union Station. Next thing you know, I'll be shipping before the mast for a voyage to Cape Horn!" This same letter contains a reference to the occultist Aleister Crowley (one of only a couple of references to the British magus in Lovecraft's correspondence), in relation to the Australian Percy Reginald Stephenson's spirited defense of Crowley in his volume *The Legend of Aleister Crowley* (Mandrake Press, 1930): "have you seen the reviews of the new book about that suave diabolist Aleister Crowley? Belknap sent me a cutting from the *Tribune*. The biographer—abetted by the reviewer—(Herbert S. Gorman, who claims to have dined with Crowley) tries to depict this reputed ally of Satan as a much-wronged and basically blameless poet—whose eccentricities are merely the harmless foibles of genius!" (Gorman, of course, was also the author of the 1927 novel *The Place Called Dagon,* portions of which may have inspired the Dunwich milieu in Lovecraft's fiction.)

Each and every letter gathered here bears witness to the varied and fascinating aspects of Lovecraft's character, from his views on communism and *Homo sapiens* in general, to his apt summing up of the pros and cons of Machen's book *The Green Round,* to the poignant description (along with pawprint) of a feline visitor to HPL's study that appears in the letter to Helen Sully of 24 November 1933. In a letter to Sully of 28 June 1934, we learn that Lovecraft favored cremation over burial—but that "life is so trivial at best that it doesn't pay anybody to worry about the ultimate disposal of his bones. What does it matter what happens to the cast-off reliquiae of any one atom in the cosmos? . . . They can dump my carcass down the sewer for all I care—I'll be out of it!"

In seeking to cheer up Helen Sully when she was depressed, his letters to her sometimes contained extended philosophical monologues on the insignificance of all mankind; one can see that Lovecraft demonstrated genuine concern for Sully's well-being, as he did with other correspondents—though his chosen method may not have been the best!

Lovecraft would never describe a "fall trip" when he could refer to an "autumnal peregrination" or a choir of old people when he could characterize them as a "septuagenary chorus." And in his style as well his subject matter lies the delight for the reader in perusing these records of his thoughts and doings.

The editors have done a sterling job in compiling and annotating this varied material. The volume is also equipped with a glossary of frequently mentioned names, a full bibliography, and a thorough index. *Letters to Wilfred B. Talman and Helen V. and Genevieve Sully* is another in the crucial series of Lovecraft's letters from Hippocampus Press and should be sought out by every avid fan of "the Old Gent."

www.ingramcontent.com/pod-product-compliance
Lightning Source LLC
Chambersburg PA
CBHW051818090426
42736CB00011B/1547